EUROPE'S
MIDDLE
AGES 565 / 1500

FOR E.R.B. AND C.E.B.

SCOTT, FORESMAN
WORLD CIVILIZATION
SERIES

WILLIAM H. McNEILL
Editor

EUROPE'S MIDDLE AGES 565 / 1500

By KARL F. MORRISON
The University of Chicago

WILLIAM H. McNEILL, *Editor*
World Civilization Series

SCOTT, FORESMAN AND COMPANY

Foreword

Two assumptions underlie the Scott, Foresman World Civilization series: first, that there is such a thing as world history and not merely the history of separate civilizations and barbarisms coexisting in different parts of the world without important relations one with another; and second, that people learn more easily and with greater satisfaction if information is organized into a more complex intellectual framework than the bald matrix of a catalogue arranged according to proximity in time and space. Interpretation, then, with all the risks of omission and individual idiosyncrasy on the part of the authors; and synthesis, with whatever risks of error on the part of the editor, are the goals for which we have striven.

In any collaborative work, a key problem is how to reconcile expertise in detail with cohesion overall. In this series each author was invited to say whatever he thought ought to be said, but only within rather narrowly defined limits of space. The overall apportionment of space was regulated by a preliminary plan for which the undersigned was responsible. The basic architecture of that plan will be apparent from the titles of successive volumes; but choice of themes and apportionment of space within each volume were left to the discretion of the various authors.

The series itself has been organized to permit its use in a number of different ways. Books two through five, along with the first and last titles, make up a course in Western civilization; and books six through nine can also be used in the same way with the first and last titles to form a course in non-Western civilization. Taken together, all ten titles constitute the basic reading for a course in world civilization, while each individual book can be used either on its own or as a supplement to a conventional world history text.

How well this procedure permitted us to achieve our goals will be for each reader to decide.

William H. McNeill

Preface

Historians frequently talk about detachment and objectivity, but fashionable ways of writing history change, at least in part, according to current pressures. In times of economic crisis, people look for economic causation in the past; in times of "imperialist" expansion, men look for the laws and institutions that preserved the great empires of antiquity. Perhaps subconsciously, historians read into former times the burning questions of their own day. Relevance is in the eye of the scholar. But ardent issues subside into ashes. Each generation of historians reads the past anew, departing sometimes very far from the views of its own teachers.

An important change has now struck European history in general and medieval history specifically. We still read works such as Bryce's *Holy Roman Empire* and G. B. Adams' *Civilization during the Middle Ages*. But studies of their vintage and later, well past the First World War, were largely introspective and political. They tended to ask: how did Europe develop its present characteristic forms of government? The experience of the last forty years has brought us to look for Europe's place in the wider context of world affairs. We are now asking: what unique conditions had, by the fifteenth century, set Europe on the path toward world dominance? Works that deal with this question and its vast net of component issues tend to be comparative by method and social by theme.

The following study attempts to answer this new question, but its main purpose is to set forth a logical framework for synthesizing present lines of inquiry. We could pose the question for discussion in this way: "were Europe's Middle Ages one or many?" I owe an abiding debt to Ernst Cassirer's brilliant book, *An Essay on Man: An Introduction to a Philosophy of Human Culture*, for the categories I have used. As for the suggested readings, I have selected books and articles to supplement information in the text and, just as important, to illustrate new methods now being developed by medievalists. Professor Darby's application of historical geography to Domesday Book and Professor Herlihy's use of quantification in his studies of Pisa and Pistoia are two examples of what I had in mind. Without wishing to implicate him in my opinions, I may also add in gratitude that this book owes much to a careful reading by Professor Herlihy.

I am also under a heavy obligation to Mrs. Joyce Sisskind, Mrs. Antoinette Blood, and Miss Margaret Lukacs, of Scott, Foresman and Co., for their unstinting help and kindness.

Karl F. Morrison

Contents

Chapter 1

The Received Tradition

INTRODUCTION

We are children of a society based on technical mastery, and when we venture to learn about Europe as it was in the period 500–1500, we set foot in territory that is both familiar and alien. The geography and, in broad outlines, the political divisions with which we have to deal are the same ones we see around us today. Cultural traits of the medieval world are part and parcel of the world in which we live. Words of the lawyer Henry de Bracton (d. 1268) are carved into the stone of the Harvard Law School, and live in the hearts and minds of those who hold that law checks the powers of government and saves the rights of men. Almost any town in the United States can boast a church in the Gothic style; many have colleges or universities; and our whole system of hospitals and charitable institutions grew out of medieval Christianity's efforts to care for the sick, the aged, and the poor.

But, if we were suddenly transported from our society into the medieval world, we would notice more than a few elements of our world in recognizable, though quaint and archaic, forms. In fact, we would have to lay aside many of our most fundamental ideas, ideas that we take for granted about right and wrong, the structure and operation of society, and even the mode and object of thought.

No less than any anthropologist, we would be stepping into a primitive, savage society, nonliterate in some times and places, semiliterate in others, and as foreign as the Maya's to the experimental science and technology that is the essence of our world.

We would have to lay aside the idea of a pluralistic society combining every aspect of man's material and spiritual life—the forces of capital and labor, social welfare and private enterprise, and the most diverse ethnic strands—and bringing them all under the single harmonizing rule of law.

1

All citizens, we like to think, stand as one before the law, whatever their religion, social standing, or ethnic background. Still, this has not been true in all modern countries; in Spain, for example, until recently Jews, Moslems, and Christians outside the Roman communion were ineligible for public office. And it is far from the medieval world when political thought—though not the actual power structure—gave the leading roles to God and the king. Social cohesion depended precisely upon inequality before the law; it rested, in other words, first upon the maintenance of the pyramid of privilege and status derived from wealth and kinship that culminated in the king, and secondly upon the ostracism of men who did not confess a particular strand of the Christian faith.

We should also have to lay aside the idea of a society that can live for long periods on economic surpluses. Granaries bursting with the ample harvests of a decade; farmers paid government subsidies to keep land out of cultivation; all this we take for granted. But the medieval world lived exactly at the subsistence level; and, with some remarkable exceptions, each community had to live largely on its own produce. Inadequate storage facilities; slow, expensive, and uncertain transport; and the most rudimentary preservatives meant that stockpiling surpluses against barren years was next to a pointless exercise, and that transport of surpluses from a region of bountiful harvest to one of famine was a game of chance. Relief of this sort was sometimes to be had, as, most dramatically, in the thirteenth century, when great quantities of wheat were shipped from the Baltic area to the Low Countries. But in most cases, reserve supplies could stave off hunger for only a few months. Heavy rains at sowing or at harvest, drought in the growing season, or blight was disastrous; and, in the later Middle Ages, we can directly connect the incidence of bad harvests with the rate of mortality.

A third predisposition we should have to discard is our mode of thought. Our modern, scientific, skeptical mind leaves little to chance and less to divine powers. We set great store by empirical knowledge; objectivity is the source and safeguard of truth. Our universe is material, operating in discoverable and constant ways according to the relativity of mass and energy. We are incredulous. Between us and medieval habits of thought stand the gigantic figures of Newton and Einstein, who changed the entire cosmology of Western science—and thus the idea of man. Given its principles, the cosmology of St. Thomas Aquinas (d. 1274) was absolutely correct; but it rested on inspired Scriptures and on faith in the anthropomorphic imagery of primitive religion, rather than on objectivity and empirical knowledge. What are fantasies to us were the realities of the medieval world in which miracles suspended the natural order of things, the supernatural blended into daily life, and the earth and very soul of man were battlegrounds for armies—visible and palpable—of angels and demons.

These are some habits of mind that are natural to us but were alien to medieval man. There are many others; but the three broad points we have mentioned may serve to show that we must be on guard against our preconceptions concerning how society is rightly organized, what resources it commands, and our most basic assumptions about man's perception of the world.

Thus far, we have spoken of "the medieval world" and "the Middle Ages." These terms hide further difficulties, and we must now turn from modern preconceptions on the broadest questions of life to some special biases long held about these "Middle Ages."

THE RECEIVED TRADITION

Our whole view of the period between the fall of Rome and the Reformation in the sixteenth century is shaped by the term "Middle Ages." We speak of it as one block of time, having special hallmarks that unify it and set it apart from classical antiquity and the modern age. This division of European history into homogeneous, chronological blocks arose among fifteenth-century Italian humanists. For them, the "middle time" was an historical unity—for some, a slough of despond—between the glories of Greece and Rome and the achievements of right-thinking men who strove to revive the corpse of classical learning. This point of view has clouded for centuries the rich diversity of medieval life. Since the period was understood as a unit, men thought of it in terms of picturesque uniformity. The sequence of barbarian invasions, extinction of learning and political order, the rise of kingdoms, the emergence of cities, and the revival of learning gave a pleasantly ordered historical progress to the scene. The humanists took the abstract naturalism of medieval art and the absence of counterpoint in plainchant as evidence of deficiency of taste and technique; the perversion of Latin and the ignorance of Greek, they thought, demonstrated the primitive character of thought. Medieval society was considered raw, if not debased. Medieval history was foreign to the refined complexities of modern life.

This was what the Renaissance humanists wished to convey when they wrote of the "middle time." The whole complex of associations sprang from and has continued to engender a view of the Middle Ages that can be compared with a purely visual and superficial experience of something foreign. People who have this historical viewpoint are rather like visitors in a strange country who cannot speak the language of their hosts. Since they can have no involvement with the natives and no basis for interpreting their experiences, they leave with one-dimensional, and often deceptively uniform, impressions. This is true even of excellent historians who choose to interpret medieval history and medieval society as a unit or evolutionary process that moved by stages toward the modern world.

The main question which we must consider is this: did Europe exist as more than a geographical unit, that is, as a society, a stylized way of life, in the Middle Ages? One would expect to find here and there a stranded ethnological rock pool, the remnant of an early invasion that subsequent events had somehow failed to blot out. We must try to see whether, with isolated exceptions, men in Europe did have a common heritage and live in much the same web of society.

The Bias in Favor of Cultural Uniformity

The issue of unity does not really concern the period before the eleventh century. The earlier history of man in Europe is part of a long process of invasion and settlement by peoples from the East. After 1100, there were, of course, invasions from the East that affected certain areas: the Mongols engulfed Russia and struck into Poland; the Turks hurled themselves into Hungary and battered at the gates of the West. But the great age of Europe as a melting pot of Asiatic invaders and Levantine cultures was past. The formative period ended when settlements were so small and so widely scattered that a few thousand invaders could completely change the cultural groupings of the entire continent. Population grew; cultures became entrenched, safe in the numbers of their adherents and in the density of settlement; and the period after the year 1000 saw chiefly the elaboration of cultural types that had already been set. Cultural diffusion, however, from the East was far from over; modes of thought that gave rise to scholastic reasoning, stores of knowledge about the physical universe, so-called Arabic numerals, and scores of other critical kinds of knowledge were to come in the next centuries.

The proposition that a unitary European culture had evolved by the eleventh century and then spread throughout Europe has been brilliantly debated. Some scholars argue that a synthesis of Roman, Germanic, and Christian elements did not mature until very late in the eleventh, or even in the twelfth century. A second opinion is that Europe became a cultural community as the Middle Ages waned in the fifteenth century. Much sound reasoning and learning stands behind each of these views.

The argument for early and sustained unity is a received tradition, our common ground. Let us examine it for a moment. The assumption of unity makes it possible to trace a coherent path of organic birth, growth, and decay. Medieval society, according to this interpretation, began and died in processes of cultural breakdown. While exact periodization varies, the disorders of the late Roman Empire gave rise to this society, and the decay of its own economic base killed it. Historians of technology close the Roman period with barbarian invasions; they see the fourth through the ninth centuries as witnessing events important for later development but no major technological advances; finally, they bracket the ensuing period, to the fifteenth century, as the golden age of medieval technology.

Scholars who approach the problem from other points of view are prepared to define shorter periods. They begin in the welter of the Roman imperial collapse, from the third century on, and close their first period with the establishment of the new empire by Charlemagne in the late eighth century. Broadly speaking, their next period runs from Charlemagne's day to the "Commercial Revolution," a time of urban and commercial growth and magnificent achievements in art, architecture, and learning. This brilliant period, they maintain, lasts through the thirteenth century until finally a series of natural disasters blighted crops, visited plague on populous and productive areas, and, along with the protracted warfare of the time, devastated wide stretches of Europe's richest territories. Trade contracted; cities dwindled in size and power; a dark perversion of mind, of which the witchcraft delusion was only one sign, settled on the West. The fourteenth century was disastrous. By the late fifteenth century, the great, dynamic world of the Renaissance was rising from the ashes of the Middle Ages.

Each advocate of this view, of course, divides the period according to his own best judgment. Many scholars would delineate more periods than the three we have mentioned; some would have fewer; but it is fair to say that they all follow this broad pattern.

The "Church Universal"

Behind the serial treatment of social, economic, and political history, proponents of unity see the transcendent bond of religion. Like the broad view of European history that we have summarized, this approach to religion has symmetry in its favor. The basic premise is that there was an entity, Christendom, which rose to power amid the chaos of the late Roman Empire, achieved its greatest extent and cohesiveness in the period c. 1050–1300, and dissolved in the disorders of the next 250 years. Again, the barbarian invasions open the story; the Wars of Religion close it.

Though bound to the different political and social groupings by many ties, Christendom, in this interpretation, transcended them. It was an interregional order, cutting across linguistic barriers with Latin as the general liturgical language, imposing a uniform standard of canon law over divergent customary laws, and crossing political divisions with the supreme moral jurisdiction of the pope, which extended to touch every aspect of life.

Indeed, the schematic division of Christendom's history into three periods rests chiefly on the acts of the Roman See. Christendom and Rome are in some measure identical. The period in which Christendom took shape and grew is defined by Rome's growth as a territorial power in Italy, by conduct of missionary activities under papal patronage, and by the gradual extension of papal jurisdiction through every level of Church order down to the parishes. As they developed their political strength at home, the Roman bishops were in the process of constructing a vast administrative order comprehending all of the clergy and an empire—composed of all Church lands—over which the popes governed as supreme administrators, judges, and legislators. European civilization, then, was a superstructure stretched across the framework of Christendom.

Much of this unity existed more in expectation than in reality during the early Middle Ages. Many challenges defied the papal claims, and the papacy's material fortunes in Italy fluctuated widely. Individual popes suffered great humiliation; the proud assertions of their predecessors mocked the feeble and unworthy men who governed Rome in the tenth century. The papacy was a tool of the Roman nobility; venality and irresponsibility dissipated its lands; its judgments were scorned abroad; and the whole powerful structure that the great popes of the ninth century had brought to fulfillment lay in ruins. The period of growth seemed then to have ended in blight, with neither flower nor fruit.

The great days of a united Christendom had yet to come. The Gregorian reform movement of the late eleventh century shook the papacy free of bondage to Roman nobility, and reestablished the credit of its judgments by purifying the life of the popes and their court and systematizing the study and enforcement of canon law. Furthermore, by means of new administrative methods, it reestablished a secure economic and political base in Italy. Imposing their moral and jurisdictional reforms on the entire Church, the reformers resumed the creation of a papal monarchy. A succession of brilliant, learned, and strong popes welded Christendom into a true administrative, jurisdictional, and legislative unity, governed by the pope through a tightly organized clergy.

This period, in which Christendom supremely gave a fundamental unity to medieval culture, reached its peak under Pope Innocent III (reigned 1198–1216). His consolidation of temporal authority around Rome; his victories over John of England, Philip Augustus of France, and rival claimants to the imperial crown; his patronage of the fourth Crusade; and his presidency over the Fourth Lateran Council (1215) all showed the medieval pope at his prime. He was a serene governor at home, an arbiter of kings abroad, commander-in-chief of military Europe, and supreme ruler of the universal Church.

The Breakdown of Christendom

But cracks had already begun to appear again in the fabric of Christendom. Philosophers had begun to reexamine the basic principles of Christianity with new techniques of reasoning imported from the Islamic world. Anticlericalism raged; heresies abounded; a non-Christian religion, Catharism, took hold of Provence and Languedoc. Christendom answered with repression: it established the Inquisition; burned heretics; and rooted out the Cathari with fire and sword in a war of more than fifty years.

Dissenters, not the papacy, heralded a new age. Having spent its great strength in local wars during the thirteenth century, the papacy limply held to its monarchic rule. Its power was challenged and bridled by kings, abused by great prelates, condemned and repudiated by pious sects that spread like locusts across Europe. Much of what survived of Christendom's unity crumbled as a result of three events: the "Babylonian Captivity" of the popes—their long residence in Avignon (1305–1378) as satellites of the

French court; the Great Schism (1378–1409), in which the rivalry of two lines of popes, one in Rome and the other in Avignon, tore the religious loyalties of Europe; and finally the Conciliar Epoch (1409–1447), in which an international council acted for a time as the true superior of the pope. The papacy irreparably destroyed its own credit for impartiality and righteousness among the faithful, and with it, the credit of the clergy as a whole. Its power and repute diminished, its administrative apparatus segmented by temporal rulers, the papacy became a Renaissance prince-dom, sunk in luxury, devoted to enjoying the earth. The unity of Christendom had vanished, and the course was set for the religious fragmentation of the Reformation.

NEW CHALLENGES TO THE TRADITION

How does this view, with its emphasis on linear development – the organic process of growth, flowering, and decay – fall short?

For all its clarity and interpretive value, this approach obscures the rich, densely woven texture of the age. The "serial history" view is really a montage, an eclectic blend of currents: the barbarian invasions which did change all Europe, the rise of cities especially in Italy and Flanders, the conflict of Church and State (especially in the dispute between the German kings and the popes), and finally, the growth of feudal monarchies in France and England. This synthesis does not keep the whole map of Europe in sight; it shifts and blends its geographical centers of gravity. By doing this, it indicates uniformity where in fact there was enormous diversity, and continuity where the history of the period shows not logical sequence, valid for all Europe, but a chaotic tracery of social experiences that varied from place to place and from age to age.

The enormous amount of research that the period has attracted, especially in the last thirty years, shows that the Renaissance idea of a "Middle Age" as refurbished by modern scholars is inadequate. Scholars sidestep the term, and the idea of uniformity it carries with it, with new phrases; *Europe Emerges, The Birth of Europe*, and *Medieval Centuries* are among the most elegant of these attempts. Scholars have confronted a vast period – longer than the life of the Byzantine Empire, and more than twice as long as the period between the Reformation and the present – in which there is no one pattern of social development. Classical feudalism in the Île-de-France, with its ordered pyramid of lords and vassals, was not the same as feudalism in Hungary; indeed, some scholars contend that Hungary never knew the fief. What is true of the conflict of Church and State in Germany does not inevitably apply to other countries. In fact, in one plausible view, Italy's peculiar social and political development makes it impossible to consider Italy part of medieval Europe at all.

Scholars are coming to the view that the dilemma of understanding what went on in medieval Europe cannot be solved by a "medieval synthesis," and that the correct approach is through a complex set of syntheses. We cannot speak of Europe as a cultural unit; we are really involved in a problem of local history, and the years that set off the beginning and the end of the "Middle Ages" are only brackets that confuse the real issues. Historians no longer concern themselves chiefly with the problems of dynasties and government at the highest level; they have come to understand that the issues we seek to define have meaning, not primarily in terms of days or years, but in terms of their relationships to each other. (The words "civilization" and "culture" are too ambiguous to describe what we are after, since, for example, we can follow recent scholars in speaking of French or Spanish or Balkan civilization or of the two civilizations in England and Italy during the thirteenth century.) Dynasties and battles have moved from the center of the historian's stage; they have given way to what Teilhard de Chardin called "the phenomenon of man."

No unique "medieval synthesis" corresponds with the facts; there was no one, evolutionary civilization in medieval Europe. The set of syntheses toward which scholarship is moving can best be described as the experience of man in Europe, empirical, improvised, and fortuitous. And of this multifaceted complex there can never be one exclusively correct history.

The World Historical Approach

Some historians have chosen to define European man in terms of world history, and to ask what place the medieval West had in the general progress of mankind. This viewpoint can tell us much. All the dominant peoples of Europe were at some stage invaders; the learned language of medieval Europe was a dead tongue — for northern peoples it was also a foreign import; and both it and the living languages of the day were written in alphabets derived from ancient Phoenicia; Christianity, the dominant religion, was alien, and its conquest of men's minds required uprooting indigenous gods, religious practices, and value systems. Medieval thinkers were very conscious that learning had passed from Egypt and Babylon to the Greeks, from them to the Romans, and thence to all the West. Obviously, the true limits of European history extend beyond the continent. The issue from the world-historical point of view is how the remote and sparsely settled western tip of the Eurasian continent slowly developed a cultivated form of life — how, in Professor Hodgson's words, the zone of "urbanized, literate civilization" expanded to include Europe — and how Europe in time surpassed the older and once far more advanced societies of the Middle East and the Orient, and finally came to dominate them. At the beginning of the period, the European peninsula was dotted with nomadic and unlettered tribes; at its end, in the fifteenth century, Russia was tentatively beginning to expand southward over the steppes, and the countries on the peninsula's Atlantic rim were sending out the forerunners of those great fleets that discovered and mastered a new world and ultimately sub-dued the fabled East. By what steps did this transformation occur? What is its setting in the broadest framework of human history?

Until the eleventh century, as we have seen, Europe was a cultural melting pot of peoples from the East. From about 1100 on, Europe moved eastward; the westward flow of culture was in a degree reversed, until, in the fifteenth century, Westerners sought to reach the East by sailing west. The Crusades took Westerners through the Balkans, the Levant, and Egypt. Nearer home, colonization pressed the borders of northern European culture to the Russian frontier.

Fundamental as this new direction was, it takes second place from the vantage point of world history: far more essential was the intensification of social orders within western Europe which made this outward expansion possible and brought its peoples to almost universal dominance. In Europe, as in no other civilized area of the world, military and commercial inter-ests evolved in sharp opposition. Medieval cities and towns were isolated enclaves in a vast forest of feudality; and feudalism in its western Europe-an forms peculiarly hampered the general growth of commerce. Though princes founded and conferred liberties upon individual commercial cen-ters, the overall picture was one of disruptive tolls, confiscation of goods, and impressment of persons. As population expanded in Europe, communi-cation became increasingly easy. Distances consequently narrowed; and the friction between commerce and feudality grew more intense. The result was a movement unique in the history of the world: the Commercial Revo-lution, the explosive effects of which brought European states to the thresh-old of absolutism and mercantilism at home and, abroad, to the threshold of Empire.

This is the general scheme of things as the world historians would have us see it. Its great value lies in tracing the course of cultural diffusion over long distances and through great periods of time; in pointing up by com-parative method the aspects of man's life in Europe that were singular; and, above all, it undercuts the received tradition of a unitary medieval society by emphasizing the dynamic forces present in the social and cultur-al divisions in Europe.

The Sociological Approach

A second body of scholarly opinion is developing which sharpens this attack by probing deeply into the complexities of life in Europe: that is, the judgment of sociologists and — especially as regards the earliest stages of medieval societies — anthropologists. Their outlook complements that of historians. A broad distinction is that historians rely ultimately on written sources, stress events — singly or in sequence — as unique steps in change, and discuss their conclusions in narrative form. Sociologists and anthropol-ogists, however, make their own sources by direct observation, deal chiefly with the broad questions of cultural unity, and state their findings in the descriptive manner of a laboratory report interspersed with narrative sections. Unable to make field observations, medievalists can be hybrids: historical anthropologists or social historians.

Just as European archaeologists, philologists, and historians in the nineteenth century uncovered the ancient cultures of the Middle East and gave them their proper place in the progress of mankind, so today scholars who approach European history with sociological and anthropological techniques are discovering for the first time the inner bonds and the vast diversity of medieval society. They have reopened the fundamental questions that earlier scholars considered settled once and for all. The issues of freedom, semibondage, and slavery are being redefined. The idea of feudalism has come under such sharp attack that more than one scholar has expressed the wish that the word could be blotted out. The origin of the lower nobility, the grounds of religious motivation, and the essential bonds of society and government are now being seen as aspects of a culture (or cultures) nearly as foreign as ancient Babylon's to that of modern Europe.

These historians need not recall the still more remote day when the hippopotamus stalked the lower Rhine and volcanoes blighted Burgundy to evoke an exotic past and a scale of change. They need only point to the normal aspects of medieval life that have vanished. The languages of some of Europe's conquering tribes—Langobardic, Vandalic, Gothic, and Old Prussian—have perished except for the smallest literary fragments. *Chansons de geste* are no longer written; they find admirers only among students of medieval literatures. Slavery, famine, plagues, piracy, brigandage, monasticism as a widely followed mode of life, and bishops as governors and generals have all subsided. How long has it been since the leper's bell was heard in the streets of Paris? How many affairs of state are now submitted to trial by ordeal? How many of our contemporaries have seen a woman burned to death for witchcraft?

For the sociologist, unlike the world historian, the essential thing about medieval Europe is not its place in the general flow of history; that place must be kept in view, but more critical is the uniqueness of man's experience and the special ways in which medieval men understood and reacted to their world. The great intellectual father of historical sociologists, Max Weber, distinguished modern life from the medieval by saying that the world had gradually been stripped of magic. He referred not merely to the magic of relics, omens, and religious or superstitious practices, but to a highly complex conviction that what was empirically true, and demonstrable by reason, could be transcended or cancelled out by a higher truth. Miracles could divert the normal course of events at every level of existence.

Thus, it is not surprising to discover that medieval men, despite their veneration of custom and tradition, had no scruples about rewriting history itself and tampering with actual sequences of events to make them suit what they believed should have happened. Indeed, when we examine medieval intellectual and legal life, we find that the roots in many places go directly back to blatant forgeries. In theology, there is the treatise of Dionysius the Areopagite, a keystone for medieval thought on the nature of God and of man's relation to Him. In Church order, the ninth-century forgeries of Pseudo-Isidore and Benedictus Levita were outstanding. In devotional matters, we find an enormous library of forged hagiographical documents, and treasure rooms throughout Europe crammed with fabricated relics. In law and political thought, one need refer only to the specious Donation of Constantine, and to the fabrications that adorned every great muniment room in the West, of which the *Privilegium Maius* forged in the fourteenth century for Rudolf IV of Austria is perhaps the best known. Nor were the forgers all obscure, embittered men. Great and learned men, archbishops of Rheims and Canterbury and Cologne, imperial chancellors, even clergy of the papal court, played the game.

How are we to draw a cultural profile of man in medieval Europe — who was bound to a religion that upheld truth above all else, who was led commercially, politically, culturally, and militarily by the clergy of that religion, and yet for whom, in every aspect of life, a capricious transcendency made it right to falsify the past?

The sociologists therefore present us with two problems: first, describing life as it really was in medieval Europe and second, studying how medieval men understood the world.

ONE RESPONSE TO THE CHALLENGES

Fortunately, sociologists also give us keys for solving these problems, or at least for setting them out in logical order for study. The substance of the work that follows is an application of their questions to medieval evidence.

It may be useful to mention the chief categories sociologists provide for drawing cultural profiles, and to suggest some issues that these points raise for the person interested in medieval history. In them, the traditional approach to medieval history receives its sharpest blows.

A New Religion in Old Societies

The first category is religion. Belief that the natural order could be, and often was, changed by divine intervention led medieval man to fill his life with rituals meant to affect the physical world, economic activities, or the social structure. Religion made him feel bigger than life; in his eyes, it gave him a handhold on his destiny. If, however, we try to set a religious norm for the age, a list of beliefs and practices essential to "the Age of Faith," we are likely to founder. Whom, or whose practices, could we choose as typical? St. Thomas Aquinas, with his vast learning and merciless reason on one hand, and his sensuous mysticism, his belief in demons and angels, on the other? St. Francis of Assisi, with his beautiful, animistic faith and his frank masochism? The Italian villagers who killed St. Romuald to keep so holy a man from leaving them and to secure for themselves a heavenly patron? The followers of the "apostolic movements" that the organized Church of the day declared heretical, with their lives of self-renunciation and, in some instances, of ritualized homosexuality?

The variety of medieval religious experience is even greater when we remember how slowly the conversion of Europe to Christianity progressed. As late as the fourteenth century, the prince of Europe's largest state, Lithuania, was a pagan; in the thirteenth century indigenous religions survived in the Baltic area, with their sacred groves, their idols, and, in some cases, their human sacrifices. Even in regions farther to the west, where the ebb and flow of belief had—far from inevitably—settled on the side of Christianity, native practices continued under a thin crust of new ritual. For example, the holy wells in England, Wales, and Alsace draw devotees to the present day. Shrines were destroyed, but the same sacred places, covered with churches, claimed the devotions of the people. Even the ancient gods survived in special areas of society's collective memory; until modern times, the English kings preserved the pagan genealogy that traced their descent from Wotan, an illuminating confusion of the god with the third-century King Woden.

For the sociologist, man's religious experience in medieval Europe is a provocative instance of a new religion in an old society. The distinctive "hall churches" of England and northern Germany, to take one example from architecture, show the survival of an indigenous type of sacred building turned to the service of the new cult. In much the same way, the great legends of medieval Europe have been seen as a popular recall of the native practices. The heroic enchanters, Morgan le Fay and Merlin, it is plausibly argued, are not the creations of overheated fancy, but the relics of ancient belief that still claimed the hearts of medieval men. Indeed, the entire Arthurian cycle has been interpreted as the bequest of a primitive natural religion and the related story of Parcifal and the quest for the Holy Grail as evidence of a secret ritual of a fertility cult. Similar views apply to the famous *Niebelungenlied,* which, though composed in the lifetime of that paragon of medieval Christianity, Pope Innocent III, sings of Siegfried, the Valkyries, and the gods of the German North.

If we are to sketch a cultural profile of medieval Europe that corresponds at all with the facts, we must discard the stereotype which equates Europe with Christendom. We must include paganism and pagan survivals in the account of man's religious experience, and try to see where further cultic or regional distinctions may be made.

Medieval Social Structure: Regionalism

The sociologists give us a second category of analysis: social structure. This is even more elusive than religion, for it includes many complex and diverse elements: the influence of neighboring peoples upon societies, the quality and range of economic activity, the scope and efficiency of technology, and most important, the ordering of society by class and by life cycle.

As in considering religion, the important thing to keep in sight here is that we are dealing with old societies in new political orders, the emerging principalities and kingdoms, that bound together tribal and subtribal groups. Attitudes toward other societies and scales of right and wrong continued the views of the tribes that invaded and settled Europe, long after the tribal structure itself had withered away. The distinctions between tribes gave rise to many intense social differences that made the progress of Europe for most of the medieval period a matter of local history. On the broadest scale, this fragmentation appears in the weakness of central government and the troublesome offspring of the conquering tribe that we call feudalism. The political center of gravity was local. Real power lay with the vassal, who often would repudiate his obligations to the lord and withdraw to his own petty domain. Kings were remote figures; the effective centers of government were not glittering royal courts, but the grim little castles that pocked the face of Europe.

This general disunity existed, however, within a framework of regional groupings that were expressed in one way by general homage to kings, and in other ways by peculiar art forms and patterns of settlement. The contrast of France above the Loire, and especially above the Dordogne, with the region south of it suggests the sort of distinctions we have in mind. North of the Dordogne, the three-field system dominated farming, and an irregularly nucleated village, often in the flatland and unwalled, was the normal settlement pattern. In the south, the two-field system dominated, and the usual settlement pattern was a compact village on a defensible position, such as a hill, with isolated buildings scattered in hedged fields. Northern France was the homeland of Gothic architecture; Romanesque is the principal style in the south, where Gothic appeared only in the fifteenth and sixteenth centuries, a timid latecomer. Customary, or "feudal," law prevailed in the North; Roman law, modified by the practices of the Visigoths, ruled the South. Northerners spoke the *langue d'oil;* southerners, the *langue d'oc.* (There is a transitional region, where the two cultures blend, as in the Limagne, where the Gothic of the town churches clashes with the predominantly Romanesque environment.)

These diverse culture traits reflect ancient social differences, and thus the impact of different influences. Equally distinct patterns appear throughout Europe—especially in Spain and Portugal, in northern, southern, and eastern Germany, and in northern, central, and southern Italy. These regional and linguistic groupings have a cohesion of their own, which corresponds with idiomatic ways of conducting life from birth to death, distinctions of class and status, forms of property tenure, and modes of commercial life.

When we think of medieval Europe, we normally think of castles and fortified cities. But medieval Europe built no fortification to compare with the Great Wall of China, nor even any like Hadrian's Wall or the German *limes.* A fortification the length of the Great Wall of China would have run from Constantinople to the Gulf of Finland, or from Paris to Athens; but Europe lacked the cultural and political unity to build one. Instead, Europe raised local walls against local enemies. The ethnic cultures which entered Europe with the invading tribes proliferated, survived the tribes, and hardened into permanent groupings that lacked a greater unity. This in itself is one of the most critical issues with which the medievalist must come to grips: why did this hardening occur? Why did prospects for cultural unification of Europe reach a specific level and then atrophy? The answer must surely lie in an examination of the impact of cultural groups upon their neighbors; and we must try to find out what gave those groups their cohesion and what barriers they found to the communication of goods, men, and ideas.

Environment

The third great key sociologists provide for setting the cultural profile of medieval man in Europe is environment. Since the sixteenth century, some historians and, more recently, sociologists have seen environment as the determining factor in culture. Other scholars assign it a permissive role, for they maintain that environment does not compel men to follow set courses, but rather offers them options that they may take up or reject. Ancient Crete became a maritime power; Corsica and Sardinia, with comparable resources and shorelines, never developed even the most modest of fleets. By virtue of excellent irrigation systems, Babylon built a high civilization with great cities and lively trade in the desert. Despite the presence of the same potentialities, Babylonia is now an arid waste.

We can perhaps steer a middle course between the environmental determinists and the "permissivists" by keeping to the instances in which man tried to take up an environmental option, only to find the topography or climate had changed. There is good reason to suppose that a considerable change in climate affected Europe during the thirteenth century. Before that time, vineyards were cultivated in England and Poland, and the Venerable Bede tells us that there was "no lack of vines" in Ireland; afterwards, viticulture as a widespread industry failed there and withdrew to what we know as more clement areas, together with other crops that require mild climate.

Perhaps the most dramatic environmental changes affected Europe's waterways, the greatest of all communication networks. Let us take these changes as paramount examples of what was at stake. The rivers of Europe changed their courses, leaving some landing stages high and dry; and some of them carried tons of silt to their mouths, ruining harbors such as those of Bruges and Narbonne and destroying the glowing prospects as a maritime center that Louis IX had envisaged for his new city, Aigues-Mortes. The unpredictable sea took its toll. Consider England. Chichester Cathedral preserves two sculpture panels allegedly from a Saxon cathedral that stood a mile from Selsey, at a site now far beneath the waves. The sea gate at Harlech castle now opens onto vast dunes; the sea itself is a half mile away. Since the thirteenth century, about a dozen once prosperous villages on Yorkshire's North Sea shore have been washed away. These examples of settlements devastated either by the sea's retreat or by its advance could be multiplied. But the fate of the Cinque Ports is perhaps most instructive of all. These five, and later seven, ports, from Dover down to Winchelsea, were important harbors for landing goods from France and Sandwich, which had been part of the Roman coastal defenses and served as the mouth of an inland waterway that ran from the Channel to London. In return for providing ships and services by agreement, they enjoyed special privileges from the Crown. A prosperous league developed, dominated by the five original members and Rye and Winchelsea, together with about thirty lesser ports. Of all these, only Dover harbor is still usable.

The sea was already lapping the market place of Winchelsea in 1262. Conditions grew worse. In February 1287, a terrifying storm drove the river Rother into a new course. Its mouth at Romney was blocked, and it entered the sea at Rye. Broomhill, a member of the league that lay between Winchelsea and Rye, vanished beneath the waves, and gradual silting destroyed Romney, Winchelsea, and Rye as seaports. They now stand about a mile from the sea, and Sandwich, ruined by another silting process, is two miles from open water.

This was the work of the turbulent North Sea, which also claimed many victims on its continental shores. The twelfth-century chronicler, Helmold, describes a storm of hurricane proportions in 1164 that flooded the entire coastland from Frisia to the lowlands of the Elbe and Weser. "Many thousands of men," he wrote, "and innumerable animals drowned." The great storms that changed the Rother's course also drove a flood along the Ems basin, drowning a city named Torum and washing away a great stretch of land with about fifty villages. Another series of storms rendered a service to the Hollanders in their efforts to reclaim land from the sea; for it closed off and filled a great bay, changing the city of Leeuwarden from harbor to inland town, but adding a vast tract of land for eventual settlement and cultivation.

The North Sea is notorious for its extreme tides and for the violence of its storms. But even in the quieter waters of the Baltic and the Mediterranean, alluvial deposits from rivers filled harbors and destroyed maritime centers.

There is more than geographical interest in these silted harbors, swamped villages, and changed river courses. What we have seen in the case of the Cinque Ports, for example, meant the total readjustment of commercial patterns in the southeast section of England. The memory of the burgesses of Winchelsea struggling with their seawalls for twenty years, hoping against hope to keep the sea out of their marketsquare, houses, and churches, evokes an admiring compassion. It was a pathos shared at the time by all tradesmen who used Winchelsea as a port of entry, by all for whom it was a center of communication and administration, and by King Edward I, whose services due from the port were in jeopardy and whose tolls from it fell by nearly one third in the year 1272–1273, and continued to decline. The major ports of southern Kent and Sussex were being driven toward extinction, a matter of the gravest possible concern. The decay of the Cinque Ports, the disasters along the continental coast of the North Sea, the silting up of harbors, and the shifting of river courses all required drastic reorientation of trade, public order, and density of settlement. They remind us in a special way that the map of Europe changed greatly during the medieval period, and they forcibly add the dimension of environment to the broad question of communication among the social structures of medieval Europe.

THE MEDIEVAL "SYNTHESIS" REEVALUATED

When we bring all these points to bear, what is left of the received tradition that argues for social and cultural unity? The greatest shortcoming of the received position is also its most fundamental assumption: that Latin Christendom was a unit whose history was inextricably bound up with the fate of the papacy. Taking Roman judgments as its norm, it classes as aberrations "heresies" that broke away from papal headship and religious phenomena which, like paganism, were altogether outside the Church. It is content to register peculiarities in liturgy and order within the Roman communion as separate members of the same biological family, with about the same effect as saying that whales and bats are both mammals. It therefore smooths over important cultural differences and idiomatic expressions of faith in the interest of a homogeneous and esthetically balanced—but sharply slanted—interpretation. The picture that emerges from modern studies of heresy in the later medieval period gives us an idea of medieval Christianity that is very different from the conventional view. Instead of having the papacy grow in stature as the keystone of Christendom to be suddenly shaken in the thirteenth century and brought crashing down in the fourteenth, we now see that the Roman communion ran neck and neck with heresy throughout the medieval period, and that they waxed in strength at the same time. Indeed, we are now beginning to understand that if anything gave a *Leitmotiv* to religious history in this period, it was not the decorous counterpoint of papal government, but the clangor of schism.

The chief flaw in the synthetic interpretation of medieval religion is this: it distorts facts by insisting on a continuous serial history. The view that seems likely to supersede it insists not on one history, but on a set of episodes or a complex set of continuous, interlocking, but separate histories.

Even so, the conventional view is the mother of the still unweaned comparative approach. It is like the exploratory trench that archaeologists dig at the beginning of an excavation to test the size and character of the

16

site; very much remains to be done. But the traditional view has given a substantial base for comparison in future work. In emphasizing the administrative, jurisdictional, and legislative order of the Church, a structure dominated by the bishops of Rome, it has given us an admirable understanding of one formalistic side of Christianity: that is, of conservative forces or what could be called religious statics—Latin Christianity as an institution.

Against this base, future scholars will compare their work on the forces of change, religious dynamics, and Christianity as a way of life. While dissenters surged against the Church's formalistic walls, many kinds of religious experience in paganism and magic flourished outside the Church; and all this we shall have to understand, not as exceptions to the rule, but as separate and autonomous rules of life.

With the illusion of religious unity dispelled, we are left with the allegation that Europe was a single political, economic, and social organism. How does this part of our tradition fare?

Its first two time brackets—the fall of Rome in the West and the establishment of the Carolingian Empire—show the geographical center of gravity for advocates of cultural unity: an axis between Flanders and Lombardy.

For the earliest age, the generalist distinction ignores all Europe beyond the Roman imperial borders of the Rhine and the Danube. We are reminded that the lands so excluded were the stage on which some of medieval history's greatest dramas were played, and that there the area of the Holy Roman Empire increased by three fifths after 1150. The vast areas beyond the *limes,* Roman military borders, did not know the crisis of imperial decay; their history falls outside the familiar pattern. Similarly, Charlemagne (d. 814) and his empire did not really matter to Muslim Europe, pagan Europe beyond the Elbe, and the part of Christian Europe that belonged to the eastern rites. Frankish affairs were peripheral to them and Charlemagne's kingdom, on the outermost edge of the world. It is perhaps misleading even in the history of the Flanders-Lombardy axis to overemphasize the great Charles' achievement as ending the period of political turmoil that the barbarian invasions opened and welding Latin Christendom into a cohesive unity. His realm was not a centrally administered, monolithic state, but a confederation of tribes, each with its own language, laws, and patterns of authority. Lombard Italy with its high level of learning and social structure and Saxony with its primitive tribal order had little in common but personal obedience to Charles. Within the Frankish lands there was enormous diversity. The East was underdeveloped and lightly populated. It fell under a new military organization of marches, which had the difficult task of ruling still savage tribes. The West, including the Rhineland, inherited the old civil order of Roman provincial culture. It had such cities as there were, and enjoyed a settled agrarian economy. Government was a local matter throughout the realm, and even Charlemagne was unable to suppress entirely the separatist movements of a bludgeoned Saxony or Bavaria, to bring the Spanish March under his effective control, or to discipline the independent strain in papal thought.

The historical, cultural, and political heterogeneity of this "imperial confederation" asserted itself in the splintering of the empire after Charles' death. Particularism triumphed.

The Commercial Revolution

The long movement called the "Commercial Revolution" involved chiefly the textile industry and, above all, the growth and use of wool. There were three great centers of this industry: in England, through the Midlands and along the east coast from Lincolnshire to London and Portsmouth; in Flanders and northern France, a rectangle with corners at Cologne, Bruges, Avranches, and Orleans; and, in northern Italy, a triangle cornering at Venice, Milan, and Florence and bending a bit to include Genoa, Lucca, and Pisa. There were other scattered centers: along the coastal fringe in south France, in northeastern Spain, and along the Rhine-Danube line. But the history of the Commercial Revolution is primarily the story of trade in cloth and raw woolens between England and the Flemish and Italian complexes.

The Baltic was a secondary center of the Revolution. There, the Hanse played the chief role, and not cloth, but the natural resources of the region — timber, grain, furs, wax, and the like — were the principal commodities. Again, we have to deal with a relatively small area, the rim of the Baltic and the coastal plain of Saxony. Behind them was a vast agricultural hinterland which was dominated by military classes, not by townsmen. The wealth of the textile centers continued and increased over a long space of time; but the greatness of the Baltic was both achieved and passed during the fourteenth century. Trade declined in the inland towns; cities to the west refused to become involved in Scandinavian politics; the age of general prosperity was slowly ending, step by step.

Did not the power and business interests of these centers spread the effects of the Revolution through the rest of Europe? Certainly, there was a diffusion of manufacturing techniques and credit institutions through city leagues like the Hanse, the Swabian League, and the Rhenish league that were organized for defense and trade.

But another effect was to sharpen regionalism. The city leagues were exclusive organizations, designed to benefit their members and to combat competition. Individual cities had guilds whose whole purpose was to monopolize every advantage of the marketplace and to exclude such alien merchants or manufacturers as they wished. Freedom to trade was severely limited in Hanse cities as it was in Venice, where aliens were forced to buy and sell and ship through the good offices of Venetian middlemen. These were extreme cases, but restrictions of the same sort, if not of the same degree, were universal. Despite their transcontinental trade, and their search for ever more distant markets, the cities remained monopolistic and insular in their economic views. *Laissez faire* was not for them.

A sharp contrast in fact set apart these few and relatively small areas of the Commercial Revolution from the great mass of agrarian Europe, ignorant of the smooth highways of capitalist economy and still following the short, narrow path of barter. The occasional peddler, the commercial buyer in search of animal products, the small hustling moneylender, and the agent of a great company farming out its weaving all brought some fruits of the movement to the countryside. But the impact of this sort of dealing was occasional, faint, and limited to areas near cities.

Lombardy, Tuscany, the northwestern corner of Europe, and the Baltic coast reaped the fruits that followed the commercial flowering, whose great—and nearly its only—beneficiaries were the cities of the plain.

Cultural and Economic Patterns

No one denies the brilliance of intellectual achievement in the twelfth and thirteenth centuries. It is hard to overrate the age that saw the birth and high development of the Gothic style, the splendid synthesis of St. Thomas Aquinas and its no less admirable rejection in the next century by William of Ockham (d. 1349), and magnificent works in vernacular literature. But here, too, it is wrong to cast a golden haze over the whole map of Europe. We have to deal with localized phenomena.

The area of pure Gothic, which we tend to think of as the "international style" of the Middle Ages, was limited. Gothic hardly touched central and southern Italy, parts of northeastern Germany, southern France, and Iberia. Where it did appear in these regions, it was translated into wholly new idioms.

The intellectual world in which St. Thomas and William of Ockham moved was in fact elitist and thus narrow. Further, our geographical axis is now extended to run from Canterbury to Rome; its center of balance is still Paris. Great cathedral schools flourished in the eleventh and twelfth centuries at Chartres and Orleans; law was taught brilliantly at Montpellier. But Paris was the fountainhead of philosophy and theology—Abelard, Gilbert de la Porrée (d. 1154), Peter Lombard (d. 1160), Richard of St. Victor (d. 1173), Otto of Freising (d. 1158), and all the major figures of intellectual activity in the twelfth century drank from it. The same was true in the thirteenth century. Oxford and Cologne were important secondary centers; Bologna became the counterpart to Paris in the study of law and theology, and a rash of new universities sprang up in northern Italy to second it.

Vernacular literature is a special case. Like any personal achievement, vernacular writings were limited in time, place of origin, and special environmental factors: for Dante (d. 1321), civil turmoil in Florence; for Wolfram von Eschenbach (fl. 1220), the life of the petty nobility at Herman of Thuringia's court; for Chrétien de Troyes (fl. 1180), the taste of the more exalted courts of Champagne and Flanders. What do they bring to our immediate concern? The wide popularity that these works enjoyed is as weighty a factor as the particular circumstances of their composition. Does this not run against an argument for regionalism by proving a broad community of taste? On the other hand, the particularist rightly answers that use of the vernacular in itself proves cultural fragmentation.

Let us now turn to the general pattern of cultural and economic decline in the fourteenth and fifteenth centuries. Did learning and commerce reach an apogee in the age of St. Thomas and then break into decline, gently about 1300 and sharply after the Black Death at the middle of the century?

Technical skills certainly saw no decline. The two last centuries of the Middle Ages saw the development of Gothic into its flamboyant stage, a style that perhaps compares unfavorably on the score of aesthetics with earlier Gothic forms, but that, at the same time, required the greatest imagination and craftsmanship. Magnificent palaces, churches, and public buildings were erected in this febrile taste throughout the predominately Gothic region and in Spain. Superb work was done in luxury goods such as tapestries, jewelry, figures in precious metals and enamels, and the like. The sumptuous courts of the dukes of Burgundy led the field in the exquisite and the ostentatious; but they had near rivals in the courts of Charles V (1364–1380) and Charles VI (1380–1422) of France, of the popes at Avignon, of English kings, and of the Holy Roman Emperors.

Furthermore, it is difficult to argue that the age of the Italian Renaissance was a time of universal decay. Dante (d. 1321) and Giotto (d. 1336), of course, died well before the middle of the fourteenth century. But Petrarch (d. 1374) and Boccaccio (d. 1375) lived until its last quarter; Brunelleschi (1377–1446) and Ghiberti (1374–1455) saw it end. There is no need to mention the giants of late fifteenth-century Italy: Leonardo, Alberti, Botticelli, and the others. England has its Gower (d. 1408), its Wycliff (d. 1384), its Chaucer (d. 1400); France, its Guillaume de Machaut (d. 1372), its Nicolas Oresme (c. 1320–1382). Ten new universities were founded in the fourteenth century; thirty-two in the fifteenth; and these had a far wider geographical distribution than earlier foundations.

The intellectual glory of these centuries was far more than the phosphorescence of decay. Whether it was less brilliant than the age of St. Thomas is a matter of subjective judgment.

Political history shows no more brilliant period than the fourteenth and fifteenth centuries, which, in Burkhardt's term, brought forth the state "as a work of art." In this period, the modern realms of Europe took shape ossifying the governmental fragmentation that survived from Europe's tribal period.

In economic history of the late Middle Ages, perhaps more than in any other field, recent studies warn us against generalization. The Hanse could be used to prove either case. It reached the height of its power and its greatest extent in the period 1356–1380, and then entered a period of "prosperous" decline. If we turn to the specific issue of depopulation, the checkerboard effect of the evidence becomes more apparent. In England, Devon and the Midlands lost heavily after the mid-fourteenth century. East Anglia, Lancashire, and Cheshire gained in population and in general prosperity. The Hurepoix, in France, was devastated; but the plain adjoining it flourished. The Upper Rhine—in the Black Forest, Württemberg, and Swabia—and parts of Thuringia saw great stretches of abandoned lands and villages; the Niederlausitz, Westphalia, and Flanders abounded in people and in wealth. Lower Lombardy thrived; Provence withered. As detailed studies accumulate, this pattern repeats itself for every region: parts of the area were depopulated, but others prospered. Generalization is all the more difficult, since decline began in different areas at different times, in some cases as far as 150 years apart. What is the emblem of late medieval economic history: the ladder that the enormously rich bankers, the Fuggers, took for a heraldic device or the abandoned village?

SUMMARY

We have been examining in this chapter the idea that Europe was a unitary society and that it followed a single course of organic growth and decline. While there is much value in this serial view, the exceptions we have mentioned indicate that it is in fact a kind of local history—a history of the Flanders-Lombardy axis—that discounts or labels as "aberrant" whatever events in other parts of Europe that do not fit the Flemish-Lombard pattern. Since Flanders and Lower Lombardy did not suffer heavy depopulation in the late Middle Ages, it looks beyond the axis for other standards at that point, perhaps to England and Tuscany. If we are prepared to say that regions outside Latin Christendom were not European (and thus that the eastern Baltic area joined Europe only after 1200, with the Christianization of the region, and that Granada became European in 1492 when the Muslim state fell to the Catholic kings); that the commercial and manufacturing center, rather than the agricultural village, was the cornerstone of medieval society; and that regional disasters of the late Middle Ages generally blighted both trade and intellect—then the view we have been discussing may stand without qualifications. But to accept that would be to ignore the rules of logic and the evidence of sociology.

If we are to understand the place of Europe in the great view of world history, and to see clearly how "urbanized, literate civilization" expanded into Europe, we must first take our cue from the sociologists and examine the religious, social, and environmental diversity of the "middle time." It is clear that this work will take us into a realm of myth and practice foreign, and in some ways repugnant, to the modern mind. We shall not find the sort of pluralistic society familiar to us, combining the most diverse forces—political, religious, and social—under a harmonizing rule of law. This was what medieval society led to, but not what it was. The stereotype of medieval Europe as a Christian and feudal unit can be laid to rest.

But should we discard the received tradition? Recent challenges to the conventional view force its modification, not its rejection. Many new studies argue for localism; older syntheses assume cultural homogeneity. Both approaches, however, overly emphasize either static conditions or uniform evolution; they tend to deal with the evidence as with stereotypes. A balanced view must rest on two elements. The first is an understanding that patterns of social evolution differed radically in different places – in Lombardy and Prussia, for example. The second is an appreciation that within each of these distinctive patterns two contrary processes were at work simultaneously: a conservative force that compacted localism, and an innovative spirit that impelled men toward a true European community. This is the sort of historical ambiguity that we see, to take one instance, at the end of our period when the growth of national churches subverted hopes of realizing a universal Church at the same time as the Conciliar Movement gave new life to those very hopes. The paradox of stratification and mingling concerns us especially; we must now look more closely at it. Because scholars agree that Europe did not know cultural unity before the eleventh century, most of our discussion will be devoted to the late Middle Ages.

SUGGESTED READING

General Bibliographies

Writing medieval history is an international enterprise, even though, for practical purposes, the reading lists that follow must be chiefly limited to works in English. Readers able to consult works in other languages will gain a fuller picture of current trends in scholarship. Bibliographies of works on national history have been compiled – such as Dahlmann-Waitz, *Quellenkunde der deutschen Geschichte,* 9th ed., 2 vols., 1931 (now being revised) – but they are all out of date. L. J. Paetow's *Guide to the Study of Medieval History* (New York, 1931, 1959; new edition in progress) inventories the principal source collections, periodicals, and some major studies.

But the only way to keep up with the increasing volume of scholarly literature is to consult bibliographical sections in major journals. The *Revue d'histoire ecclésiastique* publishes the most comprehensive of these, including books and articles in many languages and on all subjects. The *Deutsches Archiv* and the *Historische Zeitschrift* also print invaluable bibliographical data. In English, the principal sources are: The *American Historical Review, Church History, History,* and *Speculum.*

Texts in Translation

Reading source works gives spice to the study of medieval history, particularly the reading of such works as the Song of Roland, the Divine Comedy, or the great Goliardic poems. Many works have been translated into English, and the interested reader should consult C. P. Farrar and A. P. Evans, *Bibliography of English Translations from Medieval Sources,* New York, 1946. Three very important series devoted to translation are the University of Pennsylvania's

Translations and Reprints from the Original Sources of European History, Columbia University's *Records of Civilization*, and Nelson's *Medieval Classics*.

Comprehensive Studies

Three great series in English cover the Middle Ages: the *Cambridge Medieval History*, the first three volumes of the *Cambridge Economic History*, and the four relevant volumes in Methuen's *History of Medieval and Modern Europe* (in chronological sequence, by M. Deanesley, Z. N. Brooke, C. W. Previté-Orton, and W. T. Waugh). A new high-quality series, now underway, seems likely to displace the Methuen books. That is *A General History of Europe*, edited by Professor Denys Hay. Five volumes are to be devoted to the Middle Ages, and three of them have been published to date: A. H. M. Jones, *The Decline of the Ancient World*, New York, 1966; Christopher Brooke, *Europe in the Central Middle Ages, 962–1154*, New York (1964); and Denys Hay, *Europe in the Fourteenth and Fifteenth Centuries*, New York, 1966. On a smaller scale is Cornell's useful series, *The Development of Western Civilization*.

There are, additionally, a number of excellent single-volume syntheses, such as those by D. Hay, *The Medieval Centuries*, New York, 1964. R. S. Hoyt, *Europe in the Middle Ages*, New York, 1957; J. La Monte, *The World of the Middle Ages*, New York, 1949; Archibald Lewis, *Emerging Medieval Europe, A. D. 400–1000*, New York, 1967; J. B. Russell, *Medieval Civilization*, New York, 1968; C. Stephenson, *Medieval History*, 4th ed. by B. Lyon, New York, 1962; J. Strayer and D. C. Munro. *The Middle Ages, 395–1500*, 4th ed., New York, 1959.

Three very important and stimulating books in this class are: N. F. Cantor, *Medieval History, The Life and Death of a Civilization*, New York, 1963; R. S. Lopez, *The Birth of Europe*, New York, 1967; and R. Reynolds, *Europe Emerges: Transition Toward an Industrial World-Wide Society, 600–1750*, Madison, Wis., 1961.

Further Readings for Chapter I

On World History:
Hodgson, M. "Hemispheric Interregional History as an Approach to World History," *Cahiers d'histoire mondiale* 1 (1953–1954): 714-723.
McNeill, W. H. *A World History.* Oxford, 1967.
Reischauer, E. O., and Fairbank, J. K. *East Asia: The Great Tradition.* Boston, 1960.

On Periodization:
Bark, W. C. *Origins of the Medieval World.* Stanford, 1958.
Bean, J. M. W. *The Decline of English Feudalism, 1215–1540.* Manchester, 1968.
Lot, F. *The End of the Ancient World and the Beginnings of the Middle Ages.* London, 1931.
Hay, D. *Europe in the Fourteenth and Fifteenth Centuries.* New York, 1966.
Hay, D. *Europe: The Emergence of an Idea.* Edinburgh, 1957.
Lewis, A. R. *Naval Power and Trade in the Mediterranean, A. D. 500–1100.* Princeton, 1951.
Lewis, A. R. *The Northern Seas: Shipping and Commerce in Northern Europe, A. D. 300–1100.* Princeton, 1958.
Lopez, R. S. "Still Another Renaissance?" *American Historical Review* 57 (1951–1952): 1-21.
Lopez, R. S., and Miskimin, H. A. "The Economic Depression of the Renaissance," *Economic History Review* 14 (1961–1962): 408-426.

On Languages and Literatures:

Auerbach, E. *Literary Language and Its Public in Latin Antiquity and in the Middle Ages.* New York, 1965.

Bischoff, B. "The Study of Foreign Languages in the Middle Ages," *Speculum* 36 (1961): 209-224.

Bonfante, G. "Ideas on the Kinship of the European Languages from 1200 to 1800," *Cahiers d'histoire mondiale* 1 (1953–1954): 679-699.

Curtius, E. R. *European Literature and the Latin Middle Ages.* New York, 1953.

Jackson, W. T. H. *The Literature of the Middle Ages.* New York, 1960.

On Other Special Topics:

Artz, F. B. *The Mind of the Middle Ages.* Revised ed., New York, 1959.

Beresford, M. *The Lost Villages of England.* London, 1954.

Cheyette, F. L., ed. *Lordship and Community in Medieval Europe.* New York, 1968.

Cipolla, C. M. *Money, Prices, and Civilization in the Medieval World.* Princeton, 1956.

Coulborn, R., ed. *Feudalism in History.* Princeton, 1956.

Crump, C. G., and Jacob, E. F., eds. *The Legacy of the Middle Ages.* Oxford, 1926 (especially E. A. Lowe's comments on medieval scripts).

Ganshof, F. L. *Feudalism.* London, 1952.

Heer, F. *The Medieval World: Europe 1100–1350.* London, 1962.

Jones, Emrys. *Human Geography.* Revised ed., New York, 1965.

Jones, G. F. *The Ethos of the Song of Roland.* Baltimore, 1963.

Loomis, R. S. *Celtic Myth and Arthurian Romance.* Columbia, 1927.

Weston, J. L. *From Ritual to Romance.* Cambridge, 1920.

Chapter 2

Regionalism and Cultural Infiltration

The histories of China before the Revolution of 1911 and of ancient Egypt are told in terms of dynasties. The rise and fall of ruling houses gave the past its unifying theme; the regnal year—and in China the year period became an arbitrarily set space of time, short or long as the omens required—was the essential unit. In contrast, the history of the Byzantine Empire centers, not upon its dynasties, but upon the city of Constantinople itself. For the New Rome—as for the Old, whose past was reckoned in years of uniform length from the foundation of the city—its achievements shone in the religious, military, and administrative web of authority that centered on the capital. Its adversities struck in attacks upon the imperial city and in the more covert inroads of foreigners upon its trade. Its end was the fall of the city.

We can speak of China and Egypt as cultural units because their dynasties drew them together and gave them lasting bases of social cohesion. Rome and Byzantium found their cohesive elements in the life of their political and cultural capitals.

Medieval Europe, however, lacked any concrete unifying element to match these. Despite the expansion of kingdoms in the Middle Ages, Europe remained essentially a region of small principalities; and its characteristic settlement was not one great city, but the agricultural village in its many forms.

How can we explain this fragmentation? The task is all the more difficult in view of the fact that, despite great regional diversity, Western Europe in the Middle Ages did have an identity and a marked character. Very different societies flourished beyond the eastern frontiers of the Holy Roman Empire and south of the ever advancing borders of the Christian kingdoms in Spain. Geography, history, religion, language, and other cultural traits explain the curious world of Western Europe, which, although its sections had much in common, still was not a community. We turn first to the impact of geography.

BARRIERS OF REGIONALISM

Topography and Climate

Perhaps the most essential feature of European topography is dependence upon river basins as paths of transport and communication. The steppe lands sweep from Asia through Russia and come to an end in the westernmost part of the great plain of Western Europe, Belgium and northern France. From the Caucasus on, communication between this fertile, level area and the south is hindered by highlands and by great, serpentine mountain ranges that swirl through the Balkans and cut off Dalmatia, Italy, and the Iberian peninsula. In three areas these ranges act as defenses, encircling large, fertile river basins and demarking natural limits for settlement. Hungary, Bohemia, and Aragon owed their development to this condition. But, even in these three cases, natural defenses cut areas off partially from the outside, from peaceful influences as well as from hostile.

South of the great mountains, lesser ranges splintered the land. In Italy, the only extensive flatlands are in the Lombard Plain; smaller plains exist along the western coast, near Pisa, Rome, and Naples. The rest is the jagged hatching of the Apennines, with their irregular pattern of cliffs and remote valleys. In the Iberian peninsula, broad ranges running from east to west segment Spain and Portugal, leaving only an interrupted fringe of coastland along the Mediterranean, severing the entire peninsula from northern Europe, and chopping it so sharply into cellular units that even now the areas of Portugal, Aragon, and Castile preserve the distinctive characteristics that originally gave rise to their separate political orders.

Mountains impede physical communication; other geographical features affect the very quality of life. The climates of Spain range from subtropical in the south and southeast to the nine-month winter in parts of Old Castile. Italy receives its heaviest rains in the fall and early winter; the Danube basin has its maximum rainfall in June. The North Sea is turbulent; it has heavy fogs from October to March; and its high salt content, together with the warming effect of the Gulf Stream to the west, keeps it clear of ice. Its neighbor to the East, the Baltic, is by contrast normally quiet; it seldom has fogs; and its low salt content, reinforced by extremely low temperatures, allows all harbors to freeze over, some of them from November until March. The coastal plain along the North Sea, from Holland to western Germany, has a wet but clement oceanic climate; its extension along the Baltic, from Kiel eastward, has a dry, severe continental climate; ice normally closes the Rhine at Cologne only about twenty-one days each year; the Memel and the Vistula are usually frozen over for more than three months annually.

We could easily compile a long list of such contrasts: vegetation zones ranging from subtropical to arctic; snow covers varying from year-round to never; soil quality scattered from bogs to rich alluvial deposits to solid rock.

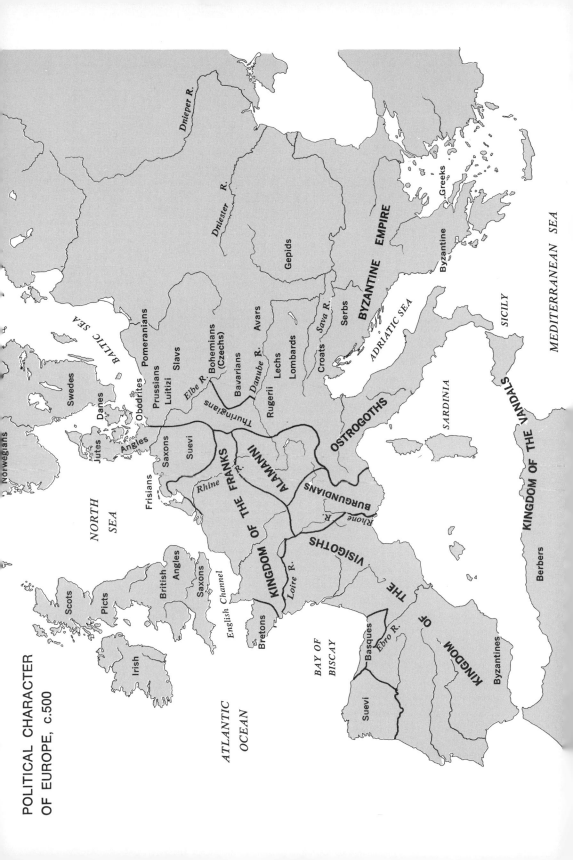

POLITICAL CHARACTER
OF EUROPE, c.500

Economic Implications

But what does all this mean? The importance of climate for commercial shipping is clear: river landings and seaports along the North Sea saw trade year-round, while their Baltic counterparts were shut for up to a quarter of the year. For broader implications, research on crop yield ratios gives a clue. The crop yield ratio tells us the proportion of grain sown to grain reaped, the return of the harvest to the investment of seed. Exact figures are of course not available for most areas before the modern period; cost accounting was not part of the medieval peasant's burden. A Dutch scholar, B. Slicher van Bath, has painstakingly gathered such evidence as there is: it begins for France, Catalonia, Tuscany, and the Lombard Plain about the year 800; for England, Ireland, Flanders, Frisia, and Holland in the thirteenth century; and for the rest of Europe, about 1500. The evidence is uneven in quality and in date; it is scattered and often inferential. Nevertheless, Professor Slicher has been able to show as regards cereal crops that Western Europe fell into four distinct yield areas. Perhaps the richest was the North Sea zone; followed closely by western and southern parts of Europe (France, Catalonia, and the Lombard Plain). Germany (that is, the area east of a line from Kiel to Strassburg), Switzerland, and Scandinavia composed a northern and central European growing area; and the lands from Czechoslovakia and Poland on, an eastern zone.

Many exceptions can be taken to these divisions. For example, the areas of Spain, Italy, and the Low Countries that had poor harvests have been left out of account. "France" means the region between the Loire, or even more the Seine, and the Rhine. Some areas in the countries mentioned — such as Switzerland — could not grow cereal crops at all. There are too many gaps in the evidence, as Professor Slicher himself says, to draw any but very general conclusions. But it would be wrong to discount the strong regionalization that the evidence does warrant. It allows us to distinguish more exactly than, for example, we could by setting olive-producing areas against lands where root crops predominated. We can say that even in the regions that produced and depended upon the same crops, variations in geography and climate made enormous differences in the proportion of investment to harvest, in the intensity and term of labor required. From this, it followed that ecology favored the small independent farmer in some areas where a small labor force brought success and the great landowner in others where much intensive labor was needed. Nature determined how crops could most advantageously be grown and harvested; the structure of society in a given area was determined largely by what produce could be grown and how labor was organized to cultivate it. Terrain was a critical element.

This partially explains why manorialism developed in some regions and not in others. There is a tendency in works of a general nature to treat the manor as a hallmark of the medieval world. In fact, as a mode of organizing labor, it suited only part of Western Europe, and of that part only sections at any given time. The work unit of the manor developed principally

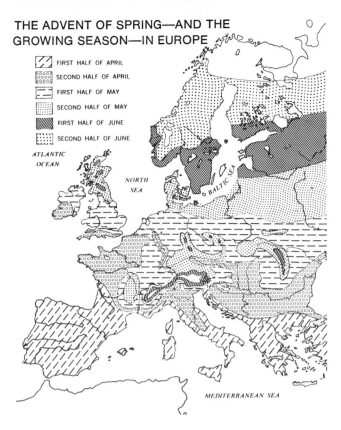

THE ADVENT OF SPRING—AND THE
GROWING SEASON—IN EUROPE

FIRST HALF OF APRIL
SECOND HALF OF APRIL
FIRST HALF OF MAY
SECOND HALF OF MAY
FIRST HALF OF JUNE
SECOND HALF OF JUNE

ATLANTIC
OCEAN

NORTH
SEA

BALTIC SEA

MEDITERRANEAN SEA

in grain-growing areas, and it produced enough food for subsistence and perhaps for small surpluses, but not enough to support large-scale trade with communities outside the manor. It belonged to a great landholder, a lord. Its essential feature was the village, and the chief business of villagers was the production of grain. The work went on all year because the seasonal rotation of crops and the heavy plow that characterized manorialism required vast fields, teams of oxen, and corps of workers. The manor was a large, isolated, self-sufficient cooperative farm.

Manorialism had no chance to develop where animal products were essential; for grazing, especially if it involved moving animals from valley to mountain pasturage in the summer, meant that villages had no stable population to tend to crop rotation. Thus, great parts of Spain, which were given over to sheep growing, and sections of Italy and the Alps, where the transhumance of cattle was a normal occupation, never knew the manor. Neither did regions that lacked broad, flat fields. Most of Italy except for the plains, the Iberian peninsula except for the extreme northeast part, and the Scottish highlands fall into this class. Terraced hillsides, poor soil, boggy land, or extremely dense forestation held the manor out of the Celtic areas (Ireland, Wales, parts of Scotland, and Brittany) and most of Scandinavia.

But more than terrain was involved. Manorialism was the answer of society at a particular level of development to the labor of food production.

It never spread widely in southern France because modes of land tenure and use there were efficiently regulated by Roman Law as it was expanded by indigenous custom; the manorial village would have been an artificial innovation contrary to existing and thoroughly viable institutions. The same is true of great parts of Italy, exhausted agriculturally even in the third century, where geography and climate were against the manor as well. Frisia, a land of villages, lacked both seigniorialism and manorialism. In Western Europe, the manor itself withered away when the object of cultivation ceased to be merely support of the manor and became production of great surpluses for trade with neighboring villages and towns. Commerce in the hands of tradesmen killed the manor there. Between 1200 and 1400 manorialism all but vanished from the areas of its classic pattern—the Low Countries, northern France, England, and northwestern Germany. And yet, just at that time, the manorial village in variant forms spread into the Baltic states, Poland, Hungary, and western Russia, where it was actually fostered by the growth of trade dominated not by a merchant class, but by the landed nobility.

Manorialism was a product of terrain acting upon society, not simply of one or the other. Furthermore, it is important to remember that, even in "manorial" areas, much land was not attached to manors; peasant alods (private lands not held by manorial or feudal tenure) were richly interspersed among seigniorial holdings.

The point to be made here is that ecology was a determining factor in the different ways medieval men organized themselves for the production of food, and consequently in the segmentation of medieval society.

Communication and Isolation

If terrain divided men, it also, in the waterways of Europe, offered them chains of communication. The Mediterranean, the Atlantic, and the northern seas were paths of travel that evaded the great mountain barriers and, as Viking exploits showed, potentially connected the ports around the whole European peninsula. From a very ancient time trade in amber had followed this route: from Samland on the Baltic, the principal source of amber, by sea into the Mediterranean. Amber traveled by other routes that followed Europe's rivers: from the Baltic to the Black Sea by way of the Vistula and the Dnieper, along the valley of the Elbe, from there down the Danube, and finally trailing the coastline to the mouth of the Rhine, down that great river, and thence along the Rhone and into the Mediterranean. Homer represents the Phoenicians as trading in amber; whether they went to the Baltic to get it is disputed.

Seas bypass the mountain ranges; rivers cut through them. Despite the formidable ranges of central Europe, the Rhine, the Elbe, and the Danube, with their tributaries, form a web of communication routes throughout the area. Similar connections exist among the Rhine and the great rivers of France; and, as the amber routes showed, the rivers were effective high-

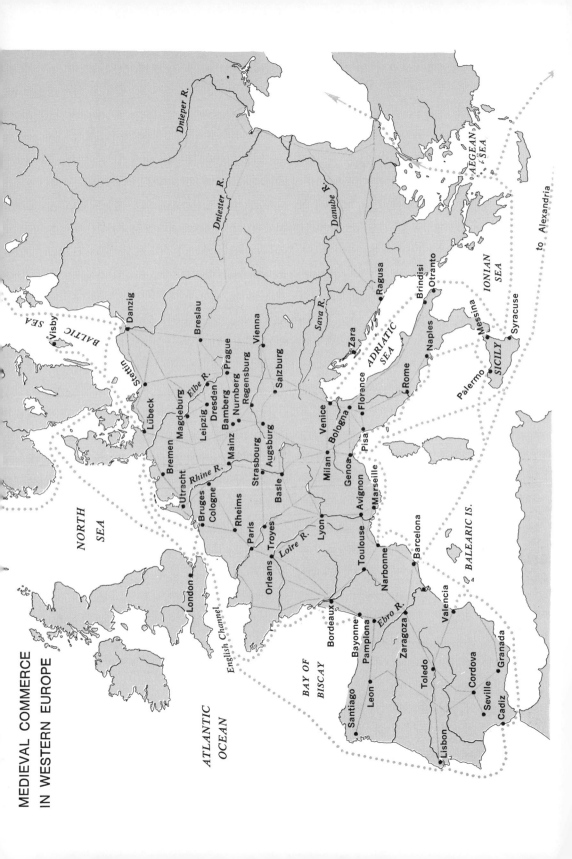

MEDIEVAL COMMERCE
IN WESTERN EUROPE

ATLANTIC
OCEAN

NORTH
SEA

BALTIC SEA

Visby

Danzig

Breslau

Stettin

Lübeck

Bremen

Magdeburg

Leipzig

Dresden

Prague

Bamberg

Nurnberg

Regensburg

Vienna

Salzburg

Elbe R.

Dnieper R.

Dniester R.

Danube R.

Sava R.

Ragusa

Zara

ADRIATIC
SEA

Brindisi

Otranto

Naples

Rome

Messina

SICILY

Palermo

Syracuse

IONIAN
SEA

AEGEAN
SEA

to Alexandria

Utrecht

Rhine R.

Cologne

Bruges

London

English Channel

Rheims

Paris

Mainz

Strasbourg

Augsburg

Basle

Venice

Bologna

Florence

Pisa

Genoa

Milan

Avignon

Marseille

Orleans

Troyes

Lyon

Loire R.

Toulouse

Narbonne

Barcelona

BALEARIC IS.

Valencia

BAY OF
BISCAY

Bordeaux

Bayonne

Pamplona

Ebro R.

Zaragoza

Santiago

Leon

Toledo

Cordova

Seville

Granada

Cadiz

Lisbon

ways between the most distant parts of Europe at every point of the compass.

There are many cryptic traces of these connections: the earliest British coins imitate a gold stater of Philip II of Macedon; stone crosses in Northumbria and Merovingian manuscript illuminations of the same period show heavy Byzantine influence, and, in fact, Merovingian illuminators took some motifs from even farther afield, from the Copts. We know that in the fifteenth century Europe's rivers connected the great financial center of Antwerp with such distant cities as Cracow and Vienna; we know that since Homeric times, the waterways had carried trade from one end of Europe to the other, indeed between Europe and the Near East, bearing both merchandise and the ideas that we see preserved in such artifacts as coins and manuscripts. The rivers and seacoasts were the avenues for all the barbarian invaders; for the Burgundians who followed the east German plain to Worms and then went up river; for the Huns who, in 451, followed the Danube to Worms, went through the great western plain to defeat on the Catalaunian Fields, and, in 454, passed through the Hungarian plain to the coast at Aquileia, and thence into the Lombard Plain. The Visigoths, the Vandals, the Magyars, and all the rest followed river basins and coastlines, both in their first invasions and, as did the Franks under Clovis, in their later campaigns of expansion.

A great network of water bound Europe together; it connected the British Isles with Byzantium, France with Coptic Egypt, the West with the steppes of central Asia. It carried small objects of great value, such as amber, and tribes of warriors with their families and baggage.

This network is one of the great creative factors in the growth of civilization in the West. But did it really make one culture? Did it override geographical barriers and differences that climate imposed on the quality of life? Did it harmonize nonmanorial with manorial areas, the regions of the grazier with those of the farmer, and produce one pluralistic society, an organic whole, instead of many different societies? The answers we seek can only come from examining the ways men bore with impediments and used their advantages; that is, from history.

Groups in the West raised formidable ethnic and political barriers against each other. When St. Augustine of Canterbury tried to enlist the old British Church in his effort to convert the Anglo-Saxons, its bishops spurned his invitation. The Angles and Saxons had seized and still held their ancestral lands, the Britons said, and they would no sooner have communion with them than with dogs. The Byzantine Princess Anna Comnena and the Russian Primary Chronicle despised the "Latin barbarians." But the Latins themselves were divided by such sentiments: Germans refusing to allow Slavs into their colonial towns; Roger II of Sicily welcoming men of all nations to his court, except Germans, whom he thought "barbarians"; English illuminators archaizing their taste by clinging to native styles rather than adopting artistic fashions of their Danish conquerors; natives everywhere—in England, Bohemia, and Poland—resenting the predominance of aliens in towns and at court. Charles V's election as king of Germany (1519) made him lord of territories throughout Europe; but it exasperated popular animosities. The Spanish nobility objected to his election on the ground that he would devote Spanish resources to foreign enterprises. The German electors, whose votes he had bought at great price, refused to allow him to wear the regalia of a Spanish king to the coronation itself; he must appear, they said, not as a foreigner, but as prince of the empire in his robes as Archduke of Austria. Even in the cosmopolitan world of the sixteenth century, Europeans did not feel themselves part of a broad cultural unit.

Every major cultural movement between the thirteenth and the sixteenth centuries was identified with town life. Gothic architecture, scholastic philosophy, the Renaissance, and finally the Reformation grew up in urban centers and spread through regular contact among towns. Still, towns flourished in various areas at different times and under different conditions; towns in one area rose to greatness at the same time as other regions saw their towns abandoned, and as still others had their first laid out. The great movements of the age therefore played out their strength in an ever-changing field.

The characters of these movements varied accordingly. Was there one Renaissance? Were there two, or even more? We think of Petrarch as a Renaissance man, but of Chaucer, his contemporary, as a medieval man. And it is commonly accepted that the movement began in northern Europe about the mid-fifteenth century, just as its impetus failed in Italy. Constant warfare in Italy from 1494 until Charles V's imperial coronation after his sack of Rome (1527), domination of Italy by the Spanish Hapsburgs, and the moral severity of the Council of Trent (1545–1564) stilled the Italian currents just as their counterparts in the north began to surge. Yet more telling, the character of learning in the north took on a distinctive cast. Far different from the Italian precursor, it lacked paganism as a font of inspiration, and neopaganism as a *Leitmotiv*. The power of scholasticism impeded humanistic license; Gothic architecture and script failed to give way before newer tastes. The whole force of the movement was political and religious, rather than belletristic and philosophical, as in Italy, and it remained a concern of the learned elite, without any broad following among the nobility or the *haute bourgeoisie*. Beside these broad distinctions, many important features gave a special stamp to the currents in each state. This segmentation of the "community of letters" corresponds with the particularistic scheme that we have been sketching.

Among many primitive divisions that set off one part of mankind from another, language stands as the most enduring and conservative sign of the ethnic group's coherence, and of its separateness from the rest of the world. The linguistic areas of Europe are perhaps the greatest surviving monuments of acts in the grand panorama of history from the remote days of the Celtic settlement, through those of the Roman Empire and the age of the barbarian invasions, and on to more recent times. England is divided linguistically into the Celtic—Gaelic, Welsh, and Cornish—and the Germanic areas. France has its Breton, Basque, and Germanic areas, as well

These two precious relics illustrate communication at the highest level among Europe's cultural groupings. The enamel plaques on the "Crown of St. Stephen," the emblem of Hungary, are of Byzantine workmanship; they probably survive from a crown sent by the Byzantine Emperor Michael VII to King Geza I about 1075. The coronation mantle of the Holy Roman Empire recalls the bond between the Islamic culture of Sicily, where it was made and to which it owes its design, and the Hohenstaufen emperors, in whose baggage it reached Germany.

Vatican Library

as the regions of the *langue d'oc* and the *langue d'oïl* with their many dialects. The Iberian peninsula knew eight languages, including Arabic, and countless dialects. The area of German hegemony was divided into Germanic, Baltic, and Slavonic districts; and a belt of oriental tongues, belonging to the Uralic family, ran through Finland, Estonia, Hungary, and Turkey. Beyond lay Russia and the Greek East. Every conqueror spread his own language; the defeated sought asylum for their culture, of which language was the sign and chief safeguard.

These divisions naturally impeded communication. In the thirteenth century Roger Bacon observed that dialects from one section of France were often incomprehensible in another district. Linguistic unity often attended or sharpened political cohesion, as when the Flemings revolted against the French and defeated them at Courtrai (1302), and when, in the thirteenth and fourteenth centuries, France assimilated French-speaking areas on the western border of the empire. At the outbreak of the Hussite Wars, the Taborites translated the Scriptures (c. 1420) and gave instruction in Czech as an emphatic rejection of German cultural dominance. There are many similar instances in which the vernacular tongue was taken as a sign of ethnic unity and/or separatism.

Nor could easy and frequent communication level these barriers, as radio and television in our own day are standardizing modes of speech and personal value systems. There were insurmountable barriers to free move ment: sheer distance, impenetrable forests, ignorance of geography, mountain ranges, and the ties of kinship. Xenophobia sped the traveler on his way and native hatred kept foreign conquerors wary. In different regions, the sense of beauty expressed in art and architecture and the sense of justice enacted by law and juridical institutions sprang from the most varied roots. Foreigners had no part in the general enterprises of framing and executing laws, levying taxes, or providing for the common defense. Outside the "community of the realm," they stood under often severe legal disadvantages. As organs of government developed, representative assemblies throughout Europe insisted that important offices be given to the native-born, and that these appointments and the conduct of state affairs be subject to scrutiny and approval by the estates. This tendency became acute in the late Middle Ages. Some governments, notably Venice, required all foreign merchants to deal through native entrepreneurs; others took special kinds of trade out of foreign hands, as, by the monopolistic Staple, England excluded aliens from wool exports. By the fifteenth century, even those most cosmopolitan institutions, the universities, fell victim to this nationalistic spirit. City-states of northern Italy required teaching scholars to be counted as citizens, bound by oath not to teach in other places, and, with some exceptions, citizens were forbidden under heavy penalties to study abroad. Throughout Europe, princes ignored or formally abolished academic privileges, forcing foreign students to assume citizens' military obligations and imprisoning them or confiscating their goods if they proved disobedient. From its foundation (1348) the University of Prague was meant to stop the drain of scholars abroad. Its regional character was marked in the four nations into which students were organized: Bohemians, Poles, Bavarians, and Saxons. Its weighting of privileges in favor of Czechs and the consequent exodus of German scholars in 1409 largely cut off the influx of foreign teachers and students. The same enthusiastic provincialization fell upon every great university except Padua, Venice's dependency. It was the essence of newer universities, such as Vienna and St. Andrew's.

These national barriers had local counterparts. A ruler's grand project for attracting settlers to a new town could founder if neighboring towns or lords opposed it as a threat to their interests. Local tolls along streams and roads, the protectionism of guilds, and banditry stifled long-distance trade.

THE BONDS OF CULTURAL INFILTRATION

Despite all these impediments, population movement was one of the most dynamic forces in our period. It added the strength and the distraction of volatility to Western life. This was only natural in generations when "war," in Keen's words, "was the endemic condition of West European society," when the constant passage of brigands, march of armies, and flight of refugees made peace a matter of legal declaration rather than an actual

This magnificently carved wagon was recovered from a ninth-century Viking burial site at Oseberg, Sweden. Though it may well have been intended to serve a ritual purpose, it is the only surviving specimen of this general type of medieval transport. *Universitetets Oldsaksamling, Oslo*

state of life. The normal rate of march in Charlemagne's day — as in St. Louis' — fell between twelve and fifteen miles per day. Frederick II (d. 1250) once made a forced march of about sixty miles in a day and a half, and, on urgent business, a royal courier in 1394 sped from Paris to Avignon in four days, or a rate of about one hundred miles a day. A few other instances of exceptional speed, achieved by cavalry under great duress, are also known. Transport by sea was faster, but more expensive. Specially engineered Venetian galleys could sail in thirty-one days between Southampton and Otranto. It might take as many as thirty-two days, or as few as eight, for a message to get from Venice to Vienna. Progress could only be slow over pirate-infested seas or narrow, unpaved roads and insecure bridges haunted by brigands; but so much the greater, then, the inducement for an occasional raid on an outlying monastery or a gratuitous attack on a defenseless village. War accounted for most of the great shifts in medieval population.

Society on the Move

There were, first of all, the warriors: the barbarian invaders of the late Roman Empire; the Saxons whom Charlemagne transported; the Vikings; and the Crusaders. The noble fighter remained an international character: the Archbishop of Narbonne, former abbot of Citeaux, who led a crushing charge against the Muslims at Las Navas, or St. Louis (d. 1270) himself, twice a crusader to the Near East. But, from the eleventh century on, a new sort of warrior appeared. When feudal services could be commuted into cash payments, the territorial princes — popes, kings, cities, and barons alike — could afford to dispense with the contractual quiddities of knight's service for short periods at stated seasons and turn to professional fighters, the "free companies" or bands of mercenary soldiers who could be hired at any time of the year for the duration of a war and who shook the dust of their homelands from their feet. Many, like the German mercenaries that became the fighting elite of cities and principalities throughout Europe, the Catalan Grand Company in Constantinople, and Sir John Hawkwood in Italy, went far afield in search of blood and booty.

On the other hand, there were the noncombatants, the captives, the camp followers, and, above all, the fugitives: the monks fleeing inland with their relics to escape the Vikings or the six hundred Holzatian families in the eleventh century who fled before their enemies and found refuge in the Harz mountains.

The Elites

Still, war and the displacements it caused were only part, perhaps the most characteristic sign, of a greater syndrome. They brought together many kinds of enterprise — social, technological, political, economic, religious—which found restless expression in other ways as well. We often represent medieval life emblematically by the peasant bound to the soil, the lord bound to the peasant, the monk immured by his vow to keep stability of place, and the townsman safely locked behind his gates and palisades. But, in fact, every class was on the move.

The formal political and religious structures of the time required much of this. For kings and princes especially, transience was the hallmark of life. Diplomatic missions between distant parts of Europe, with their sumptuous gift exchanges and imposing entourages of clergy, scholars, and warriors, connected the greater courts throughout our period. These contacts often led to marriage alliances, such as those that brought Kievan princesses to the thrones of France and the Holy Roman Empire in the eleventh century, and transformed a long series of French and German ladies into Byzantine empresses. Such marriages amounted to permanent diplomatic legations of foreign powers, for a noble bride took with her priests, artists, men-at-arms, councillors, and entertainers of every sort. The effect was sometimes profound. It brought Angevins to the throne of Hungary (1308–1387); it furnished the dynastic cause of the Hundred Years' War (1338–1461). French art and dress took on a distinct south German flavor under the influence of Isabelle of Bavaria (d. 1435); Portuguese taste was tinged with English under the patronage of many queens from Arthur's land; and English taste with Czech in the time of Anne of Bohemia, whose connections also prepared for the introduction of Wycliffism into her native country. A diplomatic network and exchange of personal and technical knowledge in this way could spread to the farthest corners of Europe, as it did in the first three marriages of Frederick II, to Constance of Aragon, then to Queen Yolande (or Isabella) of Jerusalem, and thirdly, to Isabella, John of England's daughter. (He married, less glamorously, a fourth time.)

An equally profound social trait made vagabonds of kings within their lands. For the greater part of our period, Europe knew no capital cities, permanent residences for heads of state, stable headquarters for bureaucratic machinery, or fixed depositories for the treasuries and documents of state. In the Byzantine Empire and in the Caliphates, as in nations today, rulers traveled a great deal on diplomatic visits and military campaigns. But the business of government went on in the capital which an umbilical cord of dispatch boxes connected to the migrant court. This arrangement developed very slowly in Western Europe. The absence of a money economy forced even kings to live from hand to mouth on revenues from goods that were perishable and difficult to move; and so they rode with their courts like locusts from one manor to another. There was no systematic structure of government and thus no need for a stable administrative center.

The same economic currents that set mercenary soldiers on the road clipped the government's wings. As a money economy spread and operations of government came to rest increasingly on the preservation of documents and inexorably regular chains of command, government from horseback faded away. In France, Philip Augustus began to centralize his administrative apparatus in Paris, and, also toward the end of the twelfth century, the English kings settled their exchequer at Winchester and their archives in Westminster. These were tentative and fortuitous steps. The French court itself, becoming slowly less peripatetic, finally came to rest at Versailles in the seventeenth century. England anticipated this stability by three centuries. Other states, such as Burgundy and Spain went without capitals until the sixteenth century. The Holy Roman Empire never had a formal capital, apart from the territorial seat of its current ruler.

By the nature of their office, bishops had always had permanent residential and administrative centers, and a series of temporal princes from the twelfth century until the sixteenth followed that plan. As Dr. Peyer has pointed out, not only Western Europeans, but some African tribes, South Sea islanders, and other peoples whose government depends on natural economy, have known the migrant king who is constantly moving from one homestead to the next with his train of men and sacred relics and tabernacles, showing himself to his people for their homage and veneration. Travel abroad for diplomatic or military reasons simply extended this occupation geographically.

The great bond of religion encompassed national units. We are only beginning to appreciate the relations that continued vital influences between Jewish communities of northwest Europe and the Holy Land. The role of the Christian clergy as a network of passage throughout Europe is better known. In the early Middle Ages itinerant missionaries had spread Christianity across the continent. Later clerical pilgrims, refugees, and envoys moved constantly along interlacing routes among monasteries and bishoprics; there were both exotic figures, like Patriarch Heraclius of Jerusalem, who consecrated the Templars' Church in London (1185), and less exalted men, like Abbon of Fleury who taught in the tenth century at Ramsey in England. The course of administration drew clergy to episcopal and archiepiscopal sees for schooling, ordination, and judicial business, and the mixture was all the richer when assisting prelates were by birth and breeding alien to the countries of their sees. But the network was wider. In the late Middle Ages, papal efforts to supplant local powers of Church government made the Roman curia — in Rome or at Avignon — a great clearing house of information from every corner of the western world. This effect was institutionalized because bishops normally kept permanent representatives at the papal court. Still, much earlier, in the seventh century, Rome had sent Theodore of Tarsus and the North African, Abbot Hadrian, to England, and her own hierarchic preeminence and precious relics had drawn such men as the Anglo-Saxon Benedict Biscop, who made five trips to the ancient capital.

Moreover, the great religious orders spanned Europe, bound together by administrative structures that connected the most distant and obscure priory with the mother house. Cluny set the pattern for this monastic filiation in the tenth and early eleventh centuries; it had many imitators. The founder of the Carthusian order, St. Bruno (d. 1101), who was educated at Cologne, Tours, and Rheims, preached a discipline of great austerity and seclusion; but he himself taught his way of life from Grenoble to Cala-

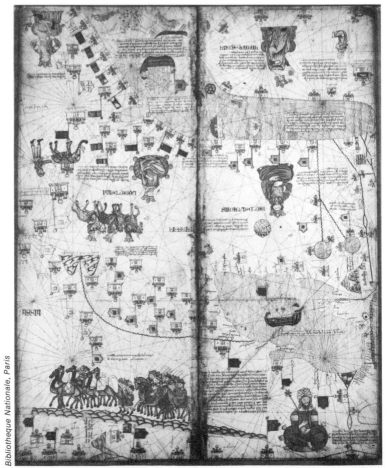

Kings, merchants, religious figures, and scholars traveled constantly and helped mingle the distinct European cultures. These pictures represent five of the most eminent travelers. Louis IX of France is shown at sea, in Cyprus, in the Holy Land, in Egypt, and in North Africa. The Polos appear en route to Cathay. St. Francis journeyed from Italy to the Holy Land, Spain, and Egypt. Erasmus knew all of northwest Europe, including England and northern Italy, at first hand. The ship represents the Levantine trade that made Jacques Coeur immensely rich and one of the most powerful men in fifteenth-century France.

bria. With similar enterprise, St. Norbert, who died as Archbishop of Magdeburg (1134), spread the order of Prémontré across northern Europe; and St. Bernard of Clairvaux's (d. 1153) followers planted literally hundreds of Cistercian houses between the Ebro and the Vistula. Tightly knit interregional governments, the great orders made their disputes international affairs; they spread their special forms of devotion and liturgical usage from one end of Europe to the other. Advocates of standardized art and architecture, they introduced alien concepts into many regions — such as the round churches of the Templars, Cistercian Gothic in northern Spain, or the Gothic church of the Franciscans in Rome. Some profoundly enhanced industrial production, as the Cistercians did in disseminating new techniques of iron manufacture. Above all, they commanded the resources of personnel that diffusion on this scale required. The Templar, Gaufredus Fulcher, in the twelfth century, was far from unique in having crisscrossed the Mediterranean several times to serve his order in France, the Holy Land, Egypt, and Spain.

Arts and Crafts

Outside the growing webs of civil and ecclesiastical government, many professions contributed to the movement of men and ideas. Two classes are so well known as voyagers that they need only be mentioned. The first is the university students, members of a great cosmos of learning — Bohemians who traveled to Bologna and returned with great skill in Roman and canon law; Spaniards who took home theological issues and techniques of reasoning from Paris; Englishmen who studied medicine at Padua — all disseminators of a common intellectual store. Merchants comprised the second class: the Jews who forged a chain of trading posts between Spain and China by way of Kiev in the early Middle Ages, the Genoese and Venetian trader-princes who appropriated the foreign commerce of the Byzantine Empire, petty merchants aiming to become great like the young Jacques Coeur, who traveled on a speculative trip to Egypt, Syria, and Cyprus (1432). Lines of trade bound the Baltic and North Sea coasts together, linked southern Germany with Italy and Spain, and tied the great wool-producing centers of England and Spain with the mills of Flanders and Lombardy. Foreign tastes, skills, and even diseases — the Black Death — traveled in the merchant's pack. A Pisan merchant, Fibonacci, contributed one of the greatest innovations of all time when he returned from North Africa having mastered the use of Hindu numerals.

But the famous travels of students and merchants were only part of a much broader scheme that reached to the lowest orders of society. Slaves, especially from the Black Sea area, were transported across the Mediterranean throughout the Middle Ages, even as late as the fifteenth century; in the period after the fall of Rome, Europe had been a hatchwork of routes for the slave trade. Peasants too — even the supposedly land-bound serfs — found work as migratory sharecroppers or tenant farmers, especially in southern France and Italy. Even in tight manorial areas, such as England where stability of population was an anchor of the economic system, there were always vagabonds to be taken on in harvest time as occasional laborers. The deserted villages in England and Germany during the later Middle Ages are monuments, not only to population decline, but also to the new ways of estate management that induced landlords to dispossess their villagers and to put them on the road. In times when men were scarce, landholders tried to check the fluidity of the work force by laws such as the English Statute of Laborers (1351), which set conditions of employment and wages. But the need for land of his own, or for a wife, drew the villager off into the outside world. Laws against this sort of movement ran contrary to traditional practice and had little permanent effect; serfs could simply flee under cover of night, or they could stay within the law, buying a valid license to leave their lord's land for a negligible yearly fine of a chicken or two, perhaps commuted into cash. The Flemish colonists in the German east, the French settlers in northern Spain, and the "men of all nations" whom St. Stephen (d. 1038) invited into Hungary were of this class. They carried with them tools and methods of cultivation far in advance of normal practices in the areas they colonized.

Men with sophisticated skills were in demand everywhere. Thus, from the thirteenth century on, Italians served as directors in monetary matters for many principalities and cities of northern Europe. Members of the Salimbene family, Sienese or Florentine, supervised Lübeck's coinage for twenty years in the fourteenth century. Wenceslaus II of Bohemia summoned three men from Florence to engineer his famous mint reform, and a great many of the frequent demonetizations in the late Middle Ages can be traced to Florentine, Genoese, or Lombard advisers. In this, as well as the related practice of banking, Boniface VIII (reigned 1294–1303) struck an apt *mot* when he observed that the Florentines were the fifth element of the earth. But, in the same way, many high offices in Italian city-states were held by Germans.

Artists and architects sought patrons abroad. Early in the thirteenth century, German artists executed stained glass windows in Assisi at the church of San Francesco; in the fifteenth century a mason from Cologne supervised building the western steeples of Burgos Cathedral. Employment of foreign craftsmen had always been part of cultivated life, as it was in the seventh century when Benedict Biscop imported French stone masons to adorn his monastic buildings in Northumbria, and, in the eleventh when Abbots Bernward of Hildesheim and Desiderius of Monte Cassino set Byzantine artists, or at least artists skilled in Byzantine design and techniques, to work on their churches. Knowledge of this sort of movement is greater for the late Middle Ages than for the earlier period, and we can sometimes trace the travels of individual artists, anonymous or known, and of bands of masons. The same circle of masons, for example, worked on thirteenth-century structures in Rheims, Trier, and Marburg. Guillaume d'Avignon with a band of French workmen was employed in the fourteenth century to build a stone bridge at Raudnitz over the Elbe, but left Bohemia without doing his job. Earlier, a sculptor worked at Rheims and Halberstadt; the courts of Anjou and Avignon employed goldsmiths from Cologne, Lübeck, and Freiburg. German printers outnumbered all others for a time in France, Spain, and Italy. One among many in Lyons used wooden blocks cut in Basel and metal type cast in Nürnberg; another ended in Lyons after migrating with his press from Germany to Italy, to Mainz again, and then to Albi. Every craft contributed to the general exchange of technical skills: peasants and monetary advisers alike; the miners who went from Saxony throughout Silesia, Bohemia, and Hungary; the workers from the Fens whom Edward I of England sent to drain marshes and channel rivers in Wales; German weavers in Florence (perhaps half of all weavers in that textile center in 1427); and the Italians who built the first paper mill in Germany (1389).

Cultural Borrowing from the East

In the diffusion of technical knowledge, Europe was debtor to other peoples. Nearly every craft or impulse toward a common store of knowledge owed much to Islam, and the origins of some innovations have been traced as far as China.

Many of these new elements entered and spread through Europe by means of writing. By the end of our period, the day of the handbook had dawned. From the thirteenth century on, and especially in the fourteenth and fifteenth centuries, the spread of technical knowledge occurred almost as much through these instructive books as through population movement. Ancient technical books had always circulated, such as Pliny's *Natural History* with its descriptions of chemical reactions; and early medieval writers contributed works on making pigments. After the twelfth century, the variety of the handbook grew increasingly wide. If one wished to learn about alchemy or animal husbandry, about architecture to make buildings or about the manufacture of guns and gunpowder to destroy them, about mining or painting, surgery, agriculture, or any other technical enterprise, even cooking, one could buy a book about it.

The prototype of the fifteenth-century handbook was oriental as, of course, were its physical components, paper and printing with movable type. The technical literature that preceded the handbook in the thirteenth century and later was prompted in large measure by the introduction of knowledge through translation of Arabic texts on alchemy and related sciences. Knowledge of geometry thus introduced—as, for example, by Adelard of Bath's (fl. 1126) translation of Euclid's *Elements*—lay behind some revolutionary developments in mechanics that prompted Gothic architecture and the growth of cartography. In the same way, Dante derived essential ideas and images from Islamic visionaries and St. Thomas Aquinas took modes of argumentation from Muslim thinkers.

But much cultural borrowing, perhaps the most essential, went on without the aid of formal treatises through personal contact and imitation. By wide travels in Spain, Italy, Sicily, North Africa, and the Levant, Adelard of Bath saw at first hand the advantages of the knowledge he made available in translation. Fibonacci learned about Hindu numerals in North Africa. Victorious crusaders returned to Europe with Saracen prisoners who as artists and architects joined their skills to those of Westerners who had mastered the techniques of Byzantine and Islamic crafts. European painted pottery and the chemical science of colors grew through imitation of Islamic wares brought from Spain and the Levant. Christians learned methods of enriching the soil, of irrigation and drainage, of channeling rivers, and bringing fresh spring water to crowded cities by observing Muslim techniques in Spain (although others, especially the Flemings, also made great independent contributions in these pursuits). Distillation, by which late medieval commercial staples such as brandy were produced, and improved ways of producing iron and steels likewise came from direct observation and imitation.

Even fundamental elements of European life were borrowed. Of the four great textile industries of our period, silk and cotton owed most to foreign imports. Silk production in the West began in 1147 when Roger II of Sicily conquered Byzantine Thebes and sent to Sicily the whole production apparatus he found there: worms, looms, and workers. The jealously guarded Byzantine monopoly was broken. Italian cities began to steal the secrets of silk production from one another, and the art spread to France and Germany. Cotton too was an Eastern importation. Genoa imported unprocessed cotton from the Levant from the late twelfth century on. Other importers followed suit. Mills sprang up in many Italian cities. In the thirteenth century, the plant itself, brought from Egypt, began to be cultivated in Spain and Portugal; and Barcelona became a major emporium for cotton cloth and raw cotton that fed the mills of southern Germany. The other two great textile industries, wool and linen, were of course indigenous to Europe. But even they profited from Eastern techniques and, in some ways, depended upon Eastern imports. The origins of the Humiliati, a religious order devoted to the skill of weaving woolen goods, are uncertain, but their extraordinary techniques which revolutionized wool production in the West can be traced to Alexandria. Dyeing linen and woolen cloth was a regional peculiarity. Even in the thirteenth century some areas, such as the regions around Strassburg and Freiburg, used no colors. But where it was practiced, in England or Spain or Italy, it depended upon alum, a material obtained almost exclusively from the Turks until the discovery of resources near Rome in the fifteenth century.

Finally, of the three inventions which in the judgment of some scholars "created the Middle Ages," one certainly and the others probably came from the East: the stirrup, which made it possible for an armored fighter to mount a horse, the horse collar (known in China in the third century B.C.), and the nailed horseshoe which together enabled efficient use of animal power, thus improving agricultural productivity and supporting an unproductive class of armored, mounted warriors. The exact dates at which these humble, but critical, innovations reached Europe are unknown; the West was using them by the tenth century.

Borrowing implies need. When one culture accepts knowledge or techniques from another, it admits a technical gap that makes borrowing useful. But the more advanced culture does not absorb the borrower. Europe's debts to eastern societies indeed are a fair caution against overemphasizing the exchanges of men and ideas that went on among the cultural groupings of the West.

A time lag in technical skills divided Europe's high barbarism from the high civilizations of the East. Let us look more closely at this aspect of cultural diffusion. Silk working machinery took six centuries to travel from China to Byzantium and five more to reach the West. In iron casting as a normal mode of production, the West followed China by 1000-1200 years. Gunpowder took four centuries and block printing six centuries to pass from the Hwang Ho to the Rhine.

The Extent of Cultural Infiltration

When all of the West's borrowings from the East were added up, the cardinal points of men's understanding of themselves and of the world around them remained basically the same. They were certainly modified in some ways. But the growth of natural history, scientific biology, geography, and astronomy were modern events, beginning in the sixteenth century.

The links of urban, literate civilization spread from China to the Pillars of Hercules; they had not yet been welded into a chain. Chance, need, and receptivity carried many material traits throughout the hemisphere. But transmission went on slowly, and the techniques that passed westward were simply ways of doing things, technical improvements — whether in modes of argumentation or in crafts — that left the framework of life unchanged. Indeed, the West's "borrowings" were in good measure "recoveries." Islam and Byzantium restored lost elements of Europe's own intellectual heritage, such as Aristotle's thought, that matched and supplemented parts of the heritage that Europe had never lost.

Cultural borrowing is normally selective: societies accept what suits their current conditions — practices that can help them do better what they already do and knowledge that explains more satisfactorily questions with which they already grapple — the stray refinement to fill a relatively superficial need.

Religious traits can move widely, as the spread of Christianity in Europe shows. But neither religious nor social traits passed on to the West from the Orient in a package with random techniques.

Though the societies of Europe and those of the East influenced each other in relatively superficial ways, they were never interdependent or essential to one another's development. Cultural diffusion from the Near East and the Orient was nothing more than that. It was not a true exchange. To be sure, many Europeans traveled widely in Islamic lands; Constantinople was a second home for Venetian and Genoese merchants; and a colony of Westerners was waiting to welcome Marco Polo in Peking.

The channels for true communication were open.

But what did the West give in return for the technical knowledge it received? Chiefly, the transport of raw goods, such as timber, enslavement of captives, destruction of a great capital in the sack of Constantinople (1204), and disruption of trade and society in the Levant through the Crusades.

There was no room in Byzantine or Islamic society—which alike considered Europeans barbarian infidels—for what the West could offer. Byzantium is a case in point.

Here and there, one does find a Western loan, as when the Palaeologi adopted the anointing of emperors at their coronations and in the time of Manuel I (1143–1180) when the emperor led his court into Western modes of dress and diversion. But ceremonial details, neatly fitted into familiar rituals, hardly shake native social order, and Manuel I's innovations received his people's answer when, at his death, they rose up and slaughtered Westerners in Constantinople.

The Byzantine capital was a great city. Its population reached about one million in the fifth century while much of the West still lived in scattered, isolated villages. Though it declined from 1204 on to about 100,000 in 1453, it still outstripped every Western city, except, perhaps, Paris and the urban giants of Italy: Milan, Venice, Florence, Genoa, Naples, and Palermo. Social life was structured under a uniform rule of law confirmed by standard patterns of child education and sustained by a money economy in which the government shared through an elaborate and well-administered tax system. Law and government centered upon the emperor. Problems of parliamentary representation, such as arose in the West, never troubled the Byzantine autocracy after the final neutralization of the senate in the seventh century. The Church normally functioned as a department of State; Byzantium offers nothing to compare with the conflicts of empire and papacy. Even the Western concept of virility found its contradiction in the Byzantine view which brought eunuchs into the highest administrative circles, to the patriarchal throne, and to regency over the empire itself. The cultural unity that all this engendered was expressed in art and architecture throughout the empire. For, not only did the tastes of the capital exert a hypnotic allure over provincial minds, but the emperor acted as a patron of the major arts and paid for churches and public buildings everywhere, having them built and decorated according to standard designs drawn up in Constantinople.

The history of the West intertwined more closely with that of Byzantium than with that of Islam. Constantinople's fall was one bitter fruit of the West's rise. But Byzantium's social traits constructed an impervious wall between the eastern empire and other peoples which allowed foreign modes of dress and behavior to enter, in much the same way as the modern West embraced Chinese designs as reinterpreted by Chippendale, or the religion of Zen modified for and by occidentals. Constantinople yearned for exotic modishness; but the pillars of society—the imperial autocracy and the laws by which it regulated every aspect of life—remained untouched.

Muslims and Westerners had corresponding walls. Indeed, the whole function of social traits is to give identity to a people, to preserve its inner cohesion from external influences, to perpetuate the whole stylized pattern of life that is a society. Such habits of mind and ways of dealing with men can only change as society itself evolves or decays.

Within the West, genuine cultural exchanges did take place. But they did not produce a cultural blend penetrating all regions. When he visited Scotland in 1435, a Sienese — the future Pope Pius II — struck the natives with amazement. They marvelled, Piccolomini said, as Italians marvel at Ethiopians or Indians, asking whence and why he had come and whether he knew the Christian faith. Furthermore, technological innovations never became instantaneously general or predominant. More than two hundred years after the introduction of gunpowder, Philip of Spain outfitted the Armada with archers as well as with heavy ordnance. Above all, the evidence that we are discussing shows that the West was in fact composed of a set of societies, rather than of only one. It was a set, and therefore bound together by some common tendencies. But precisely those currents also compacted innate differences and kept the walls of identity intact between societies.

Cultural infiltration within Europe, like the West's unrequited borrowings from the East, tended to be technical rather than social. These were immeasurably strengthened by religious diffusion through missionaries under allegiance to Rome. But religion is only one trait among many; society is both model and molder of religion. As we shall see, religion was not an irresistible bond, an irreducible common denominator in the West. It is as illogical to think of Latin Christendom as a social or cultural unit on this basis as it would be to think of all Buddhist countries, including medieval China and Japan, as under the heading of Indian civilization, or to suppress the distinctive Russian culture with the label "Byzantine."

SUMMARY

At the beginning of this chapter we asked some broad questions. Now it is time to take stock provisionally. All of the issues raised at the outset deal with communication, the problem of cultural infiltration.

Part of the story concerns the exchange of people and ideas with non-European peoples. What was Europe's place in the zone of urban, literate civilizations that stretched from France across the steppes of Asia to the Pacific?

The West received much from the East, but it lacked resources for a true cultural exchange. Had the Byzantine emperors in their prime, or the caliphs of Baghdad, given much thought to the essential nature of Western Europe, they could only have seen it as high barbarism on, or perhaps beyond, the fringe of the civilized world. There was consistently a cultural lag between the West and its more advanced neighbors. The all important theological treatise of Dionysius the Areopagite (written about 500) took about three hundred years to enter the mainstream of Western thought. Four centuries after it was written, John Damascene's *Fountain of Knowledge* gained currency in Europe through the work of Peter Lombard. Perhaps most telling of all, Aristotle's thought began to make the young white with excitement and the old, purple with rage, at the very moment when digesting and reinterpreting classical Greek scientific treatises reached the refinement of decadence among the Byzantines, who swerved from Aristotle to Plato, and among Islamic cosmologists, who subsided into a comfortable antiquarianism.

All this changed. Hemispheric diffusion — from China and Islamic lands to the West — had only the meaning that Europeans gave it by slow and idiomatic adaptation to local needs; the effects were immense. A second part of our story is cultural infiltration — in some cases, true exchange — within Europe; and this is a key to the dominance Europeans finally gained over other peoples. Thirteenth-century men rejoiced to catch up with scientific views of the pre-Christian era; but step by step, "natural philosophers" in the West advanced beyond the ancients, and even beyond the best Byzantine and Islamic thinkers. By the sixteenth century, studies of anatomy and astronomy, of man and his universe, had wrenched open the door to technical and empirical, rather than speculative, knowledge. It was the beginning of a mode of inquiry new in the history of mankind, and fruitful above anything known to earlier generations. The same progress from high barbarism to civilization marked many levels of existence in Europe between the eleventh and the sixteenth centuries. Still, as we have seen, this advance took not the form of a concerted frontal drive, but that of a thousand thrusts in different directions, finally adding up to a revolution. In some regions it hardly occurred at all. Everywhere, its momentum pressed on at a variable rate, paradoxically driving men apart by accentuating political and ethnic differences, as it brought them closer together by enhancing modes of communication and government.

Societies in Evolution

This ambiguity has been our chief interest. Thus far, we have been discussing the essential divisions and bonds among societies in Europe. We have seen that just as geography divided men, so too did cultural traits such as language. Far from being a society — a coherent, organic community with a single, stylized pattern of life — medieval Europe was an area in which many different societies lived. Those societies shared no common history as did the Chinese or ancient Egyptians; they followed utterly different ways of life; their modes of production were in some instances poles apart; they had no general base in political order or social structure.

Many essential facts are needed to fill in this sketch: the organization of kinship groups in different areas; the stratification of society in cities and towns; and the roles of groups who were not full members of medieval societies, especially that of the Jews who were excluded from citizenship and public office at every level and were thrown to the capricious and mercenary clemency of princes and kings for such protection as they had. The physical expulsion of Jews from many states in the fourteenth and fifteenth centuries merely expressed the alien role that society had forced on them from the beginning and which continued even in the western regions, such as the Italian states and Holland, where they found refuge. What were the lines of prestige and status in the separate societies? To what occupations were shame and glory attached? Further discussion is needed to illuminate these critical points.

Some things, however, are becoming clear from our survey. What we see most plainly are two apparently opposed processes going on simultaneously: on the one hand, a mingling and on the other, a compacting of ethnic groups and classes.

It is a curious fact that the idea of Europe as a cultural unit or community became current in the fifteenth century, at a time of economic incoherence, disparity in population swerves, disastrous civil wars, and splintering of the political map by thriving territorial states. Even religion, the sole great cultural bond of Europe, was on the verge of snapping.

Perhaps the ideal of Europe as one vast community shimmered before the intelligentsia as consolation in the midst of these chaotic events, a hybrid of Utopia and the Heavenly Jerusalem. But there was more to it than that.

The splintering of Europe was, from one point of view, the progress of many diverse and separate groupings toward a concrete economic and cultural blend. It was a stage in social evolution, the stage of differentiation and specialization. The growth of the interregional wool industry, to which we have referred, is perhaps the greatest example of this process. In agriculture there were many others. Some regions specialized in flax, others in dairy products, still others in various fruits. As such areas devoted more and more of their resources to the production of special crops, they relied increasingly on other regions, not only for luxury goods but even for necessities. Gascony, for example, specializing in wine production, became totally dependent on neighboring areas and on England for staples of fish and grain. Is this not evidence of an emerging interregional culture, the growth and functioning of a diversified and pluralistic society?

Many other factors point to that conclusion: the general acceptance of the maritime code of Oléron, for example, and the fact that merchants did travel widely, trade, and become rich. Cities differed in constitution, but the communes of northern Europe borrowed their general patterns of authority from the Italian city-states. Language was not an insuperable problem. Eager English and Dutch merchants aroused the Hanse's ire by sending their sons to the Baltic to learn German, Polish, and Lithuanian. Prospects of a great fortune were always worth a grammar lesson, and it is difficult for a person writing in the United States, where there are about fifty-five distinct language families and ten times that many languages, to argue that differences in language necessarily obstruct political or cultural union. Each region and indeed each village had its own system of weights and measures, often multiple systems for different products. Each state issued its own coinage, struck according to its peculiar standards of weight and metallic content. Having learned that debasement increased the profits of mintage, kings and princes from the thirteenth century on made a nightmare of monetary history with their frequent demonetizations. But merchants adapted to the different weight systems. One need look no further than the Florentine Pegolotti's notebook, or the great bankers — the Peruzzi in London, Paris, Avignon, and Bruges; the Alberti in Paris; and later the Medici in their pan-European network of offices. Coinage varied, but the wide imitation of coin types shows the greatest possible geographical field of exchange. Florence's florin found imitations in seigniorial and royal mintage throughout Italy, France, and the Holy Roman Empire, in Austria, Bohemia, Hungary, Aragon, and overseas in Achaea. Louis IX's superb *gros tournois* received the same compliment through much the same area and in Cyprus. And the sterlings of Henry III and Edward I spread a common type through northern Europe. To reach a balanced view of Europe's cultural unity or diversity, we clearly have to average out one set of facts against another.

In the fifteenth century the intelligentsia did begin to think of themselves as members of a European commonwealth of letters. Is this the familiar pattern of the elite cutting itself off from the majority, especially when we consider the national animosities to which reference has already been made? We are in the presence of social conditions that, maturing, allowed the Hapsburgs to unify much of Europe politically in the sixteenth century and that raised Erasmus to the level of a universal sage. A sense of community in the faith mustered Europe against its common enemy, the Turk, and prompted the international assemblies of the Conciliar Movement. The Emperor Sigismund traveled from Prague to Constance, and thence through France, Italy, England, and back to Constance in his effort to win general acceptance for the Council of Constance's decrees. Chaucer's English knight had fought in Bohemia, Anatolia, and Egypt. Craftsmen worked their ways in companies across the map of Europe. And yet, the Hapsburg unity rested on dynastic alliances, an agglomeration rather than a unit. What passed for religious unity had a counterweight in the growth of national churches and the spread of popular heresies. Common military enterprises, such as campaigns against the Turk, balance out against constant internecine wars. Even if we should point to the diffusion of Flemish taste in painting during the fifteenth century as a sign of homogeneity, and adduce the paintings in the collection of Isabella of Castile or on the altars of Baltic and Rhenish churches, we should be brought up short by the growth of ethnic arts and the prevalence of national scripts.

What is at issue is more than the familiar tension between fact and form that divides historians from philosophers, or, to use medieval terms, nominalists from universalists. We have confronted a number of complex social syntheses, and the question is whether they compose a blended

Coins are valuable evidence of cultural diffusion. The Rose Noble of Edward IV of England (1461–1483) bears the counter-stamp of Riga, in the east Baltic region. Notice also the type-borrowing between the *masse d'or* of Philip IV of France (1285–1314) and the florin of Edward III of England (1327–1377), which was designed by Florentine goldsmiths (1344).

whole or a miscellaneous set. Clearly, forces of cultural diffusion encompassed the entire Latin West. Just as clearly, centrifugal forces were at work sharpening the ancient divisions of mankind and giving birth to new ones. The historian, the seeker after autonomous facts, and the philosopher, whose vision rises to universal patterns, find two contrary bodies of evidence. Is it legitimate to attempt reconciliation of the contradictions in some higher unity? Taken separately, do not both the argument for cultural unity and the view of extreme fragmentation negate the facts? Let us keep these questions in mind as we turn to detailed consideration of society and religion in the medieval West.

SUGGESTED READING

Reference should be made to the preceding lists. In addition, see:

On Geographical Knowledge:
Beazley, C. R. *The Dawn of Modern Geography. A History of Exploration and Geographical Science.* 2d ed., 3 vols., New York, 1949.
Kimble, G. H. T. *Geography in the Middle Ages.* London, 1938.
Wright, J. K. *The Geographical Lore of the Time of the Crusades.* New York, 1925.

On Population Movement:
Ganshof, F. L. *The Middle Ages: A History of International Relations.* Translated by R. I. Hall. New York, 1969.
Keeney, B. C. "Military Service and the Development of Nationalism in England, 1272–1327," *Speculum* 22 (1947): 534–549.
Kibre, P. *Scholarly Privileges in the Middle Ages.* Cambridge, Mass., 1962.
Kibre, P. *The Nations in the Medieval Universities.* Cambridge, Mass., 1948.
Levison, W. *England and the Continent in the Eighth Century.* Oxford, 1946.
Oman, C. W. *The Art of War in the Middle Ages.* Reprinted, Cornell, 1953.
Newton, A. P., ed. *Travel and Travellers of the Middle Ages.* New York, 1926.
Peyer, H. C. "Das Reisekönigtum des Mittelalters," *Vierteljahrsschrift für Wirtschaftsgeschichte* 51 (1964): 1-21.
Rogers, F. M. *The Quest for Eastern Christians: Travels and Rumor in the Age of Discovery.* Minneapolis, 1962.
Smith, C. T. *An Historical Geography of Western Europe Before 1800.* New York-Washington, 1967.

On Technology:
Crombie, A. C. *Augustine to Galileo. The History of Science:* A.D. *400–1650.* London, 1952.
Crombie, A. C. *Medieval and Early Modern Science.* Vol. I, 2d ed., New York, 1959.
Hall, A. R. *The Scientific Revolution: 1500–1800.* London, 1954.

Postan, M. M. "Spread of Techniques: Italy and the Economic Development of England in the Middle Ages," *Journal of Economic History* 11 (1951): 338–346.

Randall, J. H., Jr. *The School of Padua and the Emergence of Modern Science.* Padua, 1961.

Singer, C. et al., eds. *A History of Technology.* Vol. 2, Oxford, 1956.

Thorndike, L. *A History of Magic and Experimental Science.* 4 vols., New York, 1923–1924.

White, L., Jr. *Medieval Technology and Social Change.* Oxford, 1962.

On Byzantium:

Diehl, C. *Byzantium: Greatness and Decline.* New Brunswick, 1957.

Geanakoplos, D. J. *Byzantine East and Latin West: Two Worlds of Christendom in Middle Ages and Renaissance.* New York, 1966.

Ostrogorsky, G. *History of the Byzantine State.* Oxford, 1956.

Vasiliev, A. A. *History of the Byzantine Empire, 324–1453.* 2d ed., Madison, 1952.

Vyronis, S. *Byzantium and Europe.* New York, 1967.

On Islam:

Daniel, N. *Islam and the West: The Making of an Image.* Edinburgh, 1960.

Grunebaum, G. V. *Medieval Islam: A Study in Cultural Orientation.* 2d ed., Chicago, 1966.

Southern, R. W. *Western Views of Islam in the Middle Ages.* Harvard, 1962.

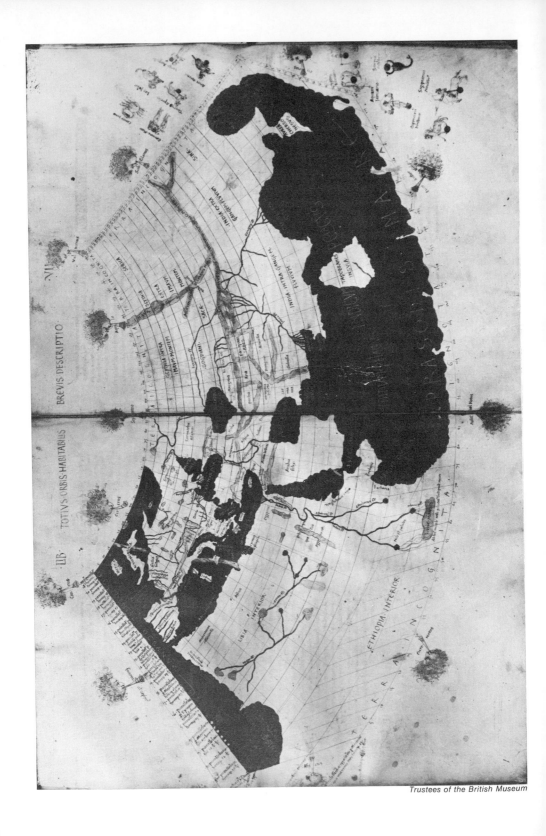

THE MANY FRONTIERS OF MEDIEVAL EUROPE

For medievalists, few historical comparisons have greater allure than that between the "Age of Settlement" in Europe (A.D. 800–1300) and the "Winning of the West" in the United States. Indeed, medievalists quickly appropriated Frederick Jackson Turner's thesis—that the frontier was the constant and dominant element in American culture from colonial days until the late nineteenth century, and that it had thereby given the United States a distinct, national character. Under Turner's influence, medievalists saw the greatness of medieval culture as deriving from the challenges and the freedom of frontier life. In the Turnerian view, the closing of the American frontier produced a revolution of the first order in economic, political, and social life. Although students of American history have had second thoughts about this causal pattern, medievalists have tried to find an analogous "closing of the medieval frontier." They hold that, after four centuries of spatial and intellectual expansion, Europeans found the limits beyond which they could not grow. By chronic speculation, they had overextended themselves. Cities contracted in population. The restrictive trade regulations that they designed to protect little corners of the world market strangled commerce and left burghers helpless before the resurgent feudal magnates. Retrenchment occurred on many levels. Lords tightened the vise of seigniorial repression. With elaborate administrative apparatus and decreased revenues, the papacy became venally obstructive and repressive, mired in greed through its extreme concern with finances and with the hierarchy as an economic structure. In corresponding straits, kings tapped every apparent source of income, evoking representative institutions out of need. Until the discovery of the New World, there could be no renewed expansion. Economy stagnated; society involuted upon itself, producing the gilded vacuity of chivalry and the moral bankruptcy of the pre-Reformation Church. Morbid emotionalism descended on intellectual life, bred of a sense that all limits had been reached.

The word "frontier" essentially raises the picture of a border between two definable territories. But when we look for one "medieval frontier," we find, not a pair, but many opposing regions. It is often considered adequate to say that expansion occurred on two fronts: an "internal frontier," which saw the settlement and cultivation of lands within the kingdoms of western Europe, and an "external frontier," which pressed the boundaries of peripheral realms out against the Moors in Spain, the Slavs in the German East, and the forces of Islam in the Holy Land.

We have already discussed the regional character of expansion movements and shown that the most elemental factors—time and terrain—varied enormously. There were also issues of motive, technique, and cultural composition. In some movements, religion gave a rallying point; in others, land hunger sufficed. In some, the systematic establishment of towns and villages, with carefully surveyed spacing between them, was an essential part of settlement. We can correctly speak of an urban frontier there. In other lands open to fresh settlement, dispersed farmsteads, estate farms, hamlets, and a variety of other patterns appeared, sometimes by plan, sometimes by chance. In a number of conquered regions, as in Valencia and the Near East, existing settlements required little or no modification. In others, such as Prussia, some native settlements were allowed to stand, while others were suppressed or appropriated and developed for alien colonists; and new villages and towns were laid out. Finally, areas had distinctive ethnic compositions. In some, as in Estonia, alien conquerors stood apart from their new subjects; they came to rule and exploit.

Ptolemy's Map. Despite erroneous data, the Alexandrine, Ptolemy (fl. 200 A.D.), used methods of projection that, recovered in the fifteenth century, led to modern cartography. The Hereford map, on page 66, represents the intervening medieval geography.

Illustration from the *Sachsenspiegel*. Much of the success of colonization depended upon the *locator*. He recruited settlers, laid out their new villages, and acted as middleman between them and their new lords. This picture shows settlement under way.

Elsewhere, as in Iberia, a cultural mingling came as a matter of course to newcomer and native. In a third regional class, settlement chiefly involved importing from neighboring districts colonists of the same cultural grouping as the natives.

Clearly, we need a classification more elaborate than "internal" or "external" frontier; we have to deal with many distinct kinds of frontiers. Curiously, this multiplicity becomes yet plainer when we see the one common strand, the unity of purpose, that ran through frontiers of every stripe: namely, the force of settlement and cultivation as an element in military defense. The Romans used the same entrenchment tactic along the Rhine-Danube frontier. In the eighth and ninth centuries, Frankish monasteries had also planted villages in defensive positions around their estates. A century later, Otto I fortified his border against the Slavs with a line of bishoprics along the Elbe from Hamburg to Prague.

Whether on those precedents, or, more likely, by spontaneous invention, medieval princes took over the same plan. Hardly any single factor illustrates the cellular structure of medieval realms, the diversity and number of Europe's "internal" frontiers, better than the strategic interspersal of fortifications and settlements along the borders of principalities and estates: Edward I's plantations along the Scottish border and his use of old and new establishments to encircle Wales, seaward and landward; the corresponding development systematically advanced by a succession of archbishops of Cologne around their new Westphalian lands in the late twelfth and early thirteenth centuries; Danish works against the Germans to the south, Norwegians to the north, and Swedes to the east; the Teutonic Order's concentration of villages and farms on the Polish border; English and Toulousan bastides on the borders of Gascony. The list could be extended indefinitely. Princes and magnates fostered this sort of development, first to check the expansion of their neighbors, drawing clear political and military lines and reinforcing them with tolls and other tariff restrictions, and, second, to construct advanced positions for attack against adjacent territories. It mattered only in extent whether the frontier region ran between kingdoms or between domains within a given realm. The motive was to divide one holding from another.

The number of such regions approached infinity. Each found its own short span on a scale of roughly five hundred years, as circumstances gave it defensive importance and its ruler the means and will to colonize it. Each lost its importance as the estate or principality it rimmed expanded, contracted, or vanished into a wider political union. Some proved to be speculative failures; others flourished. Each was in large measure a distinctive cultural unity, having, for example, its idiomatic customary and/or written laws, political — and therefore ecclesiastical — allegiance, social and military structure, dialect or language.

Verlag: Union Deutsche Verlagsges ellschaft, Stuttgart, Germany

For 300 years, Saxon rulers dominated the German frontier. The chart accounts for the early leaders of this dynasty. The effigies show Henry the Lion (d. 1195), who brought the family fortunes to their greatest height, and his wife, Princess Mathilda of England.

Roadbuilding at Bavay. Impassable roads were a great impediment to transport in medieval Europe. Road maintenance as a public function and paved surfaces for any distance outside city walls became general only after the fourteenth century. This picture shows paving techniques in fifteenth-century Hainaut.

Bibliotheque Royale, Bruxelles

The idea of an "external frontier" raises special problems. Christendom had no neat external frontier to compare, for example, with the Rhine-Danube border between the Roman Empire and the barbarians. Where was the periphery of Christendom when, for example, a king of England declared that a French king meant to destroy the Christian religion and denounced the Welsh, Scots, and Irish as pagans? In Iberia, the land of the perpetual crusade, on the other hand, religion often counted for less than sheer politics. In the ninth and tenth centuries, Christian kings leading the Reconquista occasionally appealed to the Caliph for legal decisions. Eager as they were to propagate Christianity within their lands, the kings of Castile, especially, showed remarkable tolerance in religious matters. Alphonso VI delayed conquering Toledo until its Moslem king, his friend and former protector, had died (1085). Ferdinand VIII counted the Moorish king of Granada among his most faithful vassals, and he relied especially on his Granadan forces in conquering Seville (1248), as did his successor, Alphonso the Wise, in gaining Cadiz (1262). Mudéjars, unconverted Muslims, served in the royal guard and administration. Alphonso VII gave the sense of this policy in 1135, when he had himself crowned "emperor of Spain and king of the men of the two religions." In Castile and beyond, Christians were used to living beside Muslims as neighbors. They tended to think of wars as military and political, rather than chiefly religious, exercises; and when they captured Muslim towns or districts, they normally granted terms of surrender guaranteeing the inhabitants' lives, property, and religion. They were not concerned with settlement or recolonization so much as with political control over existing farms and towns. French recruits in the Reconquista found this attitude incomprehensible. They had come to kill the infidel and seize his lands. The rift between Aragonese and Castilians, who wished to spare defeated Muslims, and Frenchmen, who hoped to annihilate them, can be traced from the late eleventh century until the decisive battle of Las Navas de Tolosa (1212). Thus, this "external frontier" in cultural terms ran between Iberia and France, not between Iberian Christians and their Muslim neighbors.

In Sicily, another arena of Christian-Muslim conflict, Frenchmen instigated the assault. But there, in contrast, prudence dictated the same religious indifference among the French rulers as had occurred among the Castilians and Aragonese in Iberia; racist and religious bigotry motivated not the kings, but their compatriot emigrés, the barons, and it ran counter to policies of state. Indeed, Sicilian history illustrates very clearly the distinction between the long process of Christianization, "extending the frontiers of Christendom," and its ultimate cause, conquest and settlement.

San Lorenzo De El Escorial

In Spain and Sicily, Christians and Muslims, even when enemies, enjoyed a shared cultural identity. This miniature shows a Christian warrior playing chess with a Saracen at a lull in the campaign, camaraderie incomprehensible to Frenchmen in the *Reconquista*

Cavalier d'or of Juan II, King of Castile and Leon (d. 1454). This vast gold coin, an artistic masterpiece, represents the chivalric ostentation of a grandson of John of Gaunt. Inspired by Spain's "perpetual crusade," love of martial splendor passed to Juan's daughter, Isabella, whose *cabelleros* conquered Muslim Granada and the Empires of America. (Size reduced.)

Bibliotheque Nationale, Paris

The Norman, Roger d'Hauteville, conquered the entire island of Sicily in thirty-one years (1060 – 1091), though he held the greater part of it inside of twenty. He and his successors had no idea of leading a war of extermination against the infidel, or of launching a *Kulturkampf*. They allowed Muslims to keep property, lands, and sometimes, castles. Most of the Norman armies, bureaucracies, and harems were Muslim. Roger refused to join the First Crusade and scorned the Crusaders' insistence that he force his Muslim troops to accept Christianity. Mosques and Muslim courts and schools flourished. Bishops and abbots recognized oaths sworn on the Koran. Norman rulers retained Muslim forms of land distribution as well as of village and central administration. Some of their coins bore Cufic inscriptions, dates from the Hegira, and the legend "Mohammed is the Apostle of God."

All this makes it perfectly obvious that Christianization was far from predominant in the Sicilian conquerors' minds. It came about slowly. Lenient as the conquerors were, the fact of conquest set off an emigration of Muslims, both from among the intelligentsia and from the farming and merchant classes. Kings richly patronized churches. They attracted prelates and secular lords from Italy and northwest Europe, and each of these alien princes brought with him an entourage of aliens who had to be settled on the land. Built up in this way, the Sicilian baronage led racist attacks against Muslims periodically from 1154 on, though the kings and the organized Church defended the persecuted. The outward flow of Arab emigrants increased.

Because of social adversity, Arabs who did not leave were forced into brigandage. For this reason, Emperor Frederick II suppressed the remaining Muslim forces and transported most of their survivors to his janissary garrison on the mainland (1243–1246).

Christianization in Sicily was thus completed about 150 years after conquest; and it resulted, not from official policy, but from the gradual enlargement of an alien elite below the level of royal administration and on many counts antagonistic to it. Frederick II won great opprobrium at the papal court for his favor toward Muslim princes and his Arab harem and janissaries. Ironically, the needs of public order in Sicily forced him to crown with victory the racist efforts of the baronage.

But in Sicily as in some Spanish provinces, the process of Christianization had exactly the reverse effect of colonization and settlement. It is true that during and just after the period of conquest, bishops, monks, and barons came with their entourages, and that unemployed mercenary soldiers from northern Europe found service there. Still, this influx did not balance the subsequent Arab emigration. Indeed, Iberia and Sicily remained populous and rich during the period of modest colonization; but they declined when the rigors of Christianization began. Then, trade stagnated; the countryside, devastated by war and banditry, was depopulated and villages were abandoned; irrigation works, essential to agriculture, fell into decay. Christianization in fact opened far greater territories for settlement than Alphonso VI or Roger d'Hauteville found. It did so by making deserts; it led to no further age of settlement. Christianization blighted these regions and ended the great age of cultivation.

The same disruption of commerce and agriculture characterized Christianization of the Holy Land in the Crusader states; it left the society of the region permanently crippled. But Islam proved sufficiently strong there, as it was not in Iberia and Sicily, to beat back the intrusive religion.

Let us look next to the northeast. Colonization extended the periphery of Christendom only in one major area of what we loosely call the German East: that is, the Baltic coastal lands between the Elbe and Lake Peipus. Poland, Bohemia, and Hungary received Christianity in the earliest stages of the "Age of Clearing"—and without the influence of hostile crusading armies and bands of Christian farmers. (It is true that St. Stephen of Hungary, himself a convert to Christianity, invited "men of all countries" to settle in his realm. But settlement and religion were distinct in that case.) The great expansion of German-speaking peoples into those three kingdoms was thus a feature of Europe's "internal" frontier, having much in common with similar developments in Gascony, for example, or Westphalia. Indeed, the Christian Boleslaw Chrobry's (972–1025) strategic plantation of German colonists on Poland's border with Pomerania, which he hoped to annex, forecast frontier strategy later used in western kingdoms and principalities.

Even in the Baltic region indicated, there was not a uniform, or simple, pattern. In Pomerania, Mecklenburg, and Silesia, Christianization was a consequence, but not a cause, of colonization. Native princes and magnates generally retained control both of their lands and of the new settlers. They granted religious freedom to colonists and allowed monastic orders, especially those devoted to agriculture—the Cistercians and the Premonstratensians—to establish houses in their territories. Christianity entered gradually, by way of the princely council and the marriage chamber, rather than by the battlefield. The Teutonic Order had the precise commission to extend the lands of the Cross by conquest. It subjected Prussia with fanatic bloodshed in a war of fifty-three years and left the blight that was also the hallmark of Christianization in Arab countries. It won Pomerelia, however, with little show of force and al-

lowed the indigenous landholders to retain their estates and religion. In Brandenburg and Ruegen, the Order mingled atrocity and conciliation.

To the larger front of eastward colonization — in Poland, Bohemia, and Hungary
— the idea of an "external" frontier does not apply at all. It seems to suit regions, in
Iberia, Sicily, the Holy Land, and the Baltic region, which passed from non-Christian
to Christian rulers. But this is correct only in appearance. In fact, the idea confuses
the fact of military expansion with one of its cultural consequences, Christianization,
though conversion was not fully achieved for many generations, not in Sicily until
the time of Frederick II and not in Iberia until the campaigns of terror and repression
in the sixteenth century. The "frontier of Christendom" therefore continued to advance long after territorial frontiers had closed, long after the age of conquest and
settlement had ended. It logically belongs to the period of economic stagnation and
social involution that Turnerians say followed the "closing of the medieval frontier."
In this light, we can perhaps understand why most of the peripheral areas we have
mentioned were already cultural backwaters by 1400, and why all of them had fallen
into economic and political decay by 1600.

"Christianization" therefore is not a sure basis for distinguishing "internal" from
"external" settlement regions; there seems to be little else to warrant such a distinction. In motives and in the use of warfare and settlement, Castilian nobles or Pomer-
anian princes differed little from Edward I in England and Gascony, and, indeed,
from the Florentines who pressed their borders to the sea. One can accept the "in-
ternal/external" distinction only with many qualifications. Whether in Castile or on
the banks of the Arno, all frontiers were ultimately "external."

We may usefully summarize this state of affairs by comparing briefly medieval
frontiers with their supposed American counterparts. The most elementary factors
are these: "Winning the West" occupied in the main a period of about eighty-three
years (from the Louisiana Purchase until the end of the cattle frontier in 1885–1886).
The entire period of settlement, from the first colonies on the Atlantic seaboard until the frontier closed, lasted nearly 290 years and involved the settlement of about
837 million acres, more than half of them after 1870. Europe's "Age of Settlement"
lasted about 500 years (800–1300) and affected an area roughly one half to two
thirds the size of the total American frontier.

Obviously, all large movements of agrarian settlement have some common features: a basis has to be struck for dealings between newcomers and natives; ar-
rangements must be made for recruiting and transporting settlers; there must be
a generally understood and accepted way of parceling out land; commercial and
governmental ties must be forged and strengthened between heartland and border
country. Beyond problems such as these, the American frontier had many divisive
features corresponding with medieval localism. There were, for example, a number of
frontiers. Students of the Wild West are prepared to agree that there were at least
two: one moved westward across the Mississippi; the other eastward from California. A sociologist might well see more: an urban frontier along the Ohio and
Mississippi valleys; an area of vast ranches in the southwest; another of dispersed
homesteads in the Missouri valley. The aggression of a young society in medieval
Iberia against an older one, more refined and decadent, has an analogue in the
struggle of Gringos against Mexicans in Texas. Though the Mississippi has not been
widely described as a frontier of Western Christendom, as has the Elbe, religion
played its ambivalent role in missionization among American Indians, as it did
among the Slavs. America had its topographical barriers — great rivers, the Rocky
Mountains, the desert of the southwest — and an enormous range of soil and climatic
conditions. It had a great diversity of languages: the Indian tongues, English,

French, Spanish, and Russian. It had a great spectrum of law, until civil law could be generally enforced, for every ranch and mining camp had its own laws and juridical procedures.

Still, we are justified in speaking of one frontier in the American West; for America had a cohesiveness that Europe in the period 500–1500 entirely lacked. From post-Revolutionary days onward, settlement of western territories fell under the government of the United States. The motive behind settlement was not to divide one territory from another, as in Europe, but to weld a territorial unit together. Local authorities counted for a great deal, and entrepreneurs, professional descendents of medieval *locatores*, did much to lay out towns and recruit settlers as speculative ventures. But, especially after the Louisiana Purchase, the federal government regulated the organization of territories into administrative districts, and the survey and distribution of land were all carried out according to standard patterns. Except for the survival of parish structure and Roman (i.e., Napoleonic) Law in Louisiana, the regular order of government and law drawn up in Washington prevailed. Moreover, the permanent successes of the Indian and Mexican Wars crowned the singleness of purpose and flexibility in deployment of military forces that this monopoly of supreme power produced. There were further advantages, such as uniformity of currency, weights, and measures; and, with the creation of the national banking system (1863), credit and banking procedures likewise followed (with modifications) one standard practice. There was none of the administrative fragmentation, the cellular political structure, or the friction of sovereignty against sovereignty that splintered medieval borderlands.

The form and supreme competence of the federal government led to another essential divergence from medieval patterns: the survival of *laissez-faire* economy. The first impulse of lord and townsman alike, before 1500, was to restrict trade by imposing tolls and protective guild regulations. A merchant taking his goods from one end of the Rhine to the other in the late Middle Ages had to pay about fifty tolls, each to a different jurisdiction. There were about two hundred toll stations along the Loire and its tributaries. Every region knew similar divisiveness. The American West lacked divisions of this sort; they would have worked against the federal government's efforts to settle a vast region by the free flow of men and goods, and against large private enterprises, such as the railroads, whose success depended on unfettered trade over long distances. An effective system of appellate jurisdiction and a marginally corrupt representative government supplied private interests with the power to beat back every major regulatory scheme. Finally, revolutionary devices for communication served governmental uniformity and freedom of movement.

From colonial days on, Americans had thought of the frontier as a solid front moving steadily westward. This view was not essentially changed by historical fact when the second front opened in California (1848). The ease and speed of verbal communication and bulk transport gave substance to the impression of a monolithic process. Topographical barriers were overcome. Extensive military maneuvers and grandiose commercial schemes that spanned the continent were executed through planned systems of routes and hatchworks of telegraph lines. Variations in languages were suppressed for governmental purposes, even in remote areas of the southwest. Sheriffs, judges, and military personnel coordinated their efforts to impose and execute a standard rule of law throughout the new territories, even in the most isolated mining camps in Colorado.

Professor O. B. Faulk, in his book *Land of Many Frontiers: A History of the American Southwest*, has cautioned against seeing the American frontier as an undifferentiated block. But, one may correctly speak of a single American frontier, as distinct from the multiplicity of frontiers in medieval Europe. In all, it lasted three-fifths as long as the European settlements, but its greatest achievements by far occupied only about eighty-three years. It thus has a preponderant chronological unity that Europe's "Age of Settlement" lacks. Moreover, it had a military, political, and cultural homogeneity totally absent in medieval Europe as a whole. There seem to be nothing more than relatively superficial analogies between the European and the American phenomena.

The Dean and Chapter of Hereford Cathedral

Hereford World Map (c. 1280). This famous map shows the world as well-informed medieval men imagined it, centered on Jerusalem, encircled by a vast ocean, and divided roughly into three parts by the Mediterranean. Ireland, Ceylon, and Paradise are islands at the outer limits, and imaginary beasts live beyond Europe.

To the contrary, the scale, not the comparison, is in error. There are indeed analogues to the temporal and cultural unities of the American frontier. We see them in the histories of individual principalities, though certainly not in any pan-European movement. The true scale of comparison lies between the American frontier and the Gascon, for example, or the Prussian. The territories of any principality, of course, were minute by comparison with the expanse of the American West. But the essential elements are sociological, not spatial. By comparing them we may hope to discover general patterns of social cohesion in the process of growth, in the peculiar territorial aggressiveness and cooperation of the frontier.

And what of the frontier's closing? In view of the wide depopulations that occurred in the thirteenth and fourteenth centuries, one cannot allege that there were simply no more lands open to settlement, as happened in the United States after about 1890. On the contrary, great tracts of land fell out of cultivation until agricultural and urban expansion resumed, in some areas during the sixteenth century, in others one or two hundred years later. It seems likely that the medieval frontiers did not close, but instead reached a developmental plateau beyond which population growth and technology could not advance them until modern times.

Chapter 3

Society

VILLAGE AND TOWN

From all that has been said, it is clear that village and town can play critical roles in helping us understand the interplay of regionalism and cultural infiltration. Indeed, some interpreters go so far as to view medieval society at its height as a sort of magnetic field dominated by the two poles of the agricultural village and the town. We have seen that there are serious flaws in the conventional image of social unity in our period. Let us now focus precisely on the evidence for and against thinking of "the medieval village" and "the medieval town" as ideal types. First, we should state the case for the affirmative side.

THE CASE FOR IDEAL TYPES

There were great variations both among villages and among towns, caused by natural differences in terrain and climate. For the village, rough or level terrain, soil conditions, and climate determined the length of the growing period, the number of crops that could be harvested each year, and the kinds of produce that could be grown. For the city, facility of transport was critical; three of the most important factors in determining the commercial potential of any town were safety and ease of inland movement, the quality of harbors, and the length of the season when transport was possible.

There were further differentiations. Some villages were settlements of graziers; some, of farmers. The old union and antipathy of Cain and Abel survived. Some cities, like Florence, were centers of banking and industry; others, like Lübeck, were international markets only; still others, like Rome, had no important industries and remained essentially local markets.

Still, a broad distinction between the two kinds of enterprise represented by the village and the town is valid and instructive. The first emphasized production; the second, marketing. In primitive society, the economic unit is also a social unit. Personal bonds, such as kinship ties, are economic relationships that impose mutual obligations: privilege is an economic institution. The functional difference between village and town was expressed in economic terms, in those complexes of rights that define any cohesive society: rights over things and rights over people and human service.

In the village, rights over land and over what was produced on the land were critical. Thus in manorial areas, what have come to be called seignorial privileges lay at the center of public order. Claims to acreage; proportional shares in harvests and in communal herds of cattle, pigs, and sheep; forest, water, and hunting rights; tariffs for the use of mills and bridges; communal rights to pasturage and to cutting turf or peat; forced labor and boon work in cropping and care for livestock — all of these things determined social relations in the manorial village.

The burden of the whole structure rested on the control of human labor. Labor was in its way more valuable than land; and this goes far toward explaining the persistence of slavery and the growth of serfdom and other servile institutions.

By contrast, personal freedom was a hallmark of the city. The catchy slogan *"Stadtluft macht frei nach Jahr und Tag"* (City air makes one free after a year and a day), epitomizes the role of the city as the creation of law, and, through its own franchises, the guarantor of individual liberty. Labor was certainly critical to the cloth manufacturers of Flanders and Italy; but the dynamics of the marketplace were different from those of the field. The manufacturers did not require a stable labor force. The demand for goods fluctuated, and, while they needed many workers when the demand was high and the stock low, they could cut back their purchases of raw materials, their rate of production, and their labor forces when demand was low and their stock surpluses were high. The manufacturing city thus required not permanent but occasional labor, workers who could be taken on or discharged at will and who in no case had permanent claims on their employer to correspond with those of the serf on his lord. The worker in the city was freer than the field laborer simply because his services were dispensable.

Important as it was, labor was less valuable than the market. Thus, the scheme of rights that regulated city life was very different from that in the village. Quality and price controls took the place of rights over land and labor. What the city had to regulate were supplies of raw materials, the transport of raw materials over long distances, the protection of goods en route, methods of computing and paying accounts, raising money for speculative enterprises, tolls and tariffs, restrictions in favor of local goods, and the like.

The social ecology of the village was thus utterly different from that of the city; and consequently, the value systems that lay behind their economic institutions differed. The villagers and the burgher attached shame, guilt, and praise to dissimilar acts and kinds of achievement. Their standards of privilege varied. We know from an early time the contempt of the townsman for the peasant and the villager's suspicion of the city slicker.

Urban and rural societies differed on almost every level of order. The guilds that regulated domestic trade and the hanse, an association in each city that oversaw foreign commerce, had as little to do with the village as the knight's fee had to do with the city.

Still, city and village existed in the same world. The town drew on the neighboring countryside for its food, some of its occasional labor, and, in some cases, its raw materials. To turn things around, the village found the city a market for its surplus labor and produce.

The question we have to treat is this: were the rights of the village harmonized on any level with those of the town? We shall have to ask whether the two kinds of settlement merged into one broader kind of social grouping locally or at a higher, perhaps truly European level.

The Village

The agricultural village is a special case, distinct, for example, from settlements that lived chiefly from mining or fishing. It was essentially a tool for cultivating the land and, in some areas, for land reclamation. Even in its palmiest days it was an isolated settlement.

We have inadequate materials for a history of the agricultural village. The earliest materials, from eighth-and ninth-century Gaul, are scattered, random allusions. Materials from the eleventh century on are much more ample. They have been studied extensively by historians who specialize in the period 1100–1300 and concern themselves primarily with northwestern Europe, England, and parts of northern Italy. But they have not been thoroughly mined by historians of the later Middle Ages, or by students of southern Europe, Scandinavia, or Central Europe. Even in English history, it is possible for Father Raftis, an eminent student of agrarianism, to observe that "the manorial village is still largely an unknown person."

In all its variations village life rested on land as the chief form of wealth and on labor as the productive force. The history of the village therefore traces the utilization of land, and, in geographical terms, it concerns two main kinds of areas: those open to settlement, where land hacked out of the forest was free of feudal tenure; and older regions, "feudal Europe" and Italy alike, where land ownership was concentrated in the hands of an aristocracy. For the student of societies, then, the critical element is the role of peasants in these different regions, something that can be defined in terms of the heading "freedom."

Entirely free men in the Middle Ages were outlaws, the dispossessed, those outside society's precisely graded levels of reciprocal obligations. A sad fate, as the Anglo-Saxon *Wanderer* poignantly shows. Within society, life was defined by reciprocal services, and the top ranks fell to the men who could choose their own lords and bear arms in their service or leave it given good cause. From this viewpoint, medieval societies were composed of unfree classes, in which rank depended on the kinds of services required and of recompense given. Even the pope was the "servant of the servants of God." Agricultural workers stood well down this ladder of privilege; slaves stood at the bottom.

Manorialism, with serfdom as its characteristic labor system, was not connected with conquest so much as with the settlement of wastelands —clearing forests, draining swamps, and in every way increasing the extent of arable land. This process of land recovery began in the Carolingian Empire about the year 800, and it continued until about 1350.

Generally, the lands open to settlement were the lands of the free peasant; servile labor tilled lands long settled, thoroughly populated, and capable of admitting new tenants only by subdividing existent tracts. There were exceptions to this rule, as for example the contrast in the country of Warwickshire between the free tenants in the north and the serfs in the south, and in the Auvergne, where the heaviest labor services fell on the most recently settled lands.

Frankish colonization, however, set the general pattern for all later developments with the "royal freemen" (Königsfreie), peasants whom the Carolingians sent as colonists beyond the Rhine, especially into Franconia. Free of all obligations except those to the king and his representatives, such men had broad rights to own property, to bear arms, and to have their legal disputes settled by royal courts. In return, their lands were subject to jurisdiction and tax assessment by the royal fisc, or treasury; the king, furthermore, could transport them to settle other areas. In time, the enfeeblement of royal powers brought these colonists to submit to other lords for protection, giving up their proprietary rights, their lands, and even their personal freedom. This pattern repeated itself again and again in Europe's frontier areas, even as the frontier advanced. It was the beginning of serfdom.

It is clear, therefore, that if the peasants' land hunger was the dynamic force in serfdom's history, it had to contend with an equally potent conservative power: the interests of the lords. In general, it is correct to say that the role of the nobility eroded between the eleventh and the fifteenth century. Wars cost them workers, crops destroyed in the field, buildings, and stock, and often left them without sufficient capital to find replacements, especially in the fourteenth and fifteenth centuries when they were caught in the pincers of inflation, which constantly raised the cost of production and brought about the decline of grain prices. Labor services declined; it was hard to find people to do them, in view of the attractiveness of fixed monetary fees. Serfs absconded under cover of night, leaving their lords' lands vacant, and even when labor services continued to be acknowledged and performed, it was difficult to assess them because of the frequent division and subdivision of peasant holdings. Worst of all was the reduction of the lords' own lands, the demesne. Lords' agents usurped tracts of land; peasants encroached on meadows and forests; and all these tenancies inclined to become hereditary. The lord himself was responsible for the dwindling of his arable lands; for he was forced to segment great stretches of the demesne among his serfs on long leases to get workers for the lands he retained; he accepted divisions by exchange and inheritance settlements; he ceded demesne rights to gain services from his peasants or protection from his own lord. All this worked to the advantage of the peasantry.

Serfs grew free; some of them grew wealthy. Their village communities became powerful. The independence of lordship that village communes won in Switzerland showed the possibilities of this trend. Then with the population decline during the fourteenth century, repression set in with temporary effects in some areas, as in England, but with devastating results in others, as in Eastern Europe where oppression of the peasantry reached its height between the sixteenth and the nineteenth centuries. It was as though the great stream of serfdom's history had forked in the fourteenth century, the Western branch leading to freedom and the Eastern, to bondage.

The process to the fourteenth century was far from smooth. Even in the eleventh and twelfth centuries, lords vehemently protested that peasants were impinging on their forests along the Lower Rhine. The thirteenth century, supposedly the great age of enfranchisement, saw remarkable steps in the other direction. Lords who had commuted labor services into fixed rents were caught in an inflationary spiral. In England, through persistent efforts over a period of fifty years, lords succeeded in closing common land to their peasants and curtailing, or even forbidding, grazing rights and such forest rights as peasants had customarily enjoyed. The forest had become rare, and therefore too valuable to be shared with the peasants or sacrificed to their wish for more arable land. Landowners in areas of Germany along the Rhine took similar actions, and in some regions —Swabia, Aquitaine, Champagne, and Burgundy—the legists' equation between slave and serf seemed likely to be realized. Repression likewise set in in parts of northern and central Italy—in Florence, for example, where peasants in the surrounding countryside, the *contado*, were forbidden to move from village to village without the city's specific permission, and the city regulated all their labor and trade.

What we call the "seignorial revival" of the fourteenth century merely intensified these trends and spread them to other areas. The series of peasant revolts during the century, all of which occurred in the most advanced and most prosperous areas of Europe, were an admonition to lords on the scene and in other regions. Repression gradually spread and became a settled policy of government in fifteenth-century Scandinavia and Eastern Europe.

The Town

We must now try to see how the town supplements our picture. Disparate as village and town were, was there some ground on which rural and urban societies could mesh into one broad social grouping? Let us see what clues the town offers.

Patterns of law and government help us. Because law gave towns their distinctive character, it must take precedence in any general survey. Like towns, villages were self-administered jurisdictional and economic units. But their law was not autonomous; its norms were, in an English term, "the will of the lord and the custom of the manor." Strong as custom was, even in nonmanorial areas—inviolable according to some thinkers—the arbitrary element of the lord's will played an inevitable role in village government. By contrast, towns, wherever they were, lived by a law different from that of the countryside. This was especially true in regions where foreigners held the cities and towns, and natives inhabited the villages. Ireland and some areas of the East settled by Germans—Kulmerland and other parts of Poland, Bohemia, and Hungary—knew such a division; but it was also a general rule in long settled areas. Despite hundreds of exceptions, historians argue that the medieval town had several essential qualities, things without which a settlement would be something other than a town: fortification, predominately mercantile or industrial commerce, and a charter of liberties. Only this last element, however, inevitably distinguished townsmen from villagers.

The great difference between town law and village custom was simply that the townsman could get on with his own work without worrying about forced labor services or unexpected requisitions. As a profession, trade was next to impossible if the merchant had to give his lord three days' service per week, more in harvest time than in other seasons, in addition to cartage, marling, and the like as the lord needed. Such services likewise disabled industrial craftsmen. The sustained and constant effort that industry needs and the regularity that marketing requires were alike impossible. Even when he could commute such services into money payments, the serf —though not the free tenant—found his life turned to the lord's profit. He could not dispose of his property without the lord's permission; he owed the lord a fine on the marriage of his daughter; he had to grind his grain at the lord's mill and bake his bread in the lord's oven, for a fee; he could not leave his manor without getting the lord's permission, and that cost a fee too; at his death, the lord claimed a death duty, a heriot. Many other restrictions hedged his freedom to move, to work for his own profit, and to dispose of his goods.

Bracton (fl. 1250) may have underestimated the restraining power of custom upon a lord's will when he wrote that a serf did not know one evening what labor he would have to do the next morning. But his comment casts into high relief the uncertainty that impeded commerce in the village.

The "liberties" of a town did away with all these claims against one's time, person, and property. Townsmen might be obliged to pay annual ground rent to their lords, and towns might owe their noble proprietors carefully defined military service and various fees—tolls, rents, profits of justice, and so forth—which were often dispensed with in return for a fixed monetary payment. But they were able to plan their lives and business enterprises and follow through. Often this power was reinforced by the freedom of the town to police itself and to try wrongdoers in its own courts and by its own laws.

All this did not amount to self-government. Occasionally, lords withdrew the privileges of towns and transferred their markets to other sites, effectively shutting down the old trading centers. Towns enjoyed relief from tolls and customs in other markets on their lords' lands, but, lacking true independence, they could not negotiate tariffs with "foreign" markets. The exactions for the benefit of the lords continued and grew, as they were renegotiated from time to time. The increased burden was passed along to aliens trading in the towns, to villagers, and to others who did business without the special franchise of citizenship. This in turn restricted commerce, and as the syndrome spread, introduced a period of relative stagnation which the town had no power to dispel.

When we think about town politics, it is right to focus on the citizenry if we are considering autonomous communes. Italy was the homeland of this sort of government, the town without a lord, the town that is in fact a lord in its own right over the backcountry. By independent growth, or by imitation of Italian precedents, some towns north of the Alps threw off the seignorial yoke and assumed communal forms of government. This is the role that we normally ascribe to medieval towns when we remember that the people of Cologne kept their lords, the archbishops, out of their see for nearly 500 years, that Bishop Gaudric had his brains dashed out when the commune of Laon rose against him, and when we contemplate the wooden cage in which the citizens of Guelinburg kept Count Albert of Regenstein for some months as punishment for infringing their liberties.

The Overlord and the Town League

But for most towns outside Italy there was another actor, a gray eminence of municipal government, the overlord. Vital as townsmen were in the history of urban growth, the towering figures in the movement were the kings, bishops, and nobles who founded towns as speculative ventures to enrich themselves and to defend their lands. With special privileges, they induced merchants and craftsmen to come and settle, to develop trade, and thus to send increasingly great wealth into lordly coffers in the form of tolls and taxes. Town walls, maintained by the burghers, were the prince's bastions. When we think about the development of urban life, we recall, not chiefly the merchants, but the great lords who were their silent partners: the Zähringer in southwest Germany; Henry the Lion (1129–1195), whose two greatest foundations, Lübeck and Munich, spanned the German-speaking world; a succession of archbishops of Magdeburg; Louis VI of France (1108–1137) and his successors; and Edward I of England.

North of the Alps, the distinction between cities that had lords and autonomous cities is not a generally useful tool. Occasionally, city-states were proclaimed according to the Italian model; but, normally, these were short-lived. More often cities in search of greater autonomy worked to throw off the yoke of a prince and take on that of a king; for royal towns generally enjoyed broader privileges and greater esteem than seigniorial.

The town without a lord was a curiosity. Thus, the valid distinction for northern Europe is not "independent" as opposed to "subject," but "free" as opposed to "enfranchised." The "free" town was a vassal of its lord; the "enfranchised" town, his possession. There were many variations. France will serve as a good example. In the south, one form of free town, the *ville consulaire*, predominated; in the north another kind, the commune, grew up. Government in *villes consulaires* was in the hands of a small board of consuls, usually twelve; in the northern commune, it fell to a body of "jurors," which varied in number between twelve and one hundred, and over which one "juror" normally presided as *mayeur*. (The northern form spread to England, and the government of mayor and aldermen in London is a relic of it.) Both consuls and jurors were elected but modes of election and terms of office varied greatly. Most French towns were "enfranchised"; they existed in every part of the kingdom. Some of them fell under the closest seigniorial scrutiny, as did Paris; others had an elective governing body and extremely wide jurisdiction; still others fell somewhere between the other two classes, having powers of municipal government but limited jurisdiction beyond rudimentary maintenance of public order.

This late medieval scene illustrates the quasi-sovereignty that local lords held over their lands, to the exclusion of central (i.e., royal) authority. The castle dominates the village; their lordships monopolize the rights to the forest and the hunt; the gallows awaits the truculent serf.

The Bettmann Archive, Incorporated

76

Whatever the variations in their degree of self-rule, the towns owed money and military services to their lords. Communes supplied at least a quarter of the men on Philip Augustus' side at the Battle of Bouvines (1214), and, given the fragmentary state of our information, they most likely sent an even higher proportion of his force. More pressing than fixed and regular payments of military service, which vassals normally rendered to their lords, and beyond even the seignorial powers reserved in individual franchises, were a number of special powers that remained in the lord's hands. Some of these were: the right to appoint some town officers, the power to make extraordinary requisitions in time of common danger and even to commandeer property in the assumption of eminent domain; the power to intervene in the commercial and political affairs of the town by granting or revoking charters to guilds and similar associations; the right to suspend municipal liberties in time of urgent need, and especially those of rebellious towns; and finally the power to renegotiate even the original "liberties" of the town.

Edward I of England held the privileges of London in suspense for thirteen years at the end of the thirteenth century. In the fifteenth century, Elector Philip of the Rhenish Palatinate declared that he could alter town laws at will. Though different in important ways, their views were related, and represented the degree to which even a town's law, the indispensable element in its life, was subject to its lord.

Some towns, to be sure, overcame this subordination by diplomacy or by force; and, in some areas, city leagues formed to defend themselves against the encircling feudality. In very different forms, these associations—the Lombard, Rhenish, and Swabian leagues; the great commercial union of the Baltic region, or Hanse; the Spanish *hermandades;* and the Swiss Confederation—sprang up where princely or royal authority ran feebly, if at all. Notably, town leagues did not occur in France or in England, where royal government, though sometimes faltering, never failed. Beside these very large confederations, smaller town leagues appeared within particular German princedoms, as in Brandenburg and Pomerania, where they won great powers in ducal government during the fourteenth century. The remoteness of effective imperial control, family squabbles that split princely dynasties, and the profound indebtedness of the princes themselves gave enhanced powers to the practical, united, and, above all, wealthy townsmen. The conditions that fostered the growth of parliamentary government in France and England therefore appeared in the Spanish and German principalities, and the responses were similar. Assemblies of the estates were called into being; townsmen held the purse strings of their princes.

But, as soon as princely government reasserted itself, leagues and the power of the estates vanished. The Lombard League is a great exception, because its members were themselves well on toward becoming independent principalities when they first united against Frederick I in 1167; they had reached that eminence when they renewed the confederation against Frederick II in 1226. The Rhenish League, including at least forty and perhaps 100 cities, was forced to disband within two years (1254–1256); it was renewed in 1381 only to be crushed by an army of nobles and knights in 1386. The Swabian League lasted ten years (1376–1386) before it went down to defeat at Döffingen. The Hanse found itself chewed away bit by bit as territorial princes, especially in the fifteenth century, forced their cities to withdraw from the League. After brilliant alliances with their kings, the *hermandades* fell prey to the nobility and began to decay from the late fourteenth century on. The Swiss Confederation never failed, because no prince was sufficiently powerful in the Alpine regions to crush it. The great days of the German Estates were over by the middle of the fifteenth century; for, by then, the reorganization of fiscal and administrative orders had restored the financial credit of the princes and given them virtually unfettered powers. Of 3000 German cities, only about eighty remained "Imperial and Free Cities" by 1500; the number ultimately dropped to about fifty, and, of these, only a few, like Ulm and Nürnberg, held sufficiently great territory to be truly independent.

The scales of force began to tip in favor of the lords in the fourteenth century; the development of national armies, greater than any urban militia, and of heavy artillery that blasted to dust the townsmen's walls, confirmed the trend. Whatever gallantry they required of knights on the field of combat, the laws of war gave no quarter to a besieged city. A victorious prince could raze its walls, confiscate all goods of its inhabitants, and put its people to the sword. A city that refused a prince's command to surrender was guilty of contumacy, and so forfeited the lives and property of its inhabitants. German princes and the kings of France and England first brought their towns to heel. The oligarchs of Holland survived until the eighteenth century. The "Free and Hanse Cities" of Hamburg, Bremen, and Lübeck lived on as vestigial remains of medieval urbanization until Hitler abolished their ancient "liberties."

The Decline of Urban Vitality

Many complex elements stood behind the ascendance of kings and princes over their towns. One was the decline in population that afflicted some regions. This trend hit some areas doubly, as in east Germany, where the population declined at the same time that the wellspring of settlers in the Rhineland dried up. Thus in 1410, the lands of the Teutonic Order counted about 730,000 inhabitants; in 1466, less than half that figure, and further reductions followed. The population likewise fell sharply in cities that earlier settlers had left: in Worms, from about 20,000 in 1300 to between 6000 and 8000 in 1500; in Hamburg, from 22,000 in 1419 to 12,000 in 1526. Sometimes the fall was sudden, as it was in 1450, when the plague killed one-third of the inhabitants of Magdeburg. Generally it was slower, as there were fewer and fewer peasants to migrate from the countryside and replenish the towns. The abandoned village had its counterpart in the shrunken town.

Furthermore, urbanism as an experiment in land speculation began to fail. Unlike early towns, which grew up organically at natural points of trade or industry — for example, at river fords or at mining sites — many of the towns founded from the twelfth century on were laid out arbitrarily without regard for geographical advantages to trade. Indeed, many were established as defensive settlements and lay on impregnable sites, isolated from the countryside. A great many bastides and small towns in southwestern Germany belong to this class of towns that had no potential for commercial growth, nor even any room for physical expansion. Some new towns were never fully built. Edward I imposed heavy fines on men who contracted to settle in his Gascon bastides and defaulted; but these measures could breathe no life into the miscarried projects. Occasionally, charters and liberties were secured and the site surveyed and partitioned, but no settlers appeared. Professor Beresford distinguishes these "abortive plantations" from "decayed plantations" and establishes the following "death rate" for the second class during the late thirteenth and early fourteenth centuries: in England the rate of failure was thirteen percent, in Wales twenty-one percent, in Gascony thirty-five percent. He has shown that, in these areas, durability was, as a general rule, greatest among the old settlements or new towns laid out on the sites of old organic villages; it was least among new foundations of the twelfth century through the fourteenth. Similar data appear in other regions, as, for example in Brandenburg and Pomerania, where the great speculative successes grew on top of old Slavic towns or villages, more exactly in the regions earliest colonized, and the new towns that lords founded as private ventures remained urban pygmies.

Finally, life in towns ceased to be as attractive to peasants as it had been. Citizenship was no longer easy to win; residence and property requirements multiplied. Guild regulations became increasingly restrictive concerning membership as well as conduct of commercial and industrial enterprises. The franchises which towns had won from their lords constricted trade outside each principality; for the greater the tax reliefs of a town's citizens, the heavier the tolls and fines that aliens had to pay. In its struggle to hold ground against English and Dutch merchants, the Hanse gave a remarkably clear example of this trend. Restriction began in 1397, when English cloth was confiscated at Danzig. By 1404, the Hanse expelled all Englishmen from its cities and forbade the importation of English cloth. In 1417, Lübeck refused to accept Dutchmen as citizens in Hanse towns, prohibited importation of Dutch cloth, and forbade expansion of the area in which Dutchmen were allowed to trade. A major stimulant to urban growth had been long-distance commerce; its basis was the freedom to travel, to trade, to become rich; but now, urban economy became protectionist and stagnant.

Students of Mamluk and Byzantine cities have shown that dominance of a city by an external, central government tends to eliminate the middle class. The urban populace then falls into two groups, the notables, who have charge of local affairs, and the lower orders. The two classes are divorced from one another and separate bonds of patronage tie each in a special way to the central authority. There is no middle class to catalyze the sentiments of the notables and those of the lower orders, and there can be no joint movement of the two surviving classes. The dangers of revolt are therefore minimal.

This is in fact the pattern that emerged in much of northern Europe during the thirteenth and fourteenth centuries, especially in smaller towns. Occasionally, the urban patriciate was expelled *en bloc*, as it was even from such illustrious cities as Mainz and Constance. The lords exercised their residual rights over enfeebled towns, and so suppressed the middle class that in some areas there was no urban middle class again until the nineteenth century. Taxes tended to suffocate municipal life, as in Brandenburg, where the tax-free nobility flourished in the countryside while a steady two-thirds of the state's total tax burden fell on the increasingly depopulated and withering towns. The nobility held all major military and political offices; they dominated such meetings of the Estates as survived; the territorial lord was sovereign. The urban republic fell beneath the prince's heel; commerce between distant towns was the victim of protectionism. The political map of Europe was atomized. An absolutist and mercantilist age had dawned.

From the typological viewpoint, we can now answer affirmatively the question of whether village and town merged into a broad social grouping. Thus far, we can say that both responded to the demographic swell that began in the eleventh century, reached a peak in the thirteenth, and subsided about 1300. (It is understood that this growth in population had various proportions in different areas and times.) The political lives of settlements in seignorial lands — whether town or village — varied from those in areas free of lordship. Both kinds of settlement were key elements in the dual migration which characterized the period 1100–1300 above all others: on the one hand there was a great migration of agricultural workers into lightly settled areas, such as parts of northern France, Bavaria, and the region east of the Elbe; and, on the other, the migration of villagers into towns. By the process of imitation, townsmen and villagers even shared some important features of municipal law; for in many areas the rules and practices of the town fanned out into the surrounding countryside and supplanted local customs, although the village never became the legal peer of the town.

We must now raise some rather serious objections to the typological approach.

THE CASE AGAINST TYPES: VILLAGES

Slavery and the Labor Force

Labor stands out as the essential feature in the case for seeing "the medieval village" as a type; but the picture is not simple. The dynamic force in the history of serfdom is the peasant's hunger for land, and, in the last analysis, the history itself can be told only in terms of how that hunger was satisfied or discounted in particular places at specific times. Every change that we have considered—the transition from slave to serf; the erosion or assertion of direct lordship; the commutation of services; and the different results of the fourteenth-century crises—turned on whether the individual lord valued land over labor, or whether he was able, or disposed, to share the land and its produce with peasants.

Only sections of the canvas have been painted, but we can see some distinct, and very complex, patterns. There are many variations. We have already spoken of the distinction between manorial and nonmanorial areas; there were a great number of other kinds of tenure in Poland and Hungary, among the Celts, in Lombard Italy, and in Spain. Settlement patterns varied, reflecting the different patterns of status, trade, and tillage.

What about the terms of bondage? Some scholars have held that the culture of the Latin West was the first in the history of the world to grow without slavery as a basic mode of production. Others point out that slavery was a normal aspect of Western life until the eleventh century, when it almost universally changed into serfdom.

This second view is generally true. The point must be emphasized, however, that slavery is a local matter. Thus, even today, patterns of slavery, as defined by the United Nations, survive in about thirty countries of the "free world." The old slave-trading routes in Africa have been reopened, and the Anti-Slavery Society of London estimates a threefold increase in chattel slavery in the period 1947–1962.

Similarly, in the medieval world some areas developed an economic system in which slavery was profitable. There are good grounds for assuming that in the ninth century at least a few slaves worked on every estate in the West. Often they counted for a small part of the labor force, and many of them were domestic workers instead of field hands. England remained a chief source of slaves from well before Pope Gregory I's famous encounter with Anglo-Saxons in the Roman market until William the Conqueror forbade the export of men for sale. In Scandinavia at the same time, and well into the twelfth century, large bodies of thralls—war captives or criminals or men who could pay their debts only with their freedom—served their Norse masters or went under consignment to foreign markets.

Here and there a particularly exotic slave emerges from anonymity, such as the Negro whom the sinister Bishop Gaudric of Laon (d. 1112) used as an executioner. But general obscurity hangs over the slave as an individual and over the institution of slavery itself.

What is clear is that the institution began to disappear completely in northwestern Europe during the eleventh century. Decline had begun as early as the tenth century in some areas, for example in northern France. The rise in cost of human chattels, perhaps also shorter supplies, and the cost and difficulty of maintaining slave labor brought this about. Even when masters bought slave laborers, they often found it profitable to give them a measure of freedom by making them servile tenants with their own houses and plots of land.

Slavery continued and flourished on the borders of this area of emancipation. A chronicler tells us that, late in the twelfth century, 700 men were for sale on any market day in Mecklenburg. A hundred years earlier, Roger d'Hauteville swelled his forces for the conquest of Sicily by offering the freebooters of Europe license to sell women and children into slavery. Late in the Middle Ages, the peasants still further to the east and in Poland enjoyed great autonomy in village government, but they could be sold into slavery on the spur of the moment if their lord wished it. Lands in the Mediterranean area saw a brisk trade in slaves throughout the Middle Ages. If slavery began to die in the north during the eleventh century, it took a fresh lease on life in the south during the late twelfth and thirteenth, especially in Spain and Portugal, when Negro slaves were imported to work on the new sugar cane and cotton plantations. Pope Clement X, in the late thirteenth century, did not evoke an archaic or moribund institution when he commanded that anyone who caught them could enslave men who supplied Muslims with materials for shipbuilding or gave them any other counsel or aid. The conqueror of Valencia, King James of Aragon, had recently sent as booty gifts of Muslim slaves to the Pope and the Roman Curia and to his fellow monarchs Frederick II and Louis IX. Slaves, chiefly from the region north of the Black Sea, were a staple of trade for the Venetians and Genoese; as late as 1466, the Emperor Frederick III conferred a special privilege on Genoese merchants, freeing them from all tolls on slaves bound for market.

Largely in the hands of these middlemen, slaves formed a normal part of the population, not only in Venice and Genoa and their colonies in Greece and Asia Minor, but also in Naples, Palermo, Marseille, Montpellier, and Barcelona. The numbers were far from small. There are sound statistical reasons for thinking that about ten percent of the 80,000–100,000 inhabitants of Genoa in 1380 were slaves. In the fifteenth century, chattel slaves in large numbers worked the fields throughout the Iberian Peninsula, especially in Catalonia, Valencia, the Canary Islands, and parts of southern France. Slaves still worked as domestic servants in Italy and even in Florence, the cradle of the new humanism. Venetian and Genoese supplies having been cut off by Turkish conquests, slaves were among the most profitable merchandise that the Portuguese and Spanish explorers sought in Africa. The old hands kept in the trade, too; for the large and prosperous Genoese colony at Seville helped make that city a major market for the Negro slave. When the Spaniards and Portuguese grafted the sugar cane plantation to the New World, they likewise transplanted slavery, the system by which labor was organized on the plantations back home; and the lucrative slave traffic began between Africa and the Central and South American colonies.

It is therefore misleading to argue that "Latin culture" evolved without a basis in slavery. When warlike nomads settle, they tend to enslave as workers captives taken in campaigns or conquered peoples. This is a general rule of life; we see it almost everywhere in newly sedentary societies that retain war as a major pastime and have extensive lands to cultivate. The masters fight; the slaves work the fields. Of course, slavery occurs in other contexts, as in ancient Athens. But this was the operative rule in western Europe during and after the barbarian invasions. It reinforced the different motivations that fostered slavery in the Roman Empire.

The point to be made here is that the trinity of conquest, settlement, and slavery was precisely the economic basis out of which medieval societies grew, that it faded away in different areas at different times, and, finally, that it survived in Mediterranean Europe well past the dawn of the modern era.

Serfdom

Let us turn to serfdom. Legists and canonists from the twelfth century on defined serfdom in terms derived from Roman Law that originally dealt with slavery. The analogy, or even identification, was far from accurate. Though under bondage to his lord, the serf could deal as a free man with the rest of the world. As a legal person, he was schizoid, and the servile part of his character often dominated or obscured the free part.

For some, greatness lay in servility's path, as it did for the so-called *ministeriales* of Germany. This condition of servitude has a curious history. The term *ministerialis* (servant) was interchangeable with *miles* (dependent warrior or knight) from the Carolingian age until the eleventh century. Differentiation then set in, region by region, until, by the thirteenth century, *ministerialis* was clearly the higher rank. The last stage ended in the fourteenth and fifteenth centuries, when the "servants" were absorbed into the lower nobility.

The curious thing about the middle period (twelfth and thirteenth centuries) is that free men and nobles renounced their liberty and rank to become *ministeriales* or the peers of serfs, both those owned body and soul and those who merely owed their lords fixed services and payments. The services demanded of *ministeriales* varied so widely from place to place, and even within given households, that it is meaningless to speak of their condition as a "class" or as a legal institution. Some *ministeriales* were powerful agents of the imperial government; others cleaned pigstys in provincial courts, hardly above the peasants who tilled the soil. Carried up by the rise of the territorial powers they served—the princely houses, episcopal sees, and religious houses—*ministeriales* became the instruments and the beneficiaries of government. In cities, where they originally acted as administrators for their lords, they either ceded their powers to the burghers or had entered the bourgeoisie themselves by the late thirteenth century. A more brilliant fate lay before them at princely courts. By usurpation of powers and lands, they cast aside bonds of service to territorial lords and themselves joined the free nobility.

Each period in the history of the *ministeriales* shows both the inaccuracy of lumping serfs with slaves and the difficulty of considering serfs as a class. Parallels occur in other countries. Even before the Norman Conquest, England knew serfs who, like *ministeriales*, performed administrative and incidental duties. It also knew serfs who owed week-work coupled with other services. There were serfs like the *ministeriales* Werner von Bolanden (late in the twelfth century) who held fiefs of forty-three princes and was himself lord of 140 vassals; some serfs were indistinguishable from the free peasantry; others lived like dogs, open to arbitrary services and exactions, hopelessly bound to their lord's caprice. Finally, there were important geographical variations; *ministeriales* did not even appear in the Slavic areas of the empire.

It misleads, therefore, to speak of serfdom as a uniform condition. It also misleads to think of serfdom as following an organic course of growth and decay throughout Europe. We have seen something similar in the spotty survivals of slavery and a hint of what lies beneath the surface in the case of the *ministeriales*. Let us now take a look at the geographical spread of serfdom and its variations from place to place.

Because the early stages of serfdom are so little known, the best question to ask, perhaps, is: "When did serfdom end?"

Regionalism in the History of Serfdom

Pockets of serfdom survived in England until the seventeenth century. The Revolution swept away larger survivals in France, including a form of serfdom in the Juras that amounted nearly to chattel slavery. From eastern Germany on through Russia, the wealthy estimated their standing in terms of the serfs they "owned" until the reforms of the last century. In parts of Spain the institution lived into even more recent times.

From the beginning, serfdom flourished where the large estate functioned as a semiautonomous legal and administrative unit. It survived longest in regions where vast estates kept that character, where town growth was stunted, and where the balance of power lay with the lower nobility, because the higher nobility salvaged little but debts from their internecine wars and the independent peasant had been driven out or reduced to bondage by the expansion of the demesne. The Baltic areas of Germany, the Austrian Alps, the Slavic East, and Aragon were the principal areas where this occurred; but there were other regions in the heart of the manorial area where the lower nobility likewise stood between prince and peasant and reduced the powers of each to his own profit. In Champagne, the Franche-Comté region, and the Vermandois, for example, the local landholders were the effective rulers, and the practices developed in the late Middle Ages that subjected serfs to arbitrary demands.

In other areas, serfdom was a rarity after about 1400, and especially after 1500. These were mainly regions where the lower nobility lost out in its power play. The steps by which this occurred in England have been most carefully studied, and it will help to look at them.

Though England knew well-developed serfdom before the Norman Conquest, neither William the Conqueror nor his immediate successors disturbed lords' jurisdiction over serfs. Indeed, royal courts refused to judge charges of serfs against their lords and justified this course on the basis of excerpts from Roman Law that dealt with slavery. If rarely, serfs were sold; they were in many cases liable to arbitrary demands; their property was vulnerable to confiscation, lawful or not. There was another side to the picture. Roman Law to be sure imposed many disabilities on slaves; it also forbade gross cruelty to them, and serfs benefited from that ancient clemency. The public character of the serf had not been effaced. He still paid taxes in his own right and served in militia levies, inquest juries, and the like. Criminal cases involving serfs came before the royal courts, and, on the royal estates, serfs enjoyed a special privilege that custom gradually extended to others: the right to appeal beyond the manorial courts of their immediate lords to the king's court.

The public character came more and more to the front in the twelfth and thirteenth centuries. The distinctions between free peasants and serfs eroded as free men got tenure of land burdened with servile services and serfs took land with "free" tenure on leases for fixed spaces of time. The distinctions grew all the less clear as services of every sort were commuted into fixed money rents, and as tenements owing servile or free service were fragmented in deals between lords and peasants and among peasants.

A severe crisis arose in the fourteenth century, when, on the one hand, the abrupt decline in population reduced the labor force thus making the services uncommuted into money payments more valuable, and, on the other, when inflation and the debasement of coinage made rents fixed in the thirteenth century next to worthless. Threatening terrifying punishments, lords took measures to renew defunct obligations, to bind serfs once more to labor services, even those long before commuted into money rents, and further to prevent day laborers from moving freely from place to place and to fix their wages. It seemed a new day in the history of oppression.

But these measures were soon abandoned. Many lords discovered that for them it was more profitable to raise sheep with small labor, than grain with much; and, far from binding laborers to the soil, they did all they could to enclose the fields and expel the peasants. Often, the repressive measures were beaten back by opposition of strong peasant communities. Repression also failed on other grounds. The law of the marketplace asserted itself. The small supply of labor and the great demand for it drove wages up, despite all formal regulations, and the lords themselves cast aside fixed wages. Most important, the peasant communities found a strong ally in the Crown. Step by step, the fifteenth-century kings took advantage of long-latent privileges and extended them, removing legal barriers between serfs and the royal courts. Ultimately, serfs could sue their lords in the king's court for trespass; the great disabilities of serfdom vanished, and the institution itself was well along the road to extinction.

This is the pattern with which we are most familiar, and which we tend to project across the entire map of Europe. Enfranchisement came perhaps earliest in Flanders and Hainaut in the thirteenth century; serfdom disappeared in the area around Paris by the mid-fourteenth century. Indeed, changes in the economic structure of Europe led lords in northern France to foster, not the village of serfs, but the colony of free peasants or *hospites* from the eleventh century on. Such settlements cleared land, made it productive, and supplied incomes in annual rent. In time, especially after the French kings adopted this usage in their *villes neuves*, the liberties of settlements of free men were guaranteed by written charters. Direct lordship gradually eroded between the eleventh and fourteenth centuries; differences among free and unfree peasants blurred; the bonds of serfdom dissolved.

But this was true only of areas where a close mercantile bond existed between cities and the countryside. In other regions, serfdom was dissolved not by formal acts of enfranchisement, but by natural evolution of the money economy and of estate management. Throughout Germany, lords compiled collections of manorial customs themselves, or, in a later practice, had the tenants of each manor assemble annually and declare their obligations orally one by one to defend themselves against undue exactions and the lord himself against usurpations by the lord's estate agents. Settlers from Flanders, Holland, and the Rhineland carried their liberties with them into colonies in northern and eastern Germany. Taught by inflation to avoid permanent cessions of land at fixed money rents, lords resorted to new cessions for set lengths of time which bound the peasant neither to lord nor to land.

Furthermore, the entire history of serfdom varied from region to region. The process was slow in some areas, for example, in Prussia. In fifteenth-century England, the process toward enfranchisement was nearly complete. Serfs could harm the lord's interest by neglect of his property; they could even leave their tenements, and, since demand for land was lightening, replacements were hard to find. Penalties were negligible; lords stood in many ways at the mercy of their tenants. Before the fifteenth century, Prussia had not known serfs that were bound to the soil. They could leave their lord and go to another, in most places at the cost of a small fine, in others with no condition at all. But in the fifteenth century, heavy restrictions began to be placed on movement at the instigation of the nobility and with the authority of the Teutonic Order. Labor services were increased; lords gained arbitrary powers, until by the end of the century they could kill a runaway serf without any legal process. Early in the sixteenth century, serfs' rights of bequest were curtailed; serfs themselves were bound to the soil.

In England, the manorial estate had seen its best, and nearly its last, day by 1500. The demesne was let out; the change to sheep farming reduced demand for labor services, and serfdom faded away. In Prussia the reverse happened. The vast estate began to come into its own in the fifteenth century. The demesne expanded to suppress and engulf indepen-

Medieval life rested squarely on the peasant, as modern life does on the consumer. The mower from the Portal of the Virgin in Notre Dame, Paris, shows the idealized laborer; the sculpture from Mainz, the brutalized serf who some medieval theologians said was inhuman and thus had no soul.

Dom-und-Diozesanmuseum, Mainz

Archives Photographiques, Paris

dent peasant holdings; cultivation of grain became increasingly important; demand for labor grew as the labor force dwindled; and serfdom of the most repressive sort developed.

Even though, in 1200, serfdom was out in Flanders and on the way out in England and the Ile-de-France, a long and important history awaited it in other regions. In 1400, it was just beginning in Prussia and the East, and one could still find intensive cultivation of the demesne and forced labor services in northern Italy, as at Genoa. In Aragon, serfdom flourished beside slavery, as it had in England before the Norman Conquest.

Still, the lords remained powerful enough to achieve the "seignorial revival" of the thirteenth and fourteenth centuries. Why was that revival transitory in some regions and permanent in others? The answer involves many complex elements. But perhaps the greatest of them is political power. Where the great estate survived as a semiautonomous unit of government, serfdom survived. Where the power of the lord over his serfs was transcended by the higher power of a prince or king, serfdom gradually died. This was the case in England, where the king's courts ultimately rendered manorial courts obsolete, and in the Rhenish Palatinate, where, in 1489, nobles protested that the Elector had transgressed their rights with his own demands on the serfs for payments and personal services, and that he was corroding their power by supporting serfs at odds with their lords. Serfdom could not survive once the principle was established that every man, free or not, owed his supreme loyalty to a power beyond the manorial lord.

Serfdom thus lingered in areas where princely or royal government was impeded, as it was for geographical reasons in the Jura and for historical reasons in the German east. In those regions, the lords were the chief beneficiaries of rural prosperity. But in other areas, the profits in taxes went to the prince or king — the territorial state.

Behind this political explanation stands a delicate web of social and economic factors, not to mention the genius of individual men or sheer chance. Moreover, much work remains to be done before we have a full picture of serfdom, and thus of the peasant village in medieval Europe. There are too many blank spaces on our map.

The fallacy of speaking of "the medieval village" as a type is apparent. Even the physical layouts of villages were visible symptoms of underlying historical contrasts; for the agricultural village followed very different periods of development. Its history in a given area was closely connected with the colonization movement. Thus, the great age of the village in southeastern Germany ended just as it began in the northeast; development in northern France, which was always relatively well cultivated, followed a completely different course from that in the lands of the Teutonic Order, where, within a century, a void was filled by the foundation of about 1400 villages and ninety-three towns. Finally, there were areas where the population was homogenous, and others where the native population on scattered farms was dominated by villages laid out according to imported plans and settled by a foreign elite.

For our purposes, it may be sufficient to have described the varieties that slavery and serfdom experienced, at the same time from place to place, and in the same place at different times. We had already seen that Europe could be divided into manorial and nonmanorial areas for geographical and historical reasons. To that we can now add that the labor bases of agricultural enterprise also varied greatly, and thus, by implication, that the societies that rested on those bases were poles apart in some essential ways.

THE CASE AGAINST TYPES: TOWNS

Town Law

Students of urban typology recognize three major areas in medieval Europe: one where Roman urban life continued unbroken through a series of mutations (as in Italy and southern France); a second where it had vanished except for vestigial remains of a highly localized nature; and a third where it had never existed. There are a great many profound distinctions beyond these.

Law was the hallmark of towns, but nothing could be more misleading than to speak of "town law" as a type. Municipal "liberties" varied from place to place; they were tailored to the individual case. They did not necessarily mean that towns were free of seignorial control; for, as we have seen, many towns and even great cities such as Paris were subject to lords. Neither did they mean that citizens of towns were inevitably free men. The catchword "Stadtluft macht frei nach Jahr und Tag" to the contrary, serfs are known in some northern French towns and in towns of southern Germany — Regensburg, Strassburg, Basel, and others — in the twelfth century. Nothing of the sort is known for northern Germany. If "Stadtluft macht frei" later became a general operating principle north of the Alps, enabling fugitive serfs to shed their bondage by residing in a town for a year and a day, many towns in thirteenth-century Italy required residence of ten years. A number of Italian cities kept the illusion of common freedom by refusing to accept serfs as citizens at all, though they might live in the town, and others accepted all serfs other than those belonging to their own citizens.

There were many variations in town laws; towns that were autonomous principalities in their own right were free even of the restrictions we have mentioned, and towns on seignorial lands differed in the degree of their subjection.

Our detailed knowledge of city laws begins in the thirteenth century. Because the volume of municipal charters, private legal handbooks, and official codifications increases greatly from then on, we can trace the genealogical development of "families" of law.

A particularly early "family" begins with the liberties of Breteuil which date from the eleventh century. Probably granted to the Norman town by William the Conqueror, as its duke, the privileges spread in England to Hereford, and thence to Wales, especially to the castle towns founded by Edward I. In France, an important series of charters for seignorial towns began with the privileges of Count Alphonse Jourdan of Toulouse for Montauban, and spread throughout the region of the *villes neuves*. More dramatic patterns appear in Germany. In the old settled areas of the west, the geographical spread of a town's laws normally reached only into the vicinity of the town itself, though sometimes towns in a broader, but still contiguous, area had similar laws. In the east, however, very elaborate patterns of descent appeared. It is mainly true that this growth occurred in broad geographical bands running eastward: Lübeck gave its law to the northern coastal areas; Magdeburg, to the central region; and a composite Bavarian and Austrian law spread through the Danube basin. Lübeck law in turn descended from the law of Soest and had the law of Cologne as its grandmother. It was thus a sibling to the law of Freiburg-im-Breisgau, which spawned an enormous brood of town laws in mining areas of Silesia, Bohemia, and Meissen. Despite its obscure origins, Magdeburg law, the widest spread of these families, gives an idea of scale: it was adopted in sixty-four Silesian towns and in about 445 towns in other areas of Poland, aside from towns in Germany proper.

More was involved in these "genealogies" than the diffusion of laws. Important as that fact was, yet more important were the lasting bonds of which it was a symptom. There were ethnic ties, shown in another way by the fact that the German dialects follow the same west-east bands as the three great law families: Low German across the north, Middle German through the central land, and High German in the south. The grain traders bound from Lübeck across the Baltic, the miners who went from Freiburg to Silesia, the salt merchants traveling eastward from Augsburg, all took their laws, their languages, and the whole complex of native practices with them. So did the Flemish colonists who settled villages along the Elbe. The German town dwellers took more than cultural traits; they took the means for keeping those traits alive. The lines of trade and communication flourished between the settlers and their homelands. In law, this communication was expressed in the practice of carrying difficult cases to the town which gave rise to one's own law. Thus, cases were carried from Breslau to Magdeburg, as a "supreme court," and from Greifswald to Lübeck.

Similar families of law grew up in the Low Countries, and along the Maas as far as Aachen; but they were far smaller than the giants of the colonial east.

The very local character of this phenomenon is illustrated — to take only two examples from among many — by Prague, which was really two cities divided by the Moldau, one under Magdeburg law and the other under Nürnberg law. A still more complex urban agglomeration developed at Brunswick, where seven adjacent settlements grew up side by side; five of these were towns each having its distinctive laws, just as it had its own walls abutting onto its neighbor's walls. Local differentiation was not always geographical. Some cities in Languedoc ruled nobles by one law and commoners by another.

Law varied from town to town, even from district to district within some towns, and from time to time, since towns occasionally changed their constitutions.

Different Urban Power Structures

"Urban typology" breaks down on other fundamental points aside from law. One could raise the generalization that Italian towns accepted nobles and knights as citizens, and that northern towns, with eminent exceptions, excluded them. But even here the rule is modified in many cases, the most distinguished being the exclusion of nobles by the popular party in Florence during the late thirteenth and early fourteenth centuries. Another general feature was that patriciates ruled towns from the Baltic to the Mediterranean, and that almost every town had to cope with a struggle for power between urban oligarchs and the lower orders. Still, these conflicts turned out differently in different places. In some towns, as in Nürnberg, the patricians won unqualified victories, crushed and abolished the artisans' guilds, and settled into a rigid, castelike system. In towns which depended on trade more than on manufacture, the patricians normally had the last word. This was the case, for example, in the Hanse cities, where such victories as the craft guilds won proved ephemeral. In other towns, the struggle ebbed and flowed. The artisans sometimes crushed the oligarchs, as they did at Cologne in 1396; and many patterns of representation, many shifts in the balance of power, were tried. Even the composition of oligarchies varied. In some towns, as in Augsburg, active businessmen, however rich, were excluded from the inner councils of government. In others, as in Lübeck, descent and wealth were criteria, not the ability to live off accumulated capital and unearned income; men of affairs also governed. In some towns, marriage into the nobility of the surrounding countryside was the way to power in municipal government; in others, it was political suicide. In some regions, as in Ireland and Estonia, towns were isolated fortresses from which foreign conquerors ruled hostile and suppressed natives. In others, they were the brightest stages of intellectual and social life for entire provinces or kingdoms.

Finally, the general suppression of urban life by princes was not a universal phenomenon. There were exceptions to this picture; for the history we have traced applies only to those areas where princes and kings mustered their forces, reorganized their finances, and incorporated the city-republic into a wider political union. Depopulation, as we have already pointed out, was a local phenomenon. Some cities, like Cologne, sustained only a temporary decline, then quickly regained their positions. Those towns were best able to preserve their liberties and to retain their republican constitutions. In Flanders and Brabant, towns remained populous and rich, and their communes survived even the repressive measures of their new overlords, the Dukes of Burgundy, in the fifteenth century. Bludgeoned by Philip the Bold in the "red sea" of Gavre (1453), the commune of Ghent lost many liberties. Still it later regained these, only to forfeit them once again in 1540, when it rose against Charles V. The towns of Switzerland likewise remained fully autonomous, and while (Venice excepted) they lost the republican form of government, the Italian city-states remained independent principalities, unless conquered one by another.

In fact, a great caution against "urban typology" exists in the structure of Italian towns. Because of very precise, local studies, we now see that the Italian "city-state" was far from being a monolithic state of the modern cast. It was rather a bundle of associations — burial societies, guilds, political factions, and, most important, families — each of which lived with its own laws, administrative order, and, in many cases, armed defenders. The great families lived in fortified palaces, exacted their own justice by public feud and private violence, and managed their domestic and foreign affairs according to their own lights. We have to deal with something rather more like a league of Mafia "families" than the urban agglomerates we live in today. Obviously, the operations of a city government as a corporate body, and its very organization varied as one family or alliance of factions or league of associations gained predominance; and thus, the constitutional history of each Italian city-state has the identity of a fingerprint.

SUMMARY

Settlement Patterns

We have now to return to the central question with which we began. We have left aside Muslim, Byzantine, and Russian European as distinct cultural groupings that lacked close and lasting interaction with the Latin West. We have been asking whether, even in the West, there was an organic, unified society, exemplified by village and town, which had one history and followed one stylized pattern of life. Little that has been said would support such a view. The labor bases of production varied from region to region and from age to age. Settlement advanced idiomatically everywhere; the organs of village and town government varied as widely as did street plans; there was not even a common failure rate for speculation in towns.

It is true that within particular regions villages and towns had a common history. Like the village, the town took root more readily in some areas than in others. There were some regions — such as the entire Italian peninsula — which never lost the thick settlement of Roman times and which consequently had no need to found new centers for trade and government. Of Italy's great cities, only Venice was founded in post-Roman times. New foundations, like Pope Alexander III's (reigned 1159–1181) Alessandria (established 1168), failed to become great political, commercial, or cultural centers. The economy of Italy therefore encouraged the expansion of existing settlements rather than the foundation of new ones. "Colonial" areas were a second kind of field. Throughout Wales, Gascony, Holland, Bavaria, east Germany, and the Slavic countries, settlers imported from other, sometimes distant, regions cleared the land and built the towns and villages that their new lords had set aside and surveyed for them. Though not a colonial area, northern France was also a region where settlement went hand in hand with town planting. Finally, some areas such as southeast Germany entered the town-planting stage after the greatest period of settlement had ended. Clearing these areas was not the town centered movement we see in such areas as the German east, where lords systematically laid out very broad settlement patterns with towns to act as administrative centers and mercantile entrepôts for outlying villages which were surveyed at the same time. In general, towns multiplied fastest and most densely where settlement came late; for there, in utter contrast with Italy, the whole scheme of market and transport facilities had to be worked out at once, and planners seem to have had the idea that if it was good to have a few towns, it would be better to have many. As a result, those were also the areas where the highest rate of speculative failures occurred.

Again, like the village, the "colonial" town or new plantation was often not carved out of primeval forest, but laid out beside or on top of an earlier settlement. Roman cities, like those along the Rhine, had a continuous history. The same can be said of settlements along the Hellweg, the road known in Roman times between Cologne and Magdeburg, where many ancient caravansaries, royal villas, and fortresses flowered into towns from the Carolingian period on. In other areas, particularly in the region of German colonization, the case was slightly different. There, if the settlement was new, it most often sank its roots into an old, even an ancient cultural ground to which it was alien. Slavic villages, castles, and markets were recast as German towns when the new settlers gained economic and political predominance through their far-flung mercantile connections, their advanced agricultural techniques, and the privileged position they enjoyed by virtue both of their own laws and of the special franchises that princes offered to foreign settlers. In some areas, as in Prussia, there were no towns before the colonial period; in others, as in Pomerania, there were not merely towns but flourishing cities. Indeed, a chronicler records that Jumne, at the mouth of the Oder, was the largest city of Europe, inhabited by Slavs, Byzantines, and many other peoples. Gnesen and Posen were important centers of trade, with many buildings of stone and several churches, before the period of colonization and Christianization began. Occasionally, the settlements testified to their mixed heritage in law, as did Danzig, where the Old City lived by native law and the New City by a German code.

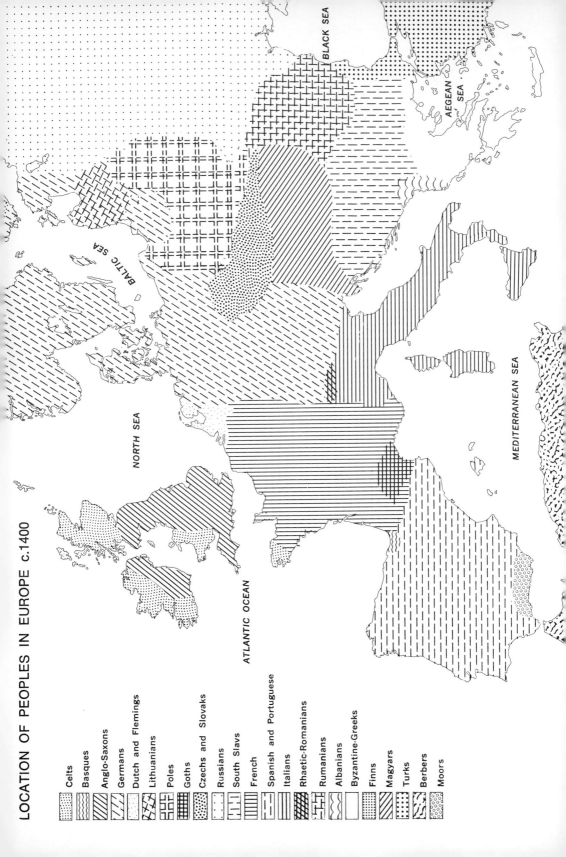

LOCATION OF PEOPLES IN EUROPE c.1400

BLACK SEA

AEGEAN SEA

BALTIC SEA

MEDITERRANEAN SEA

NORTH SEA

ATLANTIC OCEAN

Celts
Basques
Anglo-Saxons
Germans
Dutch and Flemings
Lithuanians
Poles
Goths
Czechs and Slovaks
Russians
South Slavs
French
Spanish and Portuguese
Italians
Rhaetic-Romanians
Rumanians
Albanians
Byzantine-Greeks
Finns
Magyars
Turks
Berbers
Moors

From the Pan-European viewpoint, to say this much is also to say that towns and villages throughout Europe shared no common development; that, in fact, they sank their roots into very different cultural soils, profited from indigenous histories, and expressed private aspirations. Their very forms witness the idiosyncratic character of their existence.

Town planning, like village layout, fell into distinct forms or culture patterns. Plans became standardized and multiplied, each its own kind, within given areas; settlers carried familiar settlement patterns into distant countries, and this is why, to take one instance, Flemish town plans occur in eastern Germany. We have already mentioned the difference between town plans in northern France and those in the South. There are many other clear regional types. The unwalled market town characterizes the English lowlands, parts of northern France, and the neighboring German Rhineland and southern Bavaria. The plan they share, on the whole, calls for streets radiating from a central marketplace. In southern Germany, many towns followed the "rib" pattern set by Freiburg-im-Breisgau (founded 1118), which centers on a long market street with other streets entering it at right angles. In the Baltic coastal area, other towns tended to imitate Lübeck's double-rib plan (ca. 1158). The regular grid pattern predominated in colonial areas of the German East. We could multiply examples of this genre of cultural stereotype, paradoxically both localized and spread abroad.

These patterns are not loose and disconnected facts; they reflect profound historical differences. Walls grow up in response to permanent danger from armed foemen; unwalled towns reflect freedom from that sort of danger by virtue either of geographical isolation or of an effective central government. Imitative patterns show close relations — ethnic, political, or commercial — and often symbolize dependence in legal ways. Different cultural patterns indicate different cultures; and this is demonstrated by the fact that medieval town plans can be localized geographically and ethnically.

The age of land speculation can and should be seen as a whole. Still, the whole is a composite field in which thousands of independent thrusts, some separated by two centuries and great distance, define a general trend. Every developing region had stretches of decades without founding new towns or expanding old ones, while activity went breathlessly on in other places. Some areas like the Erzgebirge in eastern Germany reached their fullest urban development in the fifteenth and sixteenth centuries, well after the speculative peak; even between the late twelfth and early fourteenth centuries, speculation went on in some areas at the same time that towns were failing in others.

In cultural origins and in areas and periods of expansion, villages and towns varied widely. Should we place greater emphasis on the local impulse than on the general trend? For the bastide dweller in late thirteenth or early fourteenth century Gascony, the important thing was that centers of trade had multiplied beyond the volume of production and that his town was strangling. It was no comfort that, a long and arduous journey away, amidst a people of strange languages and ways, new villages and towns were springing up in Brandenburg. Each area met the pattern of speculative overextension and failure in its own way and at its own time. Each city extended its walls according to immediate need, some early, others very late, some often, others but once, and others never. Each area knew a particular set of demographic problems and responded in an idiomatic way.

A great swell of population began in some European countries as soon as the effects of the Industrial Revolution began. Now, two centuries later, a similar trend appears to be launched in less-developed countries as they industrialize themselves. Clearly, some common sociological pressures are involved, and the general trend of industry plus population increase now embraces Bolivia and England. But it would hardly be maintained that the two countries have shared a common history for the last two centuries, or even that they were during that time united by the general trend that now touches them both. The industrial revolution came to Bolivia far later than to England; colonization came to the Erzgebirge far later than to Wales. We must try to steer a steady course between the analogies and mutualities that obviously exist and the very different question of a common history.

CULTURAL GROUPINGS AND PRINCES

The argument that we should think of "the medieval village" and "the medieval town" as types presents one great difficulty, aside from those already discussed. Emphasizing the revival of seignorial powers over peasants in the fourteenth century, and over cities in the fourteenth and fifteenth, presupposes general constitutional challenges and responses. This is sheer romance. There was no area where uniformity was sought more earnestly and with all possible force than in government, and none where success was less complete.

There is great sympathy among modern historians for the oppressed though nameless peasant, and fate, in its inscrutable wisdom, has continued to kindle the hearts of some with ardor for the bourgeoisie and nationalism, those household gods of the nineteenth century. A few devote their studies to royalty. In modern scholarship, the aristocrat, even of princely rank, is all too often the forgotten man; we tend to overlook the fact that kings wore the princely coronet before and while they put on the crown. And yet, in discussing whether Europe was one or many societies, we have come again and again to the lair of princes, the territorial state: it was the great beneficiary of serfdom's evolution; it was the patron and later the master of the town; it was the vessel of ethnic unity. Edward II of England gave the sense of things when he took up arms against an impending French invasion, which, he said, was meant to crush the English language, his realm, and the Christian Church. The Christian King of

France, in fighting another territorial princedom, assailed tongue, king, and religion – the great safeguards of cultural unity. The political and, therefore, the social center of gravity ultimately lay in the prince's court. This was shown most graphically in areas such as Valencia and the Baltic East, where victorious Christian minorities pushed native majorities with their separate religions, social structures, and patterns of justice, down to the level of lesser castes, and all but blotted them off the pages of history.

It was natural in an area of perpetual warfare, where fighting to the death was the dominant way of life, that the region's military chief should stand at the focal point of all great social currents. In the early Middle Ages, the instrument of this unity was the fief; increasingly, from the eleventh century on, it was the tax.

The fief transformed military associations into political agglomerations; the tax introduced the firm cohesiveness of the state. Permanent and regular tax structures failed to develop in some regions where the agglomerative form was too vigorous to wither. The Holy Roman Empire began timid experiments in general taxation as late as the fifteenth century. But the other side of the coin is that the empire's component states had developed elaborate tax schemes from an early date. The same double aspect appears in Iberia, Scandinavia, and Eastern Europe. In contrast, the papacy, Sicily, the Italian city-states, England, and France created tax systems that rank among the greatest achievements of the age. It is not mere chance that the most critical documents for social history are the meticulous official surveys put together for tax purposes, the English poll tax registers of 1377 and 1381 (which have a unique and priceless complement in the Domesday Survey of 1086) and the Florentine cadastral register of 1427 – 1428.

Papal taxation both contradicted and proved the role of the territorial state as a focus of social unity. Extraordinary levies such as Peter's Pence and the whole scheme of usual assessments that grew up as a result of the pope's right to approve accessions to Church offices cut across political borders. A substantial argument could rise on this evidence to the effect that a superior unity – the cohesion of Christendom – transcended the unifying bonds of states.

This was indeed the argument of the great medieval popes, who furthermore maintained that Christendom's unity was political as well as spiritual and that popes could depose kings and absolve subjects of their oaths of fealty. Such claims ran afoul what we may call, with a grain of salt, the inchoate national churches of England, France, and the Holy Roman Empire during the Investiture Controversy in the eleventh century. Though beaten back, they revived during the late twelfth century and reached a peak of emphasis and clear legal definition in the time of Pope Boniface VIII (reigned 1294 – 1303). In this time, the people of Europe saw the taxes that they sent to Rome turned from spiritual purposes to the papacy's interests as an Italian principality. Every great Italian war became a crusade, and the papacy devoted both normal and extraordinary revenues to fighting it. Resentment against this abuse and princely concern for territorial prerogatives finally culminated in the celebrated dispute between Boniface VIII and two kings, Edward I of England (reigned 1272–1307) and Philip the Fair of France (reigned 1285–1314). The kings meant to exclude papal tax gatherers, unless they had royal assent, and to establish their right to tax clergy as subjects, without papal assent. In their arguments and acts of force, which culminated in Boniface's humiliation and death, they refuted the papal assertions and indicated the independence and separateness of territorial states.

In this famous picture, Edward I of England (1272–1307) is shown presiding over Parliament. The presence of the Archbishops of Canterbury and York and of other prelates (on the King's right), the King of Scotland and the Prince of Wales, the temporal lords (on the King's left), and other representatives reflects Edward's determination to build the community of the realm.

"The Community of the Realm"

The spread of trade and industry throughout Europe created new sources and forms of wealth, unknown to the world of the fief. The great increase in wealth was now coming through growth of business and the accumulation of capital assets; and rulers shifted their tax burdens to benefit from this unprecedented kind of abundance. No abrupt change occurred, but step by step, in sometimes advanced, sometimes regressive, ways, kings and princes abandoned the old feudal levies and moved on to excise duties, customs tariffs, and taxes on land and movable property. By the thirteenth century, this process was well advanced in principalities from the Mediterranean to the northern seas. The great periods of tax reform came in England under Henry III and Edward I, and in France under Charles V.

New forms of wealth, including trade and industry, and the kings' chronic need for money paired to bring merchants and manufacturers into royal councils and their cash into royal coffers. The lord of lands no longer monopolized power and wealth. To enhance his rule over every scale of society, a king had to be more than a feudal suzerain; he had to be a national sovereign, and thus he had to establish a bond between himself and all those subjects who controlled material resources, a device that would involve them all in the business of government.

To do that, kings gradually added representatives of cities and towns to their councils, at first for exceptional reasons and later as a matter of course. Taxation and common danger gave birth to parliamentary institutions, but the work they undertook in fact covered the whole range of public life. In Leon, Castile, England, and the German principalities, the representatives of higher clergy, nobility, and townsmen tried to make it a general rule that the kings could impose no new taxes without their assent, that they could supervise the official conduct of royal ministers and impeach wrongdoers, and broadly that in all public affairs law was made jointly by the king and the community of subjects. In France, similar claims were made by the provincial estates and the Estates General, which first met (1302) to judge Philip the Fair's dispute with Boniface VIII over taxation.

This process more than any other welded villages and cities, townsmen and nobles, clergy and laity into true states. Under constant pressure from their princes for new levies, the various segmented elements of society realized that they had common dangers and mutual responsibilities, and that they belonged to a grouping beyond the family or town or class: "the community of the realm," as Englishmen defined it. Whether prince or king, their ruler was sovereign over them all, and his need for money gave them all the power to argue with him in order to strike bargains and enhance their positions. Edward III of England was far from unique in facing a parliament that claimed full power to assent to all direct taxes. Subjects thus saw their welfare plainest before them within the framework of the territorial state. The English parliament, the *parlements* of France, the

Spanish *cortes*, and the estates in many German principalities all saw this, and, with very different results, worked for the general cohesion of their own states and thus for political particularism.

In times of civil war and foreign danger, representative institutions claimed and exercised broader competence than in easy days. The thirteenth and fourteenth centuries were generations of almost unmitigated crisis and constant warfare. Through frequent usage, the electoral process by which representatives came to advise the king thus became a well-defined and permanent process, and the commons by right took part in royal councils and in the great affairs of state. Taxation, currency reforms, allegiance to one pope or another, patterns of jurisdiction, and much more fell under their purview. They watched over the welfare, and thus the unity, of their people.

In many cases, princes ignored the assertions of the commons, as English kings left the statutes of provisors and praemunire unexecuted. Often, they undercut coalitions by dividing and conquering them. Whenever they could, they turned the new institutional unity of their people to their own advantage. They substituted government by secret council for government by parliament as occasion offered; and their work bore fruit in the age of absolutism. Late in the fifteenth century, the Estates General asked Louis XI of France to govern without its counsel. Still, in each principality, the people as a body politic drew closer to their ruler and shrank inward from the outside world.

Political Thought and Law

At the same time, political theorists were at work rationalizing this new state of affairs. They were divided as to whether or not the ruler was absolute, the embodiment of law, and accountable only to God. Influenced by the revival of Roman Law, some theorists argued that princely government mirrored divine, and that the State was a reduced scale model of the universe. Established by God as ruler, the prince acted as God's agent and counterpart. Civil law included sacred law, as in the Roman imperial code; the rights of clergy and the privileges of all other subjects yielded to the will of the prince. Counter to this position, other thinkers argued that the welfare of the people, not what pleased the prince, was the supreme law. Indeed, the ruler represented the whole body of his subjects, and, when he violated the trust implicit in that role, he lost his claim to obedience. A prince who abused his powers was a tyrant, not a rightful governor. It was a moral duty for the people to revolt, resume the sovereign powers that they had entrusted to him, and confer them on a worthy ruler.

Thinkers did not agree on whether sovereignty rested in the bosom of the prince or in the community of the realm. But they did agree that the state was a self-contained community acknowledging no higher power outside itself. When Louis the Bavarian and his princes declared, in the fourteenth century, that papal judgment could not confer, suspend, or withdraw the imperial office, they acted on this idea. The same principles stood as a barrier between Louis and the subjects of his princes, needing only the formal confirmation that they received in the Golden Bull of 1356.

Legal thought, one of the glories of medieval life, points up this particularism. Each territory lived by its own law, and over this substructure settled a film of Roman Law from the thirteenth century on. Some states repudiated Roman Law altogether. This was normally the view of German cities, such as Lübeck and Hamburg, which considered Roman Law a device of princely government hostile to republican communes, a suspicion which the Swiss Confederation shared. And yet, the kings of England rejected Roman Law with great vehemence, upholding the common law of their people; and the kings of France and Spain considered their own statutes normative in law. Despite the heavy influence that these countries received from Roman Law, they found their supreme standards elsewhere. In the states of Italy, the laws of the Caesars held the force of a national, even an ethnic, code, which the barbarian invasions never fully extinguished. Jurists declared that the imperial code was the "common law" of the Holy Roman Empire, the classic land of the "Reception of Roman Law," where the ancient imperial statutes became normative in almost every principality. Even so, great variations remained. Roman Law had been introduced slowly during the early Middle Ages, sometimes covertly through the mediacy of Church law. For example, in courts of episcopal princes, Jews and pagans were normally tried by Roman Law instead of by the laws of the Church, to which non-Christians were of course not subject. In the thirteenth and fourteenth centuries, glossators were at work harmonizing the ancient code with Germanic temporal laws, and in the fifteenth-century Reception, this secular strand of thought combined with the older ecclesiastical strand. Each territorial state had a multiplicity of indigenous laws, and their confusion on points of procedure was a great reason for adopting the uniform standard of Roman law. Still, once the transition was made, uniformity extended only to the borders of individual states. Native laws fused with Roman in such a way as to give each territory a distinctive version of Roman Law, and in some regions — the Tyrol, Austria, and Berg — the old popular courts survived side by side with those run by Roman Law.

Degree of Politicial Consolidation

Law and legal theory, particularly the revived doctrine of sovereignty, thus followed the model and institutionalized the sociopolitical fragmentation of Europe. Fact corresponded most clearly with theory in the political segments of Italy and those of the Empire. But, if we turn to the two great kingdoms of the late Middle Ages, we see that even there the theory of territorial sovereignty obscured the fact of territorial fragmentation.

The history of England in the thirteenth, fourteenth, and fifteenth centuries is in great part a story of the struggle between kings and their magnates, of how the great nobles carved out for themselves enormous estates and vast privileges and came to hold princely powers, and of the sequence of civil wars they led in the fifteenth century. From the baronial coups against King John until Henry Tudor's victory on Bosworth Field, tension ran rife between the king, as head of the community of the realm, and the princedoms of his nobles, supported by their own extensive lands and rights and by the private armies they raised through the privileges of livery and maintenance. From the Norman Conquest (1066) until 1485, the Bishop of Durham enjoyed such sweeping palatine rights that he had his own sheriff and could exclude royal agents from his lands. As one man wrote in the fourteenth century, "The Bishop of Durham may do as he wishes, for he is as king there." The great work of the Tudors was to humble this class of quasi-independent rulers. But Henry VIII feared Stafford, whose ambitions began to be expressed in Thornbury Castle, and he cut off his head; and fear of the high nobility passed between Elizabeth and Essex at the end.

Courtesy Public Record Office, London
Despite the advance of royal centralization in England, feud and vendetta denied the king a monopoly on violence. This sketch illustrates an attempt by the royal assizes to harness private violence through the use of judicial combat under Henry III (1216–1272).

The history of the French throne provides a far more consistent process of consolidation. The slow and erratic trend, with alternating advances and compromises, began with Louis VII (reigned 1137–1180) and, most distinctly, with Philip IV. In the fourteenth and fifteenth centuries, it was especially due to the work of Charles V and Louis XI. Even Charles V faced a revolt of the nobles in his last years, and the creation of appanages, or vast estates, for scions of the royal family in the fourteenth century, carved out a new and infinitely dangerous form of principality. The retreat of France before English forces in the late fourteenth century sank royal power into the abyss. When, inspired by Joan of Arc, Charles VII (reigned 1422–1461) restored the power of his office, he took great care to construct

102

a hard-core bourgeois administrative apparatus, independent of the nobility; and Louis XI (reigned 1461–1483) enhanced this institution. At the same time, the powerful state of the dukes of Burgundy flowered and rivalled the kingdom itself in wealth and splendor. Duke Charles the Bold (reigned 1467–1477) epitomized his view and that of his peers, when he said that he would see six French kings instead of one. The danger of *Kleinstaaterei*—that is, the proliferation of small, independent states—as in the empire and in Italy, was averted. A nearly miraculous sequence of events united all the great fiefs except Flanders and Brittany in Louis XI's hands. But Burgundy's sudden collapse brought him no lasting profit. Instead, it created through lines of inheritance a vast Hapsburg territory running from Flanders down France's eastern border, an enemy with whom Louis XI's successors had to contend until the Revolution. Within France itself, the great nobility remained a festering problem until the Fronde. And this divisiveness fed on the localism of institutions; for France had 300 areas bound to distinct, indigenous legal systems, no less than the empire, and the great provinces were governed through separate assemblies of estates which had in common only subjection to the same king. Time modified, but failed to vitiate, Beaumanoir's observation that, "every baron is sovereign in his own barony."

The territorial state of the late Middle Ages was very far from monolithic autocracy, far even from the absolutism of the seventeenth and eighteenth centuries. But it was a step along the road to those patterns of government. In Brandenburg, Florence, England, and the points between, the territorial princedom became the essential unit of political and social cohesion. In Eastern Europe, this counted for less than in the West. The economic crisis of the late Middle Ages led there to the rise of the lower nobility, the institution of serfdom, and the consequent enfeebling of central authority. The balance of power between the prince and his nobles was more evenly poised.

England and France went further than other territorial states in welding many principalities into a broadly pluralistic community. Even they still faced the divisive power of the magnates. Even within their borders, they had not yet reconciled profound ethnic, linguistic, and religious differences. Such success as they won in unification hardened the political lines dividing men in Europe.

SUGGESTED READING

Reference should be made to the preceding lists. See also:

On Agrarian and Economic History:
Cambridge Economic History. Vol. 1, 2nd ed., Cambridge, 1966.
Duby, G., Translated by Cynthia Postan. *Rural Economy and Country Life in the Medieval West.* Columbia, S.C., 1968.
Latouche, R. *Birth of Western Economy.* New York, 1960.

Power, E. *The Wool Trade in English Medieval History*, Oxford, 1941.

Power, E., and Postan, M. M., eds. *Studies in English Trade in the Fifteenth Century*. London, 1933.

Raftis, J. A. *Tenure and Mobility: Studies in the Social History of the Medieval English Village*. Toronto, 1964.

Reynolds, R. *Europe Emerges*. (See reference after Chapter 1.)

Slicher van Bath, B. H. *The Agrarian History of Western Europe*, A.D. *500-1850*. London, 1963.

Slicher van Bath, B. H. "The Yields of Different Crops (mainly Cereals) in Relation to the Seed, c. 810–1820," *Acta Historiae Neerlandica* 2 (1967): 26–106.

On Towns:

Becker, M. B. *Florence in Transition*. Vol. 1, Baltimore, 1967.

Beresford, M. *New Towns of the Middle Ages: Town Plantation in England, Wales, and Gascony*. New York, 1967.

Clarke, M. V. *The Medieval City-State*. London, 1926.

Dickenson, R. E. *The West European City: A Geographical Interpretation*. 2nd ed., London, 1961.

Herlihy, D. *Pisa in the Early Renaissance: A Study of Urban Growth*. Yale, 1958.

Herlihy, D. *Medieval and Renaissance Pistoia: The Social History of an Italian Town, 1200–1430*. Yale, 1967.

Lapidus, I. M. *Muslim Cities in the Later Middle Ages*. Harvard, 1967.

Mundy, J. H., and Riesenberg, P. *The Medieval Town*, Princeton, N.J., 1958.

Rörig, F. *The Medieval Town*. Berkeley, 1967.

On Social Structure:

Bloch, M. *Feudal Society*. 2 vols., Chicago, 1960.

Darby, H. C. *The Domesday Geography of England*. 4 vols. to date, Cambridge, 1952 ff.

East, E. G. *An Historical Geography of Europe*. London, 1935.

Herlihy, D. *Medieval Culture and Society*. New York, 1968.

Granger, F. *Historical Sociology*. London, 1911.

Hilton, R. H. *A Medieval Society: The West Midlands at the End of the Thirteenth Century*. New York, 1964.

Keen, M. H. *The Laws of War in the Late Middle Ages*. London-Toronto, 1965.

Lyon, B. *From Fief to Indenture: The Transition from Feudal to Non-Feudal Contract in Western Europe*. Harvard, 1957.

Mohl, R. *The Three Estates in Medieval and Renaissance Literature*. New York, 1933.

Parsons, T. *Societies: Evolutionary and Comparative Perspectives*. Englewood Cliffs, N.J., 1966.

Verlinden, C. *L'esclavage dans l'Europe médiévale*. Vol. 1, Bruges, 1955.

On Political Divisions:

Altamira, R. *A History of Spanish Civilization*. London, 1930.

Bronsted, J. *The Vikings*. London, 1960.

Carsten, F. L. *Princes and Parliaments in Germany from the Fifteenth to the Eighteenth Century*. Oxford, 1959.

Carsten, F. L. *The Origins of Prussia*. Oxford, 1954.

Cohn, H. J. *The Government of the Rhine Palatinate in the Fifteenth Century*. Oxford, 1965.

Dvornik, F. *The Making of Central and Eastern Europe*. London, 1949.

Chapter 4

Religion: Christianity as Order

In our discussion we have found two contrary processes at work simultaneously. On the one hand, the idea of Europe as a cultural community took great strides toward becoming an accomplished fact. Scholars and philosophers throughout Europe formed an interregional "republic of letters"; the specialization of many districts in production of particular agricultural or industrial goods ended their economic self-sufficiency and bound up their welfare in a wide net of mutuality. Diversification and interdependence, sustained by improved communication and demographic increase, lay behind this side of the picture. On the other hand, we have also seen that before 1500 Europe never achieved an organic, unitary society. No more than Theodoric the Great did Erasmus know a single, pluralistic union stretching from the Baltic to the Mediterranean, and from the Vistula to the Pillars of Hercules. Countervailing forces of stratification ran against the trend toward unity: distance and natural barriers to communication; variations in social structure that sprang from the different ways men had to organize labor to wrest a living from the land; the lack of a common history, indeed, the vigor of ancient hostilities handed down in folk tale and proverb and fed by war; profound cleavages between cultural groupings, as by language and patterns of justice; and, finally, the force of territorial government, which divided Europe into jealous, antagonistic principalities and hardened cultural idioms as signs of inner political cohesion and of proud defiance of the outside world. In political terms, unification of European societies went only as high as the territorial principality.

When we turn to religion, we see much the same situation. The paradoxical coupling of mingling and stratification stands out all the more because we have grown accustomed to taking Christianity as the common denominator of medieval civilization.

SOME GREAT ISSUES

The history of medieval religion is yet to be written. Late in the nineteenth century, and again in the last three decades, scholars turned to the critical issue: the relation of religion to society, its impact on the ways men lived out their daily lives, did business, and governed. Beside the spellbinding generalizations that have often predominated in scholarly works, this approach of sociologists, or historical anthropologists, looks picayune. Its ultimate object is not to frame a composite description of medieval Christianity as a unit, but to work out a comparative history of the varieties of religious experience in the Middle Ages.

Until specialist studies have prepared the ground sufficiently for that final goal, focus brings greater rewards than a breadth of vision can. We are concerned with specific religious practices or beliefs within definable social groupings, with the responses individual men made to spiritual crises, or with concrete problems that ran throughout the history of Christianity. For the moment, the object is not to reconcile diversity and establish norms, but to examine religious groupings on their own terms, rather than against our extrapolated standards, allowing dissent to stand unmitigated and tracing its origins back not merely to abstract intellectual arguments but to profound social cleavages. What are the characteristic forms of each sect in each period of its existence? Did a religious order, such as the Cistercians or the Franciscans, have distinctive views of life that set it apart from both Christians at large and other orders? What social conditions allowed Pope Innocent III to approve the doctrine of absolute poverty as advocated by St. Francis of Assisi, and how had those conditions changed when his successors condemned it a century later?

This is the sort of question that must now be asked, and it is growing increasingly clear that the day is past when even very distinguished scholars could be content to describe in a few sentences the state of medieval religion. We have come to see that what used to be judged random deviations or pernicious heresies were absolute norms to their followers and should be analyzed in that light. Norms have multiplied.

The time is far from ripe for the great comparative study toward which scholars are working. But it is useful at different stages in the long-range process to pause and take stock. Where do we stand? What picture seems to be emerging? What place can we give religion in a cultural profile of medieval Europe?

The starting point for understanding religion as a social phenomenon is a straightforward maxim: that society, not nature, is the model of its religion. In the primitive world, uniform religious practices are perhaps the most telling symptom of an integrated society, though in more advanced, pluralistic cultures, uniformity of practices is far less important than a common attitude toward the role of religion in society. Religion begins with a particular view of man and of his place in the world. The Roman poet Lucretius wrote with great insight when he said that belief in the gods came well along in the progress of civilization — after family structure and the organization of civil government, after man had begun to cope with his environment and to sense his physical and mental limits. The root and chief feature of religion, he said, is fear. In fact, we know of no people that lacks all religious sense. But it is true that religion reflects the needs of men in a specific time; it is a device by which man tries to perform miracles, because he knows his inadequacies and fears the results they may have. The idea of how the world is run is a twin sister to the idea of man.

With this in mind, let us turn to Christianity. In the thought of medieval men, Christianity was above all a religion of The Death. It was not a cult of the dead, though it did incorporate many features of such a cult, particularly in the veneration of relics, prayers to and for the dead, and offerings of food and sustenance — either in kind or in endowments — to the saints. Medieval Christianity was partly that; it was also partly a cult of death, as witnessed by the grisly works of art and the frenetic masochism that we associate especially with the late Middle Ages. The cult of the saints, the service of "King Death," and the art of dying were integral parts of the religion. In a sense, the tomb was the cult's true symbol: the tombs of saints, breathtakingly elaborate, encrusted with enormous plates of precious metals and baskets of jewels, the objects of terrifying expense in a society that lived at the subsistence level and the goals of arduous pilgrimages; the tombs of great men and women, sumptuously carved and decorated, often preserving the images of the dead and normally placed in churches, near the wonder-working bones of the saints; the altar, the center of cult practices, the image of a tomb, and the place of daily sacrifice, ornamented with symbols of torture and death and worked in the purest and most precious materials. The world itself was in the process of dying; any moment it might perish in fire and earthquake.

There was another dimension in medieval Christianity that carried it beyond the level of a cult of the dead, or a cult of death. The death that Christianity revered was more than man's common fate, a biological end that in some way or another comes to us all, the most passive of all experiences. It was a purposive act — not a death that ends life, but the death that opens the way to life. It was redemptive death, the death of Christ, the historical beginning of the Church which was reenacted daily at the altar, the everlasting bond between the Redeemer and the redeemed, and the mystical channel of salvation. Life was death by stages; to die well was to imitate Christ in his purposive sacrifice, bearing witness to God's redemptive power, whether by negation of self-love through chastisement of the flesh, by spiritual exercise, or by the ultimate testimony, martyrdom in the act of spreading the faith.

The emphasis on death was capable of leading to the hideously macabre in private devotions. Still, the grandeur of medieval architecture, the serenity of Gothic religious sculpture, the hopes that men expressed, and the heroism of their lives show an indomitable, vital impulse. Exaltation of purposive, sacrificial death kept the Church's public teachings and ceremonies from the danger of morbidity feeding upon itself. Love transfigured death; the shadows of eternal night scattered before the splendor of the love that united God and man, the love that in Dante's metaphor moved the very stars. Death was a good leading to a greater good. The world decayed; the Kingdom of God came. The bones of the saints, sheathed in flashing gold and jewels, prefigured the day when God's holy ones would burst forth from their tombs ablaze with glory. The funereal shrouds of Good Friday fell before the radiant, triumphant joy of Easter. Death was swallowed up in victory.

Survival after death was indisputable. What was at stake was the blessed life; for, if one fell short of participating in Christ's sacrificial ministry, one reaped the wages of sin—death, not as the end of existence, but as unending existence in profound physical and spiritual torment. For medieval man, this world was full of consequences for the next. Life was a continuum; there could be no empty spaces, no gap even after biological death. Medieval Christianity had its joyous side; but the joy rose from expectation that the guilt of original sin could be atoned for and the fears lurking in every corner of life could be negated at the end. Christianity had no idea of the noble savage, no faith in the untaught and unimproved nature of man. Man's original state was brutal and lawless; then, as one writer observed, the strong preyed upon the weak, and men ate one another like cannibalistic fish of the sea. To be rude and savage was to be depraved. To be unimproved by the learning and discipline of Christianity was to be barbaric and sunk in man's natural bestiality. Men in this state were still blinded by the sin of Adam to the redemptive path of Christ.

Natural processes did not run the world. We separate man, his fate, and the material world. Medieval men filled the spaces between these three things with myth and symbols, and bound them inextricably together. The great questions of life and natural phenomena were two aspects of a great unity. Astronomy served as a kind of augury. Natural history was a branch of scriptural exegesis, heavily interlarded with fanciful beasts and allegory. What medieval men knew of physical laws came chiefly from ancient writers rather than from empirical observation, and it was modified by complete faith in supernatural powers that could for good reason suspend normal states and make the sun stand still or heal the blind. What gave it all meaning was God's great plan for salvation.

Man stood before God at the center of the universe. The physical world whirled about them, both as matter and, even more, as emanations and signs of a higher truth. As matter, it defied man's control and threatened his worldly life; as a signal of God's will, it was menacingly ambiguous. Man stood before God for His judgment. Did he stand as regenerate son or as deserving victim? The world about him gave few clues; anxiety alone was certain.

On this foundation stood the great formalistic edifice of medieval Christianity: the vast set of rituals and cult practices administered by a priestly hierarchy according to a refined and detailed body of law. The faithful were sheep to be guided, or forced if need be, in the way of salvation; their role was to obey their shepherds. If not dispelled, anxiety was at least assuaged by the repetition of liturgical formulas, the definition of piety and sin in tabooistic terms, and the establishment of a class set aside by consecration to interpret and to preach God's will. The purpose of life, the hope of salvation, was surer when stabilized and fixed in terms of ritual right and wrong, when the Church as intermediary between heaven and earth could instruct man clearly how to please and glorify his Creator, Redeemer, and Judge.

The Many Forms of Worship

The papal monarchy, of course, casts its dark shadow across the whole question of religious formalism. It should render materials for a comparative approach scarce; for the whole impulse of the papacy was to supplant local practices with Roman norms in liturgy, doctrine, and juridical procedure. In the eleventh century, the Gregorian reformers pressed this effort to an unprecedented height in their campaigns against Milanese and Mozarabic liturgies, in their claims to direct supervision of the faithful in every diocese over the heads of ordinary bishops, and in their use of legates as itinerant justices imposing Roman standards of conduct by Roman legal methods as they traveled throughout Europe. At least from the fourth century on, popes had asserted that the Church had one correct order and one legitimate form of observance — which the Apostle Peter had learned from Christ and established in the Roman Church. The Gregorians first tried to set up administrative machinery for imposing the standardization that this implied. Their work began the growth and elaboration of papal government that culminated in the jurisdiction that Innocent III actually exercised over kings and bishops, and in the international network of the Inquisition established by his successor, Gregory IX (1227–1241). One faith, one discipline, one order of government. This was the cohesive bond of Christendom.

We are only now beginning to appreciate the imprecision of this view. For example, there were numbers of liturgical uses different from the Roman. They proliferated; and, far from advancing toward a unitary pattern of worship, the later Middle Ages fell into liturgical anarchy and arbitrariness. This extreme diversity can be traced back to the two liturgical families that developed in Europe by the fifth century. One was the Romano-African which flourished in Rome and in the region around Carthage, and the other was the Gallican family with its several branches — the Old Spanish (or Mozarabic), Celtic, Milanese, and Old Frankish (or Gallican) liturgies. These rituals and the problematical Aquileian and Beneventan rites were in constant flux. Some vanished almost without trace. As it spread, the Roman order itself modified and was modified by the other orders. For example, Pippin the Short and his son, Charlemagne, forbade the Gallican liturgy in their lands and introduced Roman practice. Despite all prohibitions, native usages did survive to modify the Roman liturgy and by the eleventh century had returned the favor. The Romano-German liturgy had supplanted the old Roman practices in Italy. Liturgical reforms in the time of Innocent III and later made the Roman liturgy a legalistic exercise in which even the smallest details were prescribed. But such rigid formalism inspired diversity rather than uniformity. Even before the twelfth century distinct usages had grown up within the Roman family. The church of Lyons had its peculiar practice from the time of Charlemagne, and, in the twelfth century, some religious orders, such as the Carthusians, the Premonstratensians, and the Cistercians, began to have their own sets of liturgical rites. Three of the famous four ritual orders or "uses" of England—those of Sarum, York, and Hereford—come from this period, descendants of the use of Rouen. (The fourth "use," that of Bangor, remains entirely hypothetical.) Similar diversification occurred throughout Europe —even in Norway, where the Trondheim Rite appeared—and continued until the sweeping revisions urged by the council of Trent.

Many other variations went along with this flamboyant growth of liturgies. Calendars of the Church year varied; catalogues of saints were witnesses to local history, rather than to the devotions of a universal community. There were many parallels to the case of Winchester, which in the tenth century took on one of its own bishops, the obscure St. Swithun, as its patron and discarded Saints Peter and Paul. Latin was, of course, the normal language in the West, though oriental churches had always used vernacular languages in current or archaic forms. Still, even where Latin predominated, native languages found a place in the liturgy. Moravian churches read the entire liturgy in Old Slavonic, and in Germany, Austria, Switzerland, and the lower Rhineland, German was used in some parts of the mass. Idiomatic usages appeared in yet another way, that is, in architecture, partly because of varying aesthetic taste, and partly because different forms of worship required special settings. A liturgy that called for elaborate ceremony, with large numbers of assisting clergy, needed one kind of building. A more austere liturgy relied on a completely different ground plan for its dramatic effectiveness.

Regional Styles of Architecture

Structure and aesthetics combined to draw still sharper regional distinctions. How should God's house look? What forms of structure and ornament were pleasing to the ruler of heaven and earth, appropriate to His service, suitable to His dwelling place? We are used to answering these questions in terms of the Romanesque (c. 1050–1150) and Gothic (c. 1150–1500) styles. But in fact these styles experienced very different histories in the distinct regions of Europe, and their variations are most important evidence of separate cultural groupings. It is true that stylistic hybrids sprang up along major pilgrimage routes—churches that formed genuine interregional "families" of architectural design and decorative motifs. The most thoroughly studied of these groupings stands along the way that led through France and Spain to Compostela. But the homogene-

Late medieval Europe owed much to Islam, including knowledge of medicine and Aristotelian philosophy. That debt is expressed architecturally in these two photographs which show the cinque-foil (or five-curved) arch in its native islamic habitat (here the Great Mosque at Cordova, tenth century) and as transplanted to England in the tomb of Edward II in Gloucester Cathedral (fourteenth century).

ity of such "families" emphasizes the localism of style in places off the main roads, and in fact, it means that pilgrimage churches themselves represent a special class of "regionalized" styles.

The Romanesque family showed the idiomatic quality of religious architecture by splitting into ten major regional branches: three in Italy, five in France, one in the Rhineland, and the tenth in northern Spain. There were yet other variants, as, for example, the English style which developed from the Norman. The great domes of St. Front in Périgueux, the bristling spires of Mainz cathedral, and the classicism of Sant' Ambrogio in Milan all fall in the category of Romanesque architecture. But they also betray extreme variations in technical skills, receptivity to aesthetic influences from distant cultures (such as the Byzantine), and native canons of taste.

Even greater extremes appear when we turn to the Gothic style. Different countries received it at different times; and, in them, it followed different courses of development. For example, the Gothic age in Germany began with the building of the *Liebfrauenkirche* in Trier in 1235, although the style had by then flourished in northern France for a century. German

Before the revival of classical architecture in the late Renaissance, the dome as an architectural trait was a sign of Byzantine influence, sometimes by way of Islam. The three churches pictured here illustrate this cultural borrowing. St. Sophia in Kiev was originally built in the eleventh century. It has, however, been frequently rebuilt, and only a few of its nineteen domes are medieval. St. Front at Perigueux, France, is the greatest of a number of domed Romanesque churches built between about 1050 and 1130 in southern France. The magnificent Church of St. Anthony, at Padua (begun 1231), asserts cosmopolitanism with minarets as well as domes.

Novosti from Sovfoto

architecture therefore missed the early stage of Gothic, and entered the
race at a stage corresponding with the French "Rayonnant" or the English
"Decorated" period. Very quickly, local tastes asserted themselves and regional styles appeared both in art forms and in building materials. The
Brick Gothic, which dominated the coastal areas from Frisia to the Gulf of
Finland, the Stone Gothic that flourished in the High German area, and
the region of mixed brick and stone in Prussia and southern Scandinavia.
Similar regionalization occurred in other countries. Northern France, the
homeland of Gothic, tried for height; southern France held to quasi-

113

Romanesque taste, always suspicious of the Gothic style until it pounced upon its last great form, the flamboyant. Three distinct stylistic zones ran across Scandinavia, and Italy, except in the north and in Cistercian and Franciscan churches, ignored Gothic.

An eminent student of architectural history, John Harvey, has pointed out that the Gothic is the ultimate rejection of the dome, and it is only right to add a reference to this most obvious divergence of Western architecture from the Byzantine. Domes do occur in some isolated regions of the West, and, occasionally, well-meant attempts were even made to set a dome on a Gothic building, as at Venice in the church of Saints John and Paul (mid-fourteenth century). Itself an imitation of the Church of the Holy Apostles in Constantinople, St. Mark's in Venice set a pattern for a family of about nine churches in Aquitaine, all dating from the twelfth and early thirteenth centuries and of which St. Front was the most important member. The use of the dome or of cupolas varies widely there, as it does also in a cluster of eleventh- and twelfth-century Romanesque churches in the middle Rhineland. Aside from St. Mark's, Italy displays a series of Byzantine churches with domes, domes distributed throughout the peninsula and representing every period. The coming of the Renaissance ushered in a new age of dome building in the West. Always a law unto itself, medieval Rome ignored the dome as thoroughly as it did the Gothic style. Apart from ancient buildings converted into churches, the first domed ecclesiastical building in Rome, Sant' Augustino, was constructed toward the end of the fifteenth century.

As the Renaissance progressed, men throughout Europe came increasingly to share an idea of how a great church should look. The nearly universal spread of the dome represents this new cultural mutuality, foreign to the Middle Ages. The basilica of Old St. Peter's in Rome found few imitators; the impact of the New St. Peter's dome atop a Greek cross plan reached to every corner of Europe. The late Renaissance, the era after the Council of Trent, was also a time of standardization in liturgical usages and the whole body of regulations that governed the formalistic life of the Church. But, as we have seen, the Middle Ages was a time of luxuriant regional deviations, each a norm to itself. The popes from the eleventh century on forecast but failed to achieve the unification and general rationalization of Church order and discipline that their successors, after the Council of Trent, actually produced.

Many additional aspects of Christian practice could be cited to show that the ways churches interceded with God and displayed His glory — and thus the ways they understood God and His dealings with man — differed greatly from region to region. Local and ethnic cult practices developed; distinctive religious societies participated in and modified official worship; indigenous pagan practices incorporated into the victorious new cult set one church apart from another; local crises, such as famine or plague, and the role of clergy in local politics likewise left heavy marks. It is clear that the Middle Ages did not make a uniform response to fundamental religious needs.

AUTHORITY AND THE POPES

Cultural traits, such as the ones we have mentioned, claim an essential part in any comparative history of religion. Varying liturgies and concepts of the house of God, different calendars of saints, and even divergent Church years concern only one aspect of formalism: the Church's mediacy in devotional practices between God and man.

Behind variations of this sort was a far more critical issue: the question of jurisdiction or authority. This highly complex problem concerned religion in two ways. First, a system of authority defined members of a religion as a society; it unified them and divided them from outsiders. Second, it defined the religion's role as part of a broader, secular society, especially bringing out its attitude toward temporal government. The two functions intertwined. In the unitary view of medieval history, disputes on these points humbled the papal monarchy in the late Middle Ages and destroyed the unity of Christendom. But that fragmentation was in fact always present as both evidence and result of ancient differences in the idea of Church authority.

The roots of medieval conflicts over ecclesiastical order go back to primitive Christianity and beyond to its ancestress, the Synagogue. In the New Testament and in other writings of the Apostolic Fathers and the early apologists, several kinds of authority appear. One kind, directly borrowed from Judaism, was that of tradition, written or unwritten and confirmed by general acknowledgment and long usage. Two others that ran directly counter to tradition were the charismatic power of great leaders—prophets or saints—and the authority of some offices, such as the priesthood. To appeal to tradition was to invoke the cumulative learning and thought of all believers, past and present; to appeal to personal or official authority was to give first place to spontaneous judgments and immediate revelations of individual men.

The Apostles died, as did their followers. Eyewitnesses of the apostolic ministry also fell, and the importance of written testimonies increased. Men tried to preserve the Apostles' doctrines in writing. But, as the body of doctrinal writings grew, obscurities and apparent contradictions within it likewise multiplied. Correct ritual observance and orthodox faith depended increasingly upon true understanding of texts. But both the texts and interpretations of them varied. Tradition as cumulative knowledge did not give the single-voiced witness that men ascribed to it. Eminent teachers and, as the monarchic episcopate developed, bishops fought one another like wild beasts over articles of belief and practice.

Church and State

Constantine's conversion (c. 312) and the gradual Christianization of the Roman Empire brought the issue of authority to a new level. As long as Christianity was a persecuted sect, alien to the society in which it lived, fortuitous and improvised ways of resolving doctrinal disputes, squabbles among hunted men, made little difference to the world's rulers. Constantine, however, made these matters affairs of state. He was convinced that God would protect him and cause his reign to prosper if, through his efforts, the Church were given inner peace and unity and worldly glory.

Constantine's identification of ecclesiastical uniformity with the public weal was epochal. It catapulted Christianity from the level of an illegal and persecuted cult to that of the favored religion of a world empire. Beyond that, it opened up two problems concerning authority in the Church which have remained open questions. The more obvious one, of course, is the relation of temporal power to the spiritual, or, in the usual term, Church-State relations. What concern of the emperor were matters of faith, discipline, and hierarchic order? On what authority did he intervene in religious matters, and how far could his influence in them rightly go? Should the emperor be merely an external defender and patron, or should he be the actual head of the Church, a bishop of bishops? Could he, though a layman, consider and judge sacred things? This problem concerned the place of religion in a broader society.

The second problem involved the character of religion as a society in and of itself, its form of inner government. Temporal honors and wealth were the emperor's gift; he bestowed them liberally. But in seeking to calm controversy among Christians, he tried to impose on the churches a unity that they had never had. Constantine himself considered the faithful as a body, a community, one Church; but the scope of this misapprehension was shown by the series of schisms and controversies that began before Constantine's day and continued for the next three hundred years. Churches under persecution had grown up as autonomous institutions. Although the five patriarchal churches (Rome, Antioch, Alexandria, Constantinople, and Jerusalem) claimed headship over lesser churches in their provinces, even they had to struggle against the defiance and independent policies of their subordinates. Among the patriarchs, there was no agreement as to primacy, and the history of the patristic ages is full of their conspiracies to exalt themselves by humiliating and destroying eminent peers. Ethnic hatred of the Roman conqueror carried over into religion; most churches in Syria and in Egypt regularly followed doctrines that Byzantium had condemned. Languages and customs also divided the churches, and this is shown most clearly by the great variety of liturgical customs that sprang up in the East using vernacular languages and native cult patterns. Neither in administrative order, sentiment, nor ceremonial order was there uniformity or cohesion among believers before or after Constantine. The institution that did embrace all the faithful was not the Church, but a communion of churches. Church history until the rise of Islam, in the seventh and eighth centuries, is mainly the story of how the separate churches alternately repelled and attracted one another and gradually grew farther and farther apart.

On the one hand, then, Constantine intruded a new problem — Church-State relations — into the picture of how churches were to be governed. On

Who should have the greater power, king or bishop? A perennial problem in medieval history, this question could hardly be put more clearly than in these two pictures. The first, a plaque (made about 1200) from the door of Gnesen Cathedral, shows Emperor Otto II (973–983) investing Bishop Adalbert with the crozier, symbolizing the episcopal office. The second, the tombstone of Archbishop Siegfried of Mainz (1230–1249), shows the prelate majestically bestowing royal crowns on two diminutive kings. The different roles illustrated by these two scenes indicate the decline of royal power in Germany between the tenth and the thirteenth centuries.

117

the other, he complicated old questions of authority. Being a Christian had once meant accepting apostolic preaching as true, whether it were written or passed down by oral tradition. The disputes with which Constantine had to deal, especially the Arian conflict, raged around questions of Scriptural interpretation. They were disputes over what the Scriptures meant, not over what they actually said. Under Constantine, therefore, orthodoxy came to mean subscribing to a particular understanding of Scripture's inner meaning. Correct belief, Constantine thought, was the chief cohesive bond of the Church. If only standards of faith could be defined and crystallized in law, then the true believers would of course acknowledge them, and backsliders and proud dissenters could be forced to choose: recant or perish. Constantine would unite the Church, please God, and prosper by divine favor thus earned. This view required an authority to fix correct belief and to impose it on the unreceptive. Constantine had troops for coercion; he called the "great synod" or ecumenical council into existence for settling questions of doctrine.

Religion married politics. Correct belief became a question that put property, freedom, and even life at stake. By making it a subject of law, Constantine also prompted a change in the idea of authority among believers. Tradition came to be looked for in the decrees of synods and councils, more than in the general confession of all believers or in the common opinion of Scriptural commentators. The power to teach took second place after the power to judge. The first steps had been taken toward legalism, toward making Christianity, which was in its very nature a religion of the Book, specifically a religion of law.

Legalism always divides men. Constantine sought unity in increasingly tight definitions and increasingly severe penalties. Such unity as he could have achieved lay in compromise; but his methods in fact narrowed the grounds for compromise to such a degree that, in many cases, it was no longer possible. Tradition was being confined more and more to legalistic formulas which many could in no way accept. Jealous of their independence, the great churches refused to acknowledge one office or man as chief of the whole communion of churches, and, in fact, their constant jockeying for position effectively prevented general acknowledgment of such a head. Who spoke for all believers then? Who could fix tradition in law, define conflicts over their faith, and judge dissenters? Not any particular bishop or saint, for lack of general acknowledgment; not the emperor, most thinkers agreed, since he was a layman. Constantine set up the general council; but, as events showed, even in Constantine's own day, one council could easily overturn the decrees of an earlier one and approve beliefs that its predecessor had condemned. Moreover, the empire lacked sufficient force to impose religious standards universally, and acceptance of them ultimately became a matter of local option decided by each bishop in his diocese.

The result was chaos. The new issue of Church-State relations gave a fresh dimension to the problem of Church authority without clarifying the old questions of internal order. In fact, it exacerbated them. When the Roman Empire split under Constantine's sons and again, permanently, at the end of the fourth century, reigning emperors normally set up the creeds that they personally favored as official standards, having them duly approved by obedient synods. Contemporary emperors confessed different creeds; individual emperors changed their minds and their official creeds almost at will. For their part, many individual churches fought a double battle for their autonomy in matters of faith: on one hand, against the empire and on the other, against ambitious prelates in other sees. The result was the dismemberment of the communion of churches through schism and dissent. Resistance to an alien empire and to the aspirations of foreign prelates found natural leaders, especially in the patriarchates, the great sees that were also political centers and symbols of ethnic glory and unity. The churches of Byzantium, Syria, Egypt, Palestine, and the West went their own ways.

Religious conformity had become a sign of political submission, and rejection of the imperial creed currently in vogue a sign of civil disobedience. Until Islam engulfed Syria, Palestine, and Egypt in the seventh century, Byzantium was preoccupied with establishing religious stability through force or compromise. Despite its dangers, standardization of faith was a necessity of life.

Throughout this time, the issue of authority found yet greater complexities. Synods and councils contradicted one another; the animosity of the great sees grew keener. Though often invoked as an abstract, timeless rule of faith, tradition was rather the flexible language of politics. As the moment required, politics supplied clear answers to religion's contested issues; expedience ruled.

As subjects of the empire, the bishops of Rome had been involved from the beginning in this tortuous history of dispute and schism. They held the premier see, the only patriarchate, of the West; as the ancient capital of pagan Rome, their see claimed greater glory through its identification with Saints Peter and Paul whose bones were its principal treasure. The greater part of the West, however, fell outside the Byzantine sphere and did not share in the conflicts of this early, perhaps even premedieval, period. It began to contribute to the question of authority in the Church only in the eighth century, and through the efforts of one of its greatest figures, Charlemagne. The issues with which it had to grapple and the precedents it had to follow were familiar.

The ancient world left the Middle Ages neither a solution to the question of Church-State relations nor a distinct pattern of authority in the Church. It did leave the two issues inextricably entwined. It also showed the administrative fragmentation that could arise when standards of belief and practice were imposed without regard for regional differences or for the whole complex of cultural traits that give ethnic and national groups their identity and self-esteem.

The Papacy

What did the Middle Ages do with these thorny issues passed down from antiquity? Did they find a harmonious balance of Church and State and a smooth pattern of administrative authority that bound at least Latin Christendom into one community?

Some late medieval canonists answered both questions affirmatively. As the vicar of Christ on earth, they said, the successor and embodiment of St. Peter, the pope had power to judge any believer or any moral issue. Thus he could direct a Christian ruler whenever the prince's personal salvation or the spiritual welfare of his subjects was at stake. This meant in effect that the pope had the right to judge — and if need be to censure — a king's acts at every level of existence, and that the royal power should be wielded at the pope's direction. Kingship was an ecclesiastical office. In the allegorical language of the age, the pope held in his own right the sword of the spirit and deployed the king's sword of physical punishment.

For canonists who held this view, the pope's temporal power was the natural effect of his complete spiritual authority. The pope was the supreme judge in the Church. He exercised immediate and appellate jurisdiction. Cases could go directly to him from any part of the world, whether or not they had been tried first in another bishop's court. Beyond his judgment lay no appeal. Any issue involving sin or the possibility of sin — thus any issue — fell within his competence. Matters concerning laymen — the bonds of marriage, questions of inheritance, all disputes involving oaths — came before him as well as disputes over Church personnel or property. He dispensed all ecclesiastical privileges and many emoluments; archbishops could function as metropolitans only after receiving the pallium, the symbol of their office, from his hands; their provinces were made, divided, or abolished by his decree. He certified monastic orders as legitimate. In acknowledgment of his legal claims and powers, he received taxes from bishops, religious foundations, and laymen in every part of the Latin world.

Despite the rights of bishops, the pope held direct administrative authority over every diocese. Despite the powers of local synods and ecumenical councils, he could review their decrees and approve or reject them. Despite the force of existing law, he could grant dispensations from the rigor of the canons and correct or negate old canons and decrees of earlier popes. His legates could suspend the powers of any bishop in any degree and rule in the bishop's place. He was the architect of the Church from top to bottom. He was the sun of justice, and his brilliant rays touched even the most remote corners of the Christian world.

This was the ideological structure that Innocent III and his immediate successors brought into near reality and that the popes of Avignon nurtured to overripeness. The cornerstone of it all was the idea that man's salvation depended upon the Church as intermediary between him and God and that the pope was the Church's supreme intercessor. But above the saving function of the Church rose a great fabric of property and jurisdiction which defined salvation in terms of obedience, rather than spontaneous belief. To be against the institutions of the visible Church was to be heretical, and it is possible to define the medieval papacy entirely in terms of law and politics, without any reference to faith at all.

Indeed, the view of papal absolutism just described, which the popes in

the late Middle Ages tried to enact, is blighted by a kind of spiritual ane-
mia. Power and money reign. The extent to which religion, even in the
Roman see, was subordinate to politics is clear when we know, for example, that sixty-three percent of Pope John XXII's (1316–1334) budget went
for war and that on one day that Pope excommunicated eighty-two prelates — including a patriarch, five archbishops, and thirty bishops — for their
outstanding debts to him. Nomination to ecclesiastical office and deposition
from it, excommunication, and the remission of sins were matters of state,
or even matters of business. Nor was this new in John XXII's day. From
the tenth century on, the venality and irreligiosity of the papal Curia fed
the mills of parodists.

But the issues of Church-State relations and of authority within the
Church did not end for all people in monolithic papal autocracy. The idea
of papal monarchy was one of the great intellectual achievements of the
Middle Ages. In some ways it corresponded with the facts; under some
popes it came near realization. But it was never fully achieved. Counter-
doctrines arose expressing in one way or another the concept of tradition:
that alternate authority rested in the general witness of all believers and
that laws and offices stifled it. The idea of papal monarchy survived in the
Counter-Reformation; the opposing ideas flowered in the Conciliar Movement of the fifteenth century and its aftermath. Both are important
strands in medieval thought. Let us turn to the factors that ran counter to
the monarchist view.

ALTERNATIVES TO PAPAL MONARCHY

The popes were never fully masters in their own houses. The papal
states constituted a broad strip across Italy, the size of a great principality, and, in theory, the popes were sovereign over these states. Still, even
the most ruthless campaigns of mercenary armies in the thirteenth and
fourteenth centuries failed to match theory with reality. The urban communes of the Romagna, the city-states of Umbria and Ancona, indeed the
great nobles and the provincial towns near Rome normally acted indepen-
dently of, and often against, their lord.

Even in Rome itself, the pope had a slippery footing. One of the most
familiar figures in the Middle Ages was the pope fleeing from his see, the
shepherd harried and hunted by his sheep. In the early period, Roman
bishops suffered death, mutilation, or exile in acts of occasional violence,
scenes in the dramatic but petty struggles among powerful Roman families
or in the resistance of Romans to bishops installed by the German emperors. From the eleventh century on, the tension between Rome and its bishop
grew more institutionalized. When the Romans repudiated Gregory VII
(1084), they acted as a corporation, and the solidity of that institutional
force kept Gregory and his successors from residing permanently in Rome

for more than a decade. In retrospect, we can see that the conflicts then and in the early twelfth century were leading up to the proclamation of the Roman commune in 1143, an act of revolution against Pope Innocent II. With that, Rome joined the company of cities from the North Sea to the Mediterranean that cast off the administrative yokes of their bishops and declared their governments to be autonomous and in the hands of laymen, the citizenry, the bourgeoisie. A measure of the success of this revolt in Rome is the fact that, together with other causes, it kept Pope Alexander III out of the Eternal City for nearly twenty years of his twenty-three-year pontificate. Other cities in the papal states followed Rome's example; and great vassals of the pope usurped sovereign rights. The Patrimony of St. Peter seemed on the verge of collapse.

In Rome, the revolutionaries formed a senate of the lower classes and the minor nobility, which exercised regalian rights, such as the privilege of coinage, taxation of goods imported for sale into Rome, and control of the administration of justice.

Thus began a long, complex series of conflicts which ended at last in the fifteenth century, when the Renaissance popes dismantled the effective powers of the city's republican government and gained full control of Rome's civic powers.

That outcome was far from inevitable in our period. Even though Pope Eugenius III accepted the commune, because the Republic refused to allow his episcopal consecration otherwise (1145), he soon fled to France and raised an army to subdue his people. Hadrian IV continued the struggle by laying an interdict on the Eternal City, his own see, and between 1181 and 1187 there were three popes, all in exile. Despite a treaty between pope and commune in 1188, a reorganization in 1191–1193 stripped the pope of his revenues and powers of temporal jurisdiction.

In his efficient way, Innocent III reduced the commune's powers almost to the level of pure symbol; but republicanism survived to drive Gregory IX from the city, subject the clergy to civil courts, and curtail the powers of papal jurisdiction in Rome itself. This alternation of papal and republican rule continued into the fifteenth century, through the era of the Babylonian Captivity, when the popes asserted that it was too dangerous in Rome for them to live there. It led to the magnificent failure of Cola di Rienzi's republic (1347) and the series of early fifteenth-century revolts against papal authority. Finally, the repressive measures of Nicholas IV (reigned 1447–1455) established an autocratic government of Rome by the papacy that lasted until 1789. In the late eighth or early ninth century, a forger wrote the spurious *Donation of Constantine*. This document was intended to support astonishing claims by popes to territorial and hierarchic supremacy and to state and panoply like that of Roman emperors. Lorenzo Valla's exposure of this work as a forgery is an academic souvenir of opposition to papal sovereignty that lingered in fifteenth-century Rome.

Even in Rome and the papal states, then, the doctrine of papal monarchy had a checkered history. Expedience, force, prospects of political gain, and perhaps honest conviction gained its acknowledgment from time to time and finally won its permanent acceptance. But for nearly four hundred years, a strong counterdoctrine ran alongside the monarchist view, challenging its claims to temporal jurisdiction and, occasionally, to property. Ironically, papal autocracy won out in Rome just after the Conciliar Movement had arraigned it before all Christendom and just before the Protestant reformers in northern Europe repudiated it.

The extreme claims of the papal monarchists therefore did not correspond with the facts in the popes' own see. Were they founded in serene self-assurance or in the uncertainty and fear that breed hysterical exaggeration? Did they find resonance in the world, if not in the city? Let us see.

By the time of Charlemagne, some great and lasting barriers to a monarchic Church were clear. The whole issue of property and jurisdiction took on a special cast among the Germanic peoples because of what scholars call the "proprietary church system." Appropriation of land by conquest made the barbarians lords of the soil and of what rested on the earth. Thus, secular men owned churches and altars, and they could entrust their property to anyone. Laymen had parish churches in their gift. Kings and greater nobles had bishoprics and abbacies. Whatever their spiritual obligations to the remote and beleaguered bishop of Rome, clergy owned more immediate services to their near and powerful lords. Bishops and abbots became temporal princes in the greatness of their property and in their offices as field marshals and vice-regents. But they were still the servants of their lords, who had raised them personally to their posts and richly endowed their churches. This was generally accepted as legal and just; in the tenth century a pope sanctioned it. By right, the king stood between his clergy and any would-be monarch of a pope.

Jealous of their power and prerogatives, the Germanic clergy wished to act as third parties, playing off pope against king to serve their own advantage. Absolute domination by a king was as unattractive to the clergy as was a papal monarchy. Against kings and rival bishops the idea of papal monarchy always lay ready to hand. Many Germanic prelates opportunistically used it in one dispute and, in another, revived fortuitously and often in unpremeditated ways the ancient idea of a community of churches. Consistency was less important than political success. Churches in different regions, they argued, meet unique conditions, and thus they need special laws and institutions. Some regulations were indeed applicable to every church, but these were established by the general assent of all the faithful, expressed either by the formal acts of universal councils or by slow and tacit acceptance in practice. These were eternal laws. Papal decrees had force, not really as laws so much as authoritative interpretations of laws, and their legal relevance faded as the immediate situations which they addressed passed away. The papal court was a superior appellate court, but beyond it lay the general council, and cases had to go through a series of episcopal and archiepiscopal courts before they reached Rome. It was, therefore, neither the court of first instance in every case, nor the supreme court of appeals. Final authority lay in what patristic thinkers had called tradition — the general confession of all believers past and present — rather than in the *ad hoc* judgments of one bishop, even if he were the vicar of Christ and the successor of St. Peter.

These were the major views that conflicted again and again throughout the Middle Ages. A straight line runs from the idea of papal monarchy as framed by Charlemagne's contemporary, Pope Hadrian I, to the doctrines of Innocent III to the post-Tridentine autocracy. Another line, equally direct, connects Charlemagne, who nominated bishops, summoned and advised synods, and threatened to depose two popes, with the German princes in the Reformation who declared, *cuius regio, eius religio et reformatio eius* (he who has the region has religion and its reformation). Yet a third line carried the idea of a communion of churches from Charlemagne's bishops to the conciliarists of the fifteenth century. At times, one strand seemed to predominate over the others; at times, two reinforced one another against the third. But none of them was ever suppressed.

The Power of the Prince

A heavy shadow lay across the glittering theories of a united Christendom: the figure of the territorial prince. In the earliest days of missionary work in northern Europe, rulers had seen Christianity and, more explicitly, the Church, as one device among many for sanctioning their own power, developing effective administrative machinery, and compounding the intellectual glory and repute of their courts. Rulers never ceased to think of religion in these pragmatic, self-serving ways. We have seen the atomization of political life in the late Middle Ages due to the rise of territorial principalities. The same process deeply split the actual patterns of ecclesiastical government. The thirteenth-century Duke of Cleves, who claimed to be pope in his own lands, had his very words lifted by later dukes of Austria and inflated by Bernabò Visconti, "pope, emperor, and lord" in Milan. They all had a predecessor in Henry II of England (1154–1189), who said that, like his grandfather, he "was, in his land, king, apostolic legate, patriarch, emperor, and everything he wished." Henry VIII, as Supreme Head of the Church in England, merely continued a long and divisive convention.

In what ways did this power of prince over Church disrupt the lines of authority in the Church? Was more involved than the faulty rhetoric of calling a layman "pope" and "head of the Church"?

Let us turn to the case of England, not as a universal type, but as the most familiar of all instances. There, from the Norman Conquest on, with rare exceptions, the king was in command of the Church. In Normandy, the dukes had made themselves masters of their clergy, excluding such foreign influence of the French king and of the pope as they wished. This tradition of rule William the Conqueror extended to England. As in other kingdoms, prelates were considered servants of their temporal lord, to whom they owed military assistance and regular attendance in the royal council. Beyond this, William and his successors had sweeping powers to block and direct Church government. They could, for example, bar papal decrees and legates from their lands. They could veto decrees of local synods, and forbid the excommunication of any tenant-in-chief or royal officer. Finally, and perhaps most important, elections to bishoprics and the greater abbacies could not be held without their permission, and no such election was complete without their approval. In a famous writ, Henry II instructed the clergy of Winchester: "I command you to hold a free election, and furthermore I forbid you to elect anyone other than my cleric, Richard, archdeacon of Poitiers."

The Norman kings of England therefore exerted tight control over the selection of the higher clergy and over the policies which the clergy, set in consultation with the pope and among themselves, in diocesan or provincial synods. These powers were strongly challenged. Archbishop Anselm of Canterbury (d. 1109) preferred exile to being invested by Henry I with the temporalities of Canterbury; he denied the legality of the whole institution of lay investiture. Anselm's successor, Thomas à Becket (d. 1170) withstood Henry II when the king began to extend his powers by bringing clerics charged with criminal offenses before secular courts. At the same time, great elaboration of the royal administrative machinery bound the higher clergy, as officers of state, ever more closely to the king's service and interests. And the settlements that ended the great conflicts both with Anselm and Thomas left the king in control of episcopal and abbatial elections.

These remaining powers brought on the series of disputes that helped to lead Henry II's son John (1199–1216) to the fields of Runnymede. An election to the see of Canterbury was contested. King John provided a nominee. Pope Innocent III rejected both elections and John's nomination, proposed Stephen Langton as archbishop, forced his election, and confirmed the promotion without John's prior approval. John, in turn, rejected Langton. The struggle became intense. Innocent laid an interdict on England; John confiscated property of the clergy; Innocent retaliated with excommunication and deposition of the king. John submitted and received England itself as a fief from the Pope. In his Charter to the Church (1214), confirmed the next year by the Magna Carta, he granted the rights of free election to all churches and other religious establishments.

The Contest of Power

In this contest over familiar rights began the strongest challenge to its rule over the Church that the monarchy had ever faced. As part of his drive to centralize Church order, Innocent III corroded the authority of prelates over their own churches by nominating clergy to lesser ecclesiastical vacancies, such as canonries. Following the lead given in Langton's case, Innocent's successors undercut the power of kings over their clergy by nominating bishops to vacant sees.

Their assault on royal prerogatives came when England was most vulnerable. Henry III's long minority, with a papal legate as co-regent, and Henry's weakness, once he began to rule in his own right, allowed papal influence to supplant the king's. This process advanced by a number of devices that derived from the pope's role as judge. If an election were contested and brought before the papal Court, the pope could void the election and, as judge, exercise absolute right of appointment. The pope had the power to translate a bishop from one see to another. By these steps the popes moved, in the early fourteenth century, to appointment without election. They sent foreigners as well as Englishmen to become prelates in England. John's cession introduced a long series of royal capitulations by his son and of victories for the papal monarchy.

John, however, had set another sort of precedent by confiscating clerical property, and, in his Charter to the Church, he had modified but retained some important rights: custody of vacant churches, granting permission for elections, and confirming elections. The ascendancy of aliens whom the popes intruded into English vacancies aroused bitter resistance, especially as they introduced liturgy and laws counter to English norms. The papal collector, in charge of English provisions, was expelled. Parliament refused an enormous grant that Richard of Cornwall wished to make to the pope. When civil war began, it had as one object purging the church in England of extraneous elements.

Edward I's assertions of the royal prerogative in matters of taxation are well known. His struggle with Boniface VIII led him to deny clergy benefit of the royal courts and so to make them civil outlaws, to demand vast "gifts" in lieu of the taxes that the pope had forbidden, and to confiscate the lands of those who failed to respond. He carefully chose his points for dispute, however, and he opposed papal provision only when Boniface VIII went further than his predecessors and presumed to bestow both temporalities and spiritualities on bishops he had named. Edward refused to acknowledge such a usurpation of his authority. He forced the new bishops to renounce the objectionable terms in the papal bulls of provision before he himself granted them the temporalities of their sees. Otherwise, Edward took no exception to papal provisions. He even neglected to enforce parliamentary legislation designed to curb the practice, perhaps because papal appointments were made with his full knowledge and approval.

Meanwhile, the papal doctrine of provisions became increasingly broad. Popes had at first claimed the right to act as guarantors of free episcopal elections, providing to vacant sees the men whom relevant cathedral chapters elected. The first Avignonese Pope, Clement V (reigned 1305–1313), changed this right to approve and appoint into a right to appoint. Subsequently, election was a meaningless form. Popes ignored the electoral process and intruded their own appointees, or provided the men duly elected without taking cognizance of their elections.

Most often these appointments were made in consultation with the king; usually the papal nomination merely confirmed, in fact though not in form, the king's choice. But popular outrage at the intrusion of foreign bishops and the negation of local electoral rights sustained Edward I in his struggle with Boniface VIII; it demanded redress at the parliament of Carlisle in 1307; it routed the claims of papal monarchy during the Hundred Years' War. Despite almost constant warfare between England and France, the Avignonese popes continued to nominate French clerics to English vacancies. As enemy aliens, the bishops-designate could not take up their offices. Absenteeism sharpened national hostilities, and a series of parliamentary statutes undercut papal assertions. The Statute of Provisors (1351, 1364, 1389) purported to check papal provisions and to restore to the king his ancient rights over episcopal and abbatial elections. It declared that anyone receiving office by papal provision was liable to imprisonment and that all livings granted by the pope should be forfeited to the king. "The clamourous and grievous complaints of lords and commons" likewise produced the Statute of Praemunire (1353, with several repetitions). It ordered that if legal cases rightly fell within the competence of the king's court, they could not be taken to courts outside England (the papal Curia was meant), to the detriment of the royal prerogative and the destruction of the common law. Anyone who did so appeal was outlawed, his property forfeited to the king, and his person subject to imprisonment at the king's pleasure. Having struck aside jurisdictional ties, Parliament turned to financial ones. In 1366 it rejected a papal request for renewal of tribute payments granted by John when he received England as a fief from Innocent III. The claim, it said, was groundless; no king could make England a fief belonging to a foreign ruler without Parliament's assent, and John had lacked that.

At the same time, a long series of negotiations between popes and kings staved off the application of these statutes. The kings had what they wished; they need not endanger the substance of power by challenging ceremonial points of law. Their easy connivance continued. As a result of the Great Schism, Henry V (reigned 1413–1422) briefly allowed episcopal elections to revive and restored the archbishops as judges of them during papal vacancies. Strong popes and weak kings in the fifteenth century suppressed this practice; the series of papal provisions flowed on in a torrent. Under Henry VI (1422–1461; d. 1471) the King's Council nominated candidates; the settlement was worked out at Rome. Royal nominees were usually provided, and, under Henry VII, this became the inevitable practice. The papal monarchy had won the form but lost the essence of power over the English episcopacy.

Popular anger and royal diplomacy achieved this end. The old administrative separateness from Rome was now asserted by Parliament, rather than by the king alone. As in the days of William the Conqueror, a barrier ran across the jurisdictional lines between popes and the English church.

Paradoxically, the popes themselves paved the way for complete subjection of the church in England to temporal government. We have seen that papal provision stifled the process of episcopal election and thus removed with one blow the autonomy and the meaning of cathedral chapters. In the same way, provisions to canonries and lesser ecclesiastical offices—often on a large scale—corroded the powers of bishops to dispose of posts in their own churches and consequently to dominate the synodal assemblies through which they governed dioceses and provinces. The whole administrative elaboration of the papal monarchy had been designed precisely to reduce local autonomy and to hurl the grist of Church administration at every level into the papal mill. With the connivance or tacit approval of kings, the popes used dispensations, legatine missions, resident legates, supreme appellate and immediate jurisdiction, as well as provisions to undercut the autonomy of national clergy, to stamp it out as a semiindependent third party operating between the kingship and the papacy. Spiritually and administratively the English episcopate had lost its power of self-government to the diplomatic finesse of pope and king.

The Erosion of Ecclesiastical Privilege

As Rome's own power waned, in the Great Schism and later, the episcopate stood a nearly helpless and invitingly wealthy victim before the throne. Indeed, the subjection of the Church to civil direction grew increasingly on the point of property, that second pillar of the medieval Church. The implications of this second trend counted for more in our period than what it actually achieved. From the reign of Henry III (1216–1272) on, statutes of mortmain forbade clergy to receive fiefs without the consent of the principal lords of the fiefs; conditions of feudal tenure gave these lords important services, benefits, and the power to reclaim their lands through escheat when their tenants died, but all these advantages were nullified when the fiefs fell into the hands of an undying corporation.

Despite these severe restrictions, the clergy remained wealthy, just as, despite the parliamentary disqualification of bishops as ministers of state in 1371, prelates like Beaufort in the fifteenth century and Wolsey in the sixteenth continued to serve their kings at the highest official level. But the long series of statutes of mortmain was more than a straw in the wind of politics. Another view from the level of popular devotion reinforced it when John of Gaunt, under Wycliffe's influence, proposed to confiscate the lands of the Church, and when, in 1404 and 1410, the Commons debated the same means for relief for the poor. There was, however, nothing to compare with the secularizations that brought most of the property of Bohemian churches into the hands of nobles during the Hussite Wars. Henry VIII perfected the art of confiscation in England.

The Roman commune ultimately lost its four-hundred-year struggle against papal monarchy. England won, at the cost of lasting schism under Henry VIII. Both attacked jurisdiction and property in an unplanned and perhaps unsuspected general tendency to integrate the religious structure of an area into the political structure that governed the region. They were not concerned with the cohesion of the universal Church. That was a question of abstract theory. In fact, it dangerously subverted their aspirations. For practical political ends, the scope of cohesion reached as far as the individual state, and the great need was to suppress internal privileges and to exclude or curb foreign influence if it endangered local order.

We must pay special attention to this development in the empire. There the territorialization of the Church was even more striking than in England; it involved, not only enfeebling the episcopate by pope and prince, but also the detachment of many bishops from primary allegiance to the king-emperor and their subjection to territorial lords.

The balance between princes and clergy passed through two periods: the first, lasting until the eleventh century, when bishops acted as independent rulers in their own sees and princes were subject to the king; the second, ending in the fifteenth century, saw bishops lose their autonomy and their princely station to secular lords.

There were exceptions to this rule: the three episcopal electors of Mainz, Trier, and Cologne kept their original eminence, and ecclesiastical princedoms continued to be created until 1889 in Austria and until 1919 in Czechoslovakia. But even these great sees fell under sometimes heavy temporal direction. (The episcopal princedom as a temporal government was abolished by Pope Pius XII as late as 1951.)

In general, the German episcopate had an institutional unity before the twelfth century that rested on common obligations to the king. When the Gregorian reform shattered the king's power to nominate bishops, this bond dissolved, and authority over Church property and personnel devolved upon the nobility. The Gregorians' objects had been to cast off the royal power to present candidates for election and to make free election by clergy and people the true path to office, rather than an empty form. By the Concordat of Worms (1122), which ended the Investiture Conflict in Germany, the Gregorians acknowledged the king's legitimate right to invest freely elected bishops with the temporalities of their churches. But in time even that remnant of the old unity disintegrated.

Elections became the monopoly of cathedral chapters, and the chapters themselves were dominated by local dynasties. In this way, bishoprics were objects of family politics, treated with the same monopolistic care as other properties. Late in the fifteenth century, for example, members of the Wittelsbach family normally held the sees of Cologne, Magdeburg, Freising, Münster, Regensburg, and Strassburg. Several devices confirmed local dynasts in this preponderance. One was sheer wealth. A second was the office of ecclesiastical "advocate." As "advocates," lay lords defended and represented a church in secular affairs in return for revenues and lands which, with the advocacy, became hereditary. Their chief functions were military, and, by force of arms and unobtrusive usurpation, they gradually subverted the independence of the churches that they were meant to defend. Clergy of the churches which they "defended" were obliged to attend their councils and to provide them with both extraordinary and usual taxes. At last, they gained the right of advowson itself, the right to present clergy for ecclesiastical benefices at lower levels, or even, in many instances, at the level of the episcopate.

Although the Gregorian reform in the late eleventh century had overturned the old proprietary church system, territorial lords thus continued to function on new legal grounds as lords of churches in their lands. The implications of this became perfectly clear when lords other than the king began to invest bishops with their temporalities. Aside from an isolated example in tenth-century Bavaria, the first prince who exercised this function was Henry the Lion, to whom the Emperor Frederick Barbarossa granted the right to invest bishops of the new sees that Henry founded east of the Elbe. Later, the monarchy's weakness encouraged other princes to usurp the same powers.

Step by step, the princes beat back the authority of pope and of king alike, until, as in tenth-century France, the nobility controlled most churches outside the king's hereditary lands. Even where this formal development did not occur, episcopal sees were often so thoroughly under the influence of temporal princes as to be political satellites of the princely court.

The long English dispute over papal provisions had counterparts in almost every German principality. These disputes too ended in a compromise which in fact consolidated the princes' powers over the clergy in their lands. Sealed by treaties such as the Concordats of the Princes (1446–1447) and the Concordat of Vienna (1448), the victory of territorial government enabled princes to prevent papal bulls or briefs from being published in their petty realms and to forbid or allow under set conditions the preaching of indulgences.

As in England, the clergy had been weakened by the centralizing efforts of the papacy and by the efforts of lay lords to tap its wealth by taxes and to curtail its acquisition of property through statutes of mortmain and similar devices. Henry II's abortive attempt to bring criminal clerks before secular courts had successful parallels throughout the German states. The clergy lost heavily in cohesion and repute when the princes took for their own courts much that had formerly been claimed for clerical jurisdiction and hastened erosion by allowing appeals from Church to prince on the ground of "abuse of ecclesiastical authority." Their elections thus determined by the favor of the prince, their wealth curtailed by the prince and subject to his disposal, and their courts impugned, bishops found themselves hamstrung even in the exercise of their spiritual offices and discipline. Temporal rulers controlled many appointments to the lower clergy. Their consent was necessary before bishops could perform visitations or in any way supervise secular or regular clergy or religious foundations.

The effect of all this appears in one especially obvious symptom: the meeting of synods, the chief organ of episcopal government. Though canon law required frequent synods, diocesan and provincial synods almost ceased to be held. In Mainz' jurisdiction, for example, only eight provincial synods met between 1239 and 1455; in Brandenburg, only 18 diocesan synods met in more than three hundred years (1174–1512). This rarity of meeting was not even paralleled in Gaul, when Church order all but collapsed; the Merovingians held at least fifty-four episcopal councils in the sixth century alone.

The ambitions of popes and temporal lords atrophied institutions of local Church government and, as in England, ultimately left the Church and its property at the disposal of the territorial prince. Indeed, secularization of Church lands began in Brandenburg, as in Bohemia, before the end of the fifteenth century. The proverbial Duke of Cleves had his counterpart in every other great principality.

In every region the same pattern emerges, though with important variations: in England; in the states of the Empire; in Scandinavia; in Portugal; in the Spanish kingdoms, where Alphonso the Wise of Castile (1255) went so far as to remove his kingdom from surveillance by the papal inquisition and to grant the inquisitorial office to national authorities; in the Italian city-states, some of which had pioneered in taxation of clergy and restrictive statutes of mortmain; in the realms of Naples and Sicily; and in France, where kings destroyed the medieval papacy in the person of Boniface VIII, dominated the popes of Avignon, and gave the first impetus to the Conciliar Movement.

Everywhere, princes tried to check their loss of services and income by mortmain and to curtail the jurisdictional privileges of Church courts, in short, to make clergy citizens first and servants of the pope second. Everywhere, the spirit of universalism in the papal monarchy challenged national or ethnic identities and was rebuffed. When, by papal provisions, the popes intruded foreigners into vacant offices, they excited deep popular animosities, even in Italy where there were violent protests against the French prelates, especially legates and provincial governors, sent down by the Avignonese popes. Indeed, national consciousness fired and prolonged the Great Schism. The demand of the Romans, in 1378, for a Roman or at least an Italian pope, led to the election of Urban VI. When Urban refused to go back to Avignon, the French cardinals decided that it was more important to go home than to stand beside the pope they had elected, consecrated, proclaimed, and assisted in official business. They declared Urban's election void, elected a cousin of the French king as pope, and with him returned to Avignon.

At every stage in the Schism that followed, and in the later councils, decisions about which pope to follow and which conciliar decrees to accept were made at the level of the territorial princedom. Was the pope at Avignon or the pope at Rome the true successor of St. Peter? Each king or prince decided for himself, often in conference with his parliament or Estates. Kings and assemblies could change their minds. After accepting Benedict XIII as true pope, France withdrew from his obedience (1398), returned to it (1404), and again withdrew from it (1408), finally declaring neutrality on the particular issue of who was pope and affirming "the ancient liberties of the Gallican church." Denounced as antipope by most of Europe, Felix V still mustered the approval of Savoy, the Swiss communes, and a few German principalities. Should the Council of Basel be accepted as orthodox, or condemned as schismatic and heretical? Pope Eugenius IV repudiated it. France accepted it and, with the Pragmatic Sanction of Bourges, made its decrees national laws. Most German princes agreed to stay neutral. To assert neutrality in any of these issues was to say that the Church could exist without a pope.

It was no wonder that the Council of Constance organized itself into nations, drawing on the two fonts of political reality and the "national" organization of universities, or that, when Pope Martin V undertook to end the Schism, he chose to do it in a series of three concordats for Germany (including the Empire, Poland, Hungary, and Scandinavia), the Romance nations (France, the Spains, and the Italian states), and England.

One of the great ironies of history was that hardening national divisions in the West occurred at this moment; for in a series of inspired and dramatic acts, the papacy reconciled its differences with many Eastern churches and reunited with them. It concluded peace with the Byzantines at the Council of Ferrara-Florence (1438), in the presence of the Emperor John Palaeologus, and separate unions with Christians in Armenia, Egypt, Ethiopia, and the Near East followed in the next seven years. Many of these settlements had no lasting practical effect. But, for a time, the hope for a universal Church, a true community of faith, revived and grew potent in the affairs of men.

And yet, these far-flung unions belied the ancient and now institutionalized divisions in the West itself. This fragmentation of authority in and over the Church did not spring suddenly upon the Latin world in the late Middle Ages. Many of the issues involved had matured in the primitive Church; Constantine the Great added new questions and new dimensions to old ones. Afterwards, disputes presented the same problems in different combinations, with varying emphasis, or in unprecedented social contexts.

SUMMARY

On points of authority, religion divided men, rather than uniting them. What role could the temporal ruler properly have in Church government? Was the Church itself a communion of churches or an organic whole? Consequently, did localism or monarchy rule it?

Politics and religion were inseparable. The struggles in Rome and the papal states and the English disputes show that. The protracted conflicts between empire and papacy betray the same tension between opportunism and integrity both in the sphere of government and in that of faith. The bishops who stood beside Louis the Pious in the ninth century and threatened to excommunicate Pope Gregory IV when he moved against the emperor were spiritual ancestors of a large family: the prelates who composed the Ottonian State-Church and ratified their kings' depositions and nominations of popes; the bishops who excommunicated and deposed Gregory

VII in defense of their king, and, incidently, of their own privileges; Frederick II's episcopal supporters excommunicated by the pope in 1240, whose view the Bishop of Brixen summed up when he ground the papal bull into the dust with his heel.

Fragmentation of Church order within the empire was part of its political fragmentation. The ascendant princes imitated their king in his powers over the clergy, and stood, as he had stood, between the pope and the churches in their lands.

There were many crucial divisions beyond those we have mentioned. Some cut across national lines, as in the religious orders. The great nineteenth-century historian William Stubbs wrote of England, but his description applies equally well to the rest of Europe: "The seculars hated the regulars; the monks detested the friars; the Dominicans and Franciscans regarded one another as heretics; the Cistercians and the Cluniacs were jealous rivals; matters of ritual, of doctrine, of church policy – the claims of poverty and chastity, the rights and wrongs of endowments – the merits of rival popes, or of pope and council – licensed and unlicensed preaching, licensed and unlicensed confession and direction – were fought out under the several standards of order and profession. And not less in the politics of the kingdom."

The medieval Church had many centers of cohesion beside prince and pope, and many groupings and regroupings, even within individual orders, such as the Franciscans. All of them raised the issue of right order in the Church.

But the three great antagonists were pope, prince, and bishop. Issues among them determined in great measure the outcome of lesser disputes, precisely because, as we have seen, they fought out the question of Church order as part of a broader problem of governmental authority. Their disputes involved the cohesion of society itself.

The world of ideas exists in the world of men. Administrative orders and theories of government alike are built up cumulatively by trial and error, from the thrust of one power and the feint of another on concrete issues, matters of life and death. On the one hand, the authorization and preaching of the Crusades expressed the high claims of the doctrine of papal monarchy. On the other, the Crusades' actual failure to keep the Holy Land, the papacy's use of them against Christians, fiscal abuses that attended them, and a widespread conviction that murder and robbery could not save souls had the contrary effect: the papal tiara was smeared with scorn. The divisions of ecclesiastical authority that we have observed sprang from a similar interplay of theory and actual effect. They rose from matters discussed in the last chapter: distinctive histories, disparate kinds of commercial growth, various degrees and centers of political force, indigenous variations in language and other social bonds. Political order – and thus the ways in which the issue of Church-State relations arose – also expressed this diversity. Such profound divisions could not be smoothed over with a mere doctrine of unity, and the elaborate structure of jurisdiction that the medieval popes developed failed to suppress them.

It has been argued that the Great Schism, and especially the Conciliar Epoch, ended "the idea of papal ecumenicity." As we have seen, they in fact continued disputes that ran back in an unbroken line to Charlemagne and indirectly to Constantine the Great. The papacy had known many disputed elections that ended in schism—there were four in the twelfth century alone. It had known some prolonged interregna, when the qualified electors could not agree upon a pope. Conflicts arising from papal elections had given rise to a distinguished series of synods and councils, of which those that met in the disputes between empire and papacy were but one branch.

The essential problems and the divisive results of the fourteenth- and fifteenth-century movements were new only in magnitude. Forces of ethnic and national unity had collided many times with the organs and doctrines of papal monarchy. But the episcopacy no longer stood as a third party between pope and king, except in theory. Even in Spanish kingdoms, where they retained vast powers, the interests of the higher clergy had fused with those of the nobility, and, when threatened from without, they sprang to defend national identity. So much the more in other countries, such as England and the German principalities, where administrative centralization by pope and prince had stripped bishops of their autonomy. The episcopate had complicated, perhaps even modified, early conflicts. Now, without it, papacy and territorial state came face to face.

How could the disputes be settled? To every solution the territorial state held the key. Should one pope be accepted and the other cast aside? Should each state hold its own synods to judge? If an ecumenical council were held, would its decrees bind even those not represented in it? Who would decide whether its decrees were binding at all? The answers lay in the heart of the prince and in the counsel he took with his subjects.

For this reason, the Great Schism and the Conciliar Movement were divisive beyond other conflicts. The old questions now coursed through new balances of power and some new institutions. More interests were involved than those of king, bishop, and pope—the separate interests of townsmen and barons, and the collective interests of the community of the realm; and these interests, protected and nurtured by laws and representative practices, made religious authority their problem, almost their prerogative. As in the time of Constantine, the Council was counter-productive. It brought men of strongly opposed views together, but, in requiring them to consider inflamed issues, it crystallized differences, exasperated intransigence, and drove men apart.

Thus far, we have considered conflicts over points of authority. The divisions we have noticed occurred among men who accepted, on balance, the formalism of the medieval Church as useful and necessary channels of salvation. Hierarchy, sacraments, privilege—a Church of property and temporal jurisdiction—was beyond dispute for them, however hotly they fought over particular issues.

But many rejected this structure altogether. For them, authority itself, not aspects of it, was the great stumbling block. The schisms and other conflicts discussed earlier were clerical affairs. They involved the laity only at the exalted diplomatic level of Church-State relations. What the laity believed did not really matter. Even the Conciliar Epoch excluded nearly everyone but the clergy. Theorists of the conciliar movement gave temporal princes, however great their real influence, an insignificant part in healing the wounds of Christendom. To ordinary laymen, they gave no role at all.

To protest against authority in the Church was to challenge clerical monopoly of belief. This is precisely what Martin Luther did on the morning of December 10, 1520, when he burned Pope Leo X's bull threatening to excommunicate him, the standard book of canon law (the *Decretum Gratiani*), and the principal collection of papal decrees. He defied all the authorities of the visible Church and repudiated the laws that sanctioned them. Neither pope, nor cardinals, nor general council could define the faith. Each believer was a priest; ultimate authority lay in his own reading of the Scriptures, in his own conscience. This rejection of formalism had a history as ancient as that of clerical schism. We must now turn to that aspect of medieval Christianity.

SUGGESTED READING

Reference should be made to the following lists.

On the Papacy:
Addison, J. T. *The Medieval Missionary: A Study of the Conversion of Northern Europe, A.D. 500–1300.* New York, 1936.
Barraclough, G. *Papal Provisions.* Oxford, 1935.
Cantor, N. F. *Church, Kingship and Lay Investiture in England, 1089–1135.* Princeton, 1958.
Mollat, G. *The Popes at Avignon, 1305–1378.* New York, 1963.
Moynihan, J. M. *Papal Immunity and Liability in the Writings of Medieval Canonists.* Rome, 1961.
Setton, K., ed. *A History of the Crusades.* 2 vols. to date, Philadelphia, 1955 ff.
Sullivan, R. E. "The Papacy and Missionary Activity in the Early Middle Ages," *Medieval Studies* 17 (1955): 46–106.
Tellenbach, G. *Church, State and Christian Society at the Time of the Investiture Contest.* Translated by R. F. Bennet. Oxford, 1940.
Tierney, B. *Foundations of the Conciliar Movement.* Cambridge, 1955.
Waley, D. P. *The Papal State in the Thirteenth Century.* London, 1961.
Zema, B. "Economic Reorganization of the Roman See During the Gregorian Reform," *Studi Gregoriani* 1 (1947): 137–168.

On General Questions of Authority in the Church:
Morrison, K. F. *Tradition and Authority in the Western Church: 300–1140.* Princeton, 1969.
Ullmann, W. *The Growth of Papal Government in the Middle Ages.* 2nd. ed., London, 1962.

On Church-State Relations:

Alfoldi, A. *The Conversion of Constantine and Pagan Rome.* Translated by H. Mattingly. Oxford, 1948.

Cheny, W. A. "Paganism to Christianity in Anglo-Saxon England," *Harvard Theological Review* 53 (1960): 197–217.

Jones, A. H. M. *Constantine and the Conversion of Europe.* London, 1948.

Kern, F. *Kingship and Law in the Middle Ages.* Translated by S. B. Chrimes. Oxford, 1939.

Morrall, J. B. *Political Thought in Medieval Times.* London, 1958.

Morris, C. *Western Political Thought.* Vol. 1, London, 1967.

Setton, K. M. *Christian Attitude Toward the Emperor in the Fourth Century.* Columbia, 1941.

Tierney, B. *The Crisis of Church and State.* Englewood Cliffs, N.J., 1964.

Wilks, M. *The Problem of Sovereignty in the Late Middle Ages.* Cambridge, 1963.

On Art and Architecture:

Clapham, A. W. *Romanesque Architecture in Western Europe.* Oxford, 1936.

Conant, K. J. *Carolingian and Romanesque Architecture, 800–1200.* Harmondsworth, 1959.

Frankl, P. *Gothic Architecture.* Harmondsworth, 1962.

Harvey, J. *The Gothic World: 1100–1600: A Survey of Architecture and Art.* London, 1950.

Hauser, A. *The Social History of Art.* London, 1951.

Panofsky, E. *Gothic Architecture and Scholasticism.* New York, 1957.

Prevsner, N. *An Outline of European Architecture.* 4th ed., Harmondsworth, 1953.

Smith, E. B. *The Dome: A Study in the History of Ideas.* Princeton, 1950.

TOOLS OF THE TRADE

History is a synoptic craft. It surveys man's experience in the world over a period which we now know to be in excess of two million years, and it aims to sum up man's achievements in the struggle for physical survival and in the drive, which sets man apart from other animals, to conceptualize himself and the world around him. The great advantage of medieval studies over work in other periods of European history is that it gives this synoptic quality free rein. Because the entire storehouse of materials is comparatively small, the medievalist can examine the whole in a reasonable space of time. The totality of culture lies before him: art, drama, music, theology, law — all the achievements and aspirations of man in a brilliant age.

Let us look at a few of the auxiliary sciences on which medievalists rely. Two branches of knowledge not limited to medieval studies have chiefly enriched our information about man's physical environment in the past. The earlier of the two, archaeology, grew out of the late medieval humanists' search for artifacts of classical antiquity, especially for works of art. As it became a true science, archaeology experienced a shift in orientation. The esthetic sense that had inspired humanistic diggers was not lost; but it yielded pride of place in the late nineteenth century to an interest in past societies that went beyond the sculptor's workshop and thus demanded wide schemes of classification and precise methods of excavation and study. Men realized that it was as important to discover stages in the growth of technical skills as it was to establish the sequence in the growth of man's ideas of beauty. Archaeology had passed from esthetic to historical sensibility.

In the nineteenth century, two auxiliary sciences (as distinct from techniques) grew up to establish precise dates of archaeological sites, and thus the sequence of culture. The greater of these, stratigraphy, examines the strata, or layers, of settlement deposits at a given site. The guiding idea behind stratigraphy was drawn from eighteenth-century geology, which demonstrated that the earth's surface consisted of distinct layers that had been laid down in chronological sequence, each one on top of its immediate predecessor. Every archaeological site has its own history of settlement and therefore a stratification as distinctive as a fingerprint. Stratigraphy as a science, and the general dating pattern it was eventually able to establish depended on a broad comparison of sites from the same eras. But it ultimately required meticulous layer-by-layer digging of every site and careful examination of all associated materials, especially pottery.

In the main, medieval archaeology has gained its richest harvests not from the tombs of kings, but from settlements and churches; and here knowledge has come largely from stratigraphy. Archaeology has shown that literary descriptions of the destruction of Roman towns, such as Mainz and Cologne, by invading barbarians were greatly exaggerated. There were on the whole no vast conflagrations, no silent streets inhabited only by ravening wolves. Town life continued, perhaps on a reduced scale; but no catastrophic rupture separated the cities of the late Roman period from those of the eleventh century. Slavic settlements which German colonization suppressed have come to light, with sophisticated fortifications and settlement plans which, without archaeology, would have remained unknown. Thanks to excavations in such cities as Magdeburg, Gnesen, Breslau, Cracow, and Prague, we now appreciate that, contrary to the prejudiced accounts of German chroniclers, the Slavs were capable of building substantial structures in stone, and that Christianity reached the East long before the German colonists. To take another example: chroniclers dismissed the trading posts of Haitabu and Birka with a few lines, but modern archaeologists have established the historical features of those settlements, so critical for Baltic trade, and even for exchange of Byzantine and Islamic goods, in the ninth and tenth centuries.

Christian archaeology—the study of church architecture—has also played a remarkably distinguished role. Nearly every major church in northwestern Europe has had its subterranean secrets scratched away layer by layer, revealing what can be known of its architectural chronology. The genealogy of many churches, especially in the Rhineland, has thus been traced past successive structures in the Middle Ages to primitive Christian cemeterial churches, and finally to Roman burial places. Some, like Chartres, have been found to rest on pagan shrines antedating Roman occupation.

Perhaps one of the most dramatic chapters in medieval archaeology has been written at Cluny. At its last rebuilding, the church of that Burgundian monastery, perhaps the richest and most influential in all Europe from the late tenth until the early twelfth century, was intended to be the largest in Christendom. It survived until the French Revolution. Although Europe claimed Cluny as one of its greatest architectural treasures, revolutionists demolished the vast church and its dependent buildings, except for a few remnants. In a remarkable series of excavations, Professor K. J. Conant and his associates have uncovered the ground plans of two successive churches built by the monastery on adjacent sites and of one chapel which may have been the community's first sanctuary. Through these discoveries, and after further excavations into the outlying buildings, we can now in some measure grasp the crescendo of Cluny's prosperity and recover the breathtaking splendor for which Cluny was praised, envied, and reviled.

These archaeological renderin[g] suggest the growth of Cluny in [its] greatest period, when it head[ed] an order of about 1450 monas[tic] houses. Notice especially the sc[ale] of the earlier monastic chur[ch] Cluny II (955-c. 1010) as oppos[ed] to that of the later Cluny III (108[4] –1130), which was large enou[gh] to hold the entire Cluniac ord[er]

from CAROLINGIAN AND ROMANESQUE ARCHITECTURE by K. J. Conant, 1959, Penguin Books, Inc.

From Speculum XXIX, 1954, pa[ge]

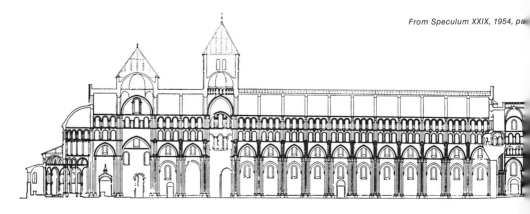

A second auxiliary science, besides stratigraphy, that now helps date archaeological discoveries is numismatics, the study of coinage. Actually, the study of ceramic wares is of more general use to archaeologists, since the pottery sequence continues from neolithic times to the present. The shape of a vessel or tile, its decoration, and its glaze can often date a site to the century, sometimes to the half-century. Coins, however, are able to provide still more exact dating, since their inscriptions give certifiable dates: witness, for example, the consular years of Roman emperors or the year of the Hegira stamped into Arabic dirhams. Some series lack exact dates of any sort, but individual coins from them can often be dated inferentially. To take one case, a coin of Charlemagne bearing the imperial title must have been issued between his coronation at Rome in 800 and his death in 814. If all other associated materials are compatible, a coin — or better, a number of coins — can date site occupation with fair to exact precision.

Just as stratigraphy instructs by dating, and also by the association of coeval materials, the importance of numismatics goes beyond questions of chronology to broader social connections. Even in classical antiquity, coins were valued and collected for their beauty of design and, in some cases, for their commemoration of great men or events. These motives continued to work on men throughout the Middle Ages, and a sense of their historical value, as well as their intrinsic worth, made coin collections normal adjuncts of libraries. Petrarch, in fact, tried to deduce the political customs of early Rome from its Republican coins. Pleased by the success of his work, he declared that every good library should have a coin cabinet. During the sixteenth and seventeenth centuries, many works, illustrated with line drawings, were published discussing ancient and medieval coins. But numismatics as a discipline, with its own rigorous methods and goals, began only in the late eighteenth century with the work of J. H. von Eckhel.

Courtesy C. E. Blunt, F.B.A.

A gold coin from the time of Offa (757—796). When this unique coin came up for auction in London recently, it was seen as authentic only by numismatists, who recognized it from a seventeenth-century engraving. The fact that it was struck in gold when coinage in northern Europe was almost exclusively silver gives it exceptional value even beyond that suggested by its age and high artistic quality.

We now understand that every aspect of coins can enhance our understanding of past societies. Since mintage was always considered a prerogative of sovereignty, a study of legal aspects illustrates the actual division — licit or not — of political authority. We can describe from numismatic evidence the struggle of French kings during the twelfth and thirteenth centuries to stamp out seigniorial mintage as part of their effort to establish the Crown's supreme authority; and the privilege of minting gold coins, acquired legally by the German Electoral Princes in 1356, stands as a symptom of the permanent fragmentation of authority in the Empire. Who reaped the profits of mintage? Did they go entirely to the king, to the local bishop or count, or to a number of officials? This casts light on the economic aspects of political privilege within societies. The physical qualities of coins likewise tell us much. The symbolism of types and the assertions of legends are positive evidence of political mythology and claims. The imperial bust and eagle on Frederick II's *augustales* are emblems of his drive to recapture for himself the territorial breadth and the unquestioned sovereignty of Augustan Rome. Grandiose aspirations more than nostalgia explain why English kings kept the title "King of France" on their coins until 1800, more than 200 years after they lost their last foot of soil in France. Examining metals used in mintage, metallic content, and weight of issues provides data about such essential matters as the economic fluctuations that drove gold coinage out of Western Europe between the ninth and the twelfth centuries and produced the debased coinages of the late Middle Ages. Study of denominations is the surest way to describe the complexity of monetary systems; it provides a measure of the change from barter to monetary economy between the tenth and the thirteenth centuries. Finally, a close scrutiny of where coin hoards were buried in a given era, and of their contents, provides evidence of the scope of cultural diffusion.

To draw evidence about past societies from coins, numismatists have developed increasingly refined techniques. Among the most recent of these is the nuclear activation process for testing metallic content without destroying or scarring coins. But the most important technique is still, as it was in Petrarch's day, comparison of coins from the same epoch. Until very recently, comparative methods depended upon line engravings — which could reflect artistic license more than the state of the coin — and costly travel by scholars to visit private and public collections. The technical refinement of photography, coupled with colotype engraving, has given great impetus to numismatics in the twentieth century by placing large bodies of reliable photographic evidence easily within the grasp of students.

The contributions of archaeology, with its auxiliary branches of stratigraphy and numismatics, have considerably enriched our knowledge of medieval societies. Numismatics entered the scene at the dramatic moment when archaeology at medieval sites began: in 1653, when by chance a workman opened the tomb of a Merovingian king, Childeric I (d. 481 – 482), at Tournai. Much has been dispersed; but remaining evidence gives priceless testimony to the artistic achievement and religious character of the king and his followers. Precious metals abounded: a purse of one hundred gold coins and a box containing 200 silver pieces (not official mintage), three hundred gold cicadas (crickets or bees) sewn onto Childeric's cloak, personal ornaments including a bracelet and buckles in gold, and other treasures went with Childeric to the tomb. Equally important were his sign of office, a signet ring with a portrait of the king, and a ritual offering paralleled in other contemporary burials and consonant with what we know of Germanic paganism at a later date: the head of Childeric's horse, heavily ornamented in gold and silver. Even in this early discovery, establishing the date of burial and the ethos of the buried depended to an important degree on numismatic evidence, as, indeed, it did when a great ship burial (without a corpse) came to light at Sutton Hoo in England two centuries later (1939).

Discoveries of this sort have forced us to abandon the idea that barbarian kings lived in relative penury, and that descriptions of the lavish use of gold in early sources, as in *Beowulf*, expressed overheated barbaric imaginations. We now credit such information as the story that Chilperic I set his daughter off on the road to Spain with fifty cartloads of treasure as marriage settlement, and the contention that the personal fortune of an Ostrogothic princess amounted to forty thousand pounds of gold. Discoveries from later times have persuaded us to accept as literal truth the enormous sums that, according to chroniclers, the Norse raiders extorted—seven thousand pounds of silver on one occasion. Our whole understanding of the magnitude precious metals held in early medieval commerce—and indeed of the quantity of gold and silver available for trade of all sorts—has consequently changed.

Geography is the second great branch of knowledge that instructs us about the physical environments of the past. While archaeology was growing into a science and propagating auxiliary disciplines, geographers were developing other skills for studying man's physical history. Using the mathematical techniques of late medieval cartographers, mapmakers in the sixteenth and seventeenth centuries were able to bring together the vast knowledge gained in the Age of Exploration, and, for the first time, to see the earth's surface as a set of geographical systems divided by mountain ranges, river valleys, and seas. Until the late seventeenth century, what we know as specialist fields, such as geology, climatology, and anthropology, still fell under the rubric "geography"; and the impact of terrain and climate on human movements led some professed geographers to emphasize history and archaeology over mathematical geography itself.

Aerial photography provides important data for the medieval archaeologist. This photo shows Bentley Grange, Emley, in England (Yorkshire, West Riding). The mounds are iron pits left from diggings which flourished between the twelfth century and the mid-fifteenth. They could be plotted on a map by surface inspection, but the photograph proves that extensive and well-established farming took place on the site before iron working began. The spoil heaps were piled on top of the marks of ridge-and-furrow plowing.

Dr. J. K. St. Joseph, Cambridge, England

By the eighteenth century, however, a clear distinction had been drawn between history, which sought to establish connections in time, and geography, which focused on spatial relationships. The great task of regional geographers in the last century and a half has been to work out the methodological implications of that distinction. The essence of the regional concept is that regions have a cohesion sustained and expressed by a number of spatially related factors. To be sure, there is a hierarchy of larger and smaller regions. But all regions are held together by a consciousness of regional identity among their inhabitants. Nature provided environmental factors with which man had to cope; regions were defined by man's use of those elements, and by the irrigation lines he laid, the commercial routes he cut out, the kinds and immediacy of communication he set up between one village and others. Encouraged by the increased attentiveness to evolution that Darwin aroused, the regionalists thus argued that, as methods of using space and communicating changed, the contours of regions changed; regions appeared and vanished. Culture and civilization were not imposed in a mechanical way by environment. Rather, man extracted them from nature by his aspirations and technical skills, all constantly in flux.

The measure of a region was man; the region's dimensions and cohesion came from human associations and changed as man's use of the environment—and thus his social bases—shifted. Religion, the structure of society, esthetic and moral achievements, wars, and the whole intellectual life of man fell outside the view of regionalists. What mattered about social institutions was, not their structure, but their function in enabling man to work and communicate.

The historical geographer shares some essential techniques with scholars in time-oriented disciplines, especially in archaeology. Archaeology provides physical descriptions of settlement plans, evidence of successive habitation eras, implements, ornaments, foodstuffs, and other data essential to the geographer's work. Both archaeologists and geographers have richly profited from the use of Carbon-I4 dating and of pollen analysis to test the nature and changes of vegetation cover. Aerial photography, too, proved its usefulness to historical geography in 1922, when it revealed a prehistoric field system near Winchester. Archaeologists had already experimented with the technique, beginning with photographs from balloons late in the nineteenth century; and photographs taken from box kites over the Sudan just before World War I established the method's usefulness to students of the past as well as to military strategists.

With philologists, geographers share another essential technique: study of place names. If you look even cursorily at a map of England, you will see that many place names derive from languages other than English. There are, for example, the Norwegian Somerby, the Latin Colchester, the French Beaulieu. Almost any region will provide a similar assortment. Chicago bears a garbled form of an Indian name; not far away are Joliet and La Porte (French), Ypsilanti (Greek), Warsaw, El Paso, and Rome. Each name tells something about the history of the place. The examples cited all indicate the ethnic origin of dominant groups when the settlements received their present names. Other place names describe spatial relations (e.g., Mile End), religious association (St. Ives), topographical features (Rawmarsh), vegetation (Broomfield), major industries (Sapperton, "village of the soap-makers"), and so forth.

Like any other sort of evidence, place names must be studied with great care. But, because they arose spontaneously, survive remarkably, and give a wide statistical sampling, they can tell a great deal about the time and circumstances of a settlement, the origin of the people who named it, their major business and environment, and, finally, their position, early or late, in the history of settlement within a broad region. Though other kinds of evidence may be fragmentary or entirely lacking, the science of place names has established precisely such data as settlement periods and patterns and the origins of colonists in prehistoric and Frankish Gaul, southwest Germany, and Spain and Portugal.

Historians from Herodotus' day to the present have considered geography the handmaid of history. Historical geographers reverse the roles, and, with their emphasis on spatial patterns and processes, they have made enormous contributions to our understanding of the Middle Ages. One has only to consult the exhaustive study of geography in eleventh-century England which Professor Darby and his associates have recently made to appreciate our debt to geography's muse. Historical geographers, or scholars inspired by them, have described medieval field systems; settlement patterns and the speed and ecological effects of colonization in the German East; explanations for the curious fact that some regions were settled with compact villages and others with dispersed homesteads; and a full and innovative appraisal of the very complex impulses behind the Viking invasions.

Thus far, we have left aside one kind of evidence essential both to archaeologists and historical geographers: written sources. Literary remains gave substance to much of the work we have been describing. De Rossi's epoch-making studies of the early Christian cemeteries and catacombs in Rome relied heavily on writings from the second and third centuries, and especially on descriptions of Rome set down by pilgrims in the seventh and eighth centuries. Numismatists rely on official documents for the regnal years from which they date ancient and medieval coins, and for evidence concerning the ideologies that coin types were meant to express. The original impetus behind modern geography came from fresh recourse to Ptolemy's *Almagest* in the late Middle Ages, and recent geographers search documents, as Professor Darby has investigated the *Domesday Book*, to establish legal aspects of agricultural and industrial production.

But historians consult written sources from a distinctive point of view. Together with archaeologists and geographers, they want to know as fully as they can how men lived in past times; together with archaeologists and geographers they read ancient documents to conceptualize the past. Unlike them, however, historians also study writings to know how peoples in the past conceptualized their present. Historians go beyond man's technological skills, his techniques of physical survival, and his material creations such as sculpture and street plans. They also wish to understand man as a thinking, social animal, and to deal with his spiritual aspirations and his battles in the fields of ethics and reason. Knowledge of this sort rests essentially on written evidence.

For most people, the manuscript is the Middle Ages' chief emblem, and it is true that great bodies of evidence for medieval studies remain unpublished. Study of manuscripts, indeed, began at about the same time as study of the Middle Ages, and a number of auxiliary sciences have developed for their critical evaluation. Until the eighteenth century, archives were organized badly, if at all. In a royal court or at the Roman Curia, recent materials might be arranged by year or by administrative region. In 1727, Pope Benedict XIII decreed that every bishop must preserve and classify his archival materials and make every effort to recover lost records. This decree and corresponding efforts by temporal rulers, to say the least, had incomplete effects. Governmental archives outside the chief administrative centers were treated with the same neglect as were private records; they consisted of boxes containing jumbled evidence of any sort and date—victims of mildew and fire, nests for mice, and raw material for bookbinders.

This was the daunting picture when the "father of Christian archaeology," Onofrio Panvinio, went searching for manuscripts in the sixteenth century. Somehow, the great body of forged material had to be separated from genuine documents, and the valid evidence put into chronological sequence and appraised.

These needs gave birth to the twin sciences of diplomatics and palaeography. The narrower of the two, diplomatics, focuses on the critical analysis of legal records, such as charters, deeds, official proclamations, and private agreements drawn up and witnessed by notaries. Medieval lawyers took great pains to distinguish false charters from authentic ones. The burden of their arguments, however, rested largely on evidence external to the disputed documents, such as whether the act in question was conceivable in view of the alleged parties' legal circumstances and whether it was substantiated by other contemporary or subsequent acts. Occasionally, internal elements of structure were invoked, but, before the advent of printing, no scholar had access to a body of materials sufficiently large and varied to allow a comparative approach to the evolution of legal forms.

The cornerstone of this new approach was laid by Jean Mabillon (1632–1707), a Benedictine of the Maurist congregation, in his book *De Re Diplomatica* (1681). An eminent scholar had attacked the traditions of Mabillon's monastery, St-Germain-des-Prés, by declaring false the documents by which Merovingian kings were thought to have established and fostered the monastery. The seriousness of the case against the privileges and the implications for St. Germain led Mabillon to a six-year study for the purpose of developing tests of authenticity drawn from the internal evidence of the documents themselves. Work since the seventeenth century has greatly elaborated and refined diplomatic techniques (including sphragistics, the study of seals), especially under the influence of two institutes founded in the nineteenth century, the École des Chartes (1821) and the Institut für Oesterreichische Geschichtsforschung (1854, reorganized 1878). The essential point that Mabillon demonstrated remains unchanged: legal documents are cultural traits. As the variety and volume of legal business increase, institutions for dealing with them ramify and specialize, and the documents they generate, as part of their legal processes, reflect those changes. Kinds of documents, formulaic terms, and methods of attestation all had distinct lifetimes, begun in need and ended when new requirements and usages had superseded them. Each chancery, each reign, each period in the history of every legal district, had peculiar and definable practices, and, once discovered, these were tests of the authenticity of documents.

By his *De Re Diplomatica*, Mabillon also laid claim to the title "father of palaeography," though the word "palaeography" was first used by his confrère at St-Germain-des-Prés, Bernard de Montfaucon (1655–1741), in a pioneering study of Greek manuscripts (*Palaeographia graeca*, 1708). Under the influence of fledgling schemes of biological classification, Mabillon was convinced that Latin handwriting had specific characteristics reflecting the epoch and locale of the writer. He therefore set about organizing scripts into genetic families descended from four major national hands: Gothic, Lombard, Frankish, and Anglo-Saxon, each of which, he argued, had broken, through degeneration, into a number of regional groups. Opponents of this view argued that all Latin scripts descended from Roman hands; its advocates elaborated Mabillon's views into an extremely rigid and intricate system of stereotypes. During the nineteenth century, philologists' efforts to establish families of languages strengthened, if also reoriented, the idea that scripts fell into quasi-biological families. But the first book to consider all Roman hands — and thus all possible ancestors of the medieval scripts in classical antiquity — appeared in 1921 (Luigi Schiaparelli, *Scrittura Latina nell'età Romana*). Palaeographical research was retarded by difficulty in reproducing facsimiles of manuscripts. The introduction of photography and photoengraving in the late nineteenth century partially solved the

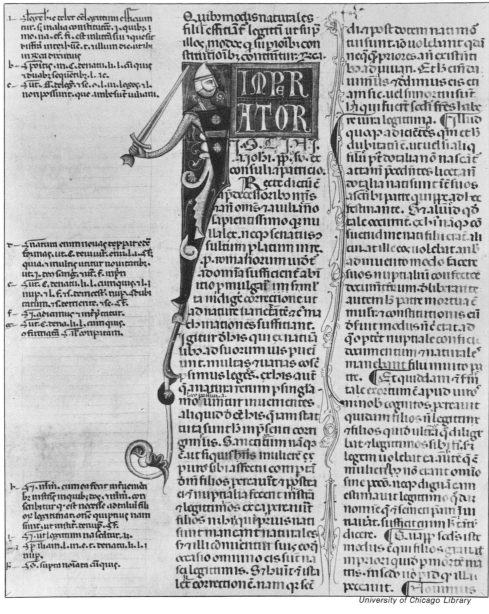

The codex from which this illustration comes, a copy of Justinian's *Institutes* with glosses (c. 1240), is a superb example of the care with which Bolognese scholars studied and transcribed legal texts. The ornamentation of *Imperator* ("emperor") recalls Rom. 13:4: "But if thou do that which is evil, be afraid; for he beareth not the sword in vain; for he is the minister of God. . . ."

problem, though this form of reproduction long remained unsatisfactory in important details (e.g., in capturing different shades of ink) and almost prohibitively expensive. These difficulties have not yet been entirely overcome, although the invention of microfilm and other photographic techniques has alleviated them and brought material before scholars in unprecedented bulk. E. H. Lowe has given a magnificent yardstick for palaeography's comparative method in his *Codices Latini Antiquiores*, a series whose purpose was to classify every manuscript written before the year 800 and to give a photograph of specimen lines from each. The same techniques are now being used in series devoted to later manuscripts.

The issue of genetic families has now been largely resolved, thanks both to the comparative method, which Mabillon and his contemporaries knew, and to the greatly increased body of material available to scholars in the last century. It is clear that the early national hands represented stages in development which were superseded — differently in various places — by subsequent periods in which Carolingian minuscule on the whole pre-empted the field. From this hand, invented at the court of Charlemagne and derived from Roman scripts, descended two main lines: the various Gothic scripts, which were widely used between the twelfth and the seventeenth centuries, and the Italic hand, a cursive script developed by Italian humanists in the late fourteenth and fifteenth centuries. From these two lines in turn sprang all modern scripts in Western Europe, each breaking off from the parent stock according to a peculiar set of historical circumstances.

The scholars of the sixteenth and seventeenth centuries were not only concerned with analyzing documents. They worked with all vigor to print them, and thus to make them known beyond the private rooms where they lay, and to preserve them from rat, fire, and man. In this brilliant age of scholarship, the leaders were clerics, worthy successors of the monks who in the darkest days of the barbarian invasions kept alive love of the learned arts. The Jesuit Bollandists in Antwerp, devoted especially to hagiography, and the Maurists led the field both in the auxiliary sciences of chronology, archaeology, numismatics, diplomatics, and palaeography and, just as important, in the publication of manuscript sources, with valuable critical apparatus. (To be sure, there were lapses from antiquarian grace even in those houses as when, in 1645 and 1656, the monks of St-Germain-des-Prés plundered the tombs of the Merovingian King Childeric II, his wife, and their infant son and sold the rich tomb offerings.)

The magnificent achievements of these scholars are apparent from the footnotes of scholarly works in our own day, as indeed are our debts to three of their followers: Giovanni Domenico Mansi (1692–1769), Ludovico Antonio Muratori (1672–1750), and especially Jean Paul Migne (1800–1875), whose enormous labors made available in "reprint editions" the whole of Greek ecclesiastical literature in the period A.D. 120–1438 and of Latin between A.D. 200 and 1216.

It was natural that the critical examination and publication of texts gave great impetus to a science which had become second nature to priestly scholars: philology. Even in classical antiquity, men had used collation of manuscripts to weed out scribal error and the study of etymology, the history of words, to establish an author's meaning. These techniques passed from the Alexandrine critics to the Romans by the second century B.C., thence to Church Fathers, and from them to medieval scholars. For a thousand years, men acted on ancient examples as transmitted in technique by Cassiodorus, who insisted on purifying texts by collating them, and Isidore of Seville, who fathomed inner meaning by etymological argument.

The first great advance beyond these techniques to true philology, a science based on comparing the content and structure of languages, came in the fifteenth and sixteenth centuries. Printing put Scriptural texts in Greek, Latin, and Hebrew before the learned public, and this in turn led to the establishment of three eminent trilingual colleges — Corpus Christi (Oxford), the University of Alcalá, and the Collège des Lecteurs Royaux (later the Collège de France). An attempt to create such institutions had been made, without conspicuous success, in the fourteenth century; given flesh and blood in the three later colleges, the longstanding desire for collation of Scriptural texts came to life. Comparison of texts became a matter, not merely of collating versions in one language, but also of putting the same Scriptural texts in different languages side by side to determine relative age and reliability. The second kind of collation was canonized in the great polyglot bibles of the sixteenth and seventeenth centuries, the earliest of which came directly from the studies of Alcalá. By the seventeenth century, some philologists were saying that the books of The Law, the Old Testament, issued from an unplanned and convoluted process, rather than from the immediate and purposive revelation of God. Historical growth with all its vagaries, contradictions, and misunderstandings undermined both the anagogical design that theologians had confidently drawn between the Pentateuch and the Gospels, and the ethical standards that they thought that design sanctioned. Europe's discovery of Sanskrit in the eighteenth century produced yet greater changes in the West's presuppositions about itself. Comparative methods yielded reason to think that Sanskrit, Latin, and Greek were related tongues derived from the same primitive language, which no longer existed. The idea of an Indo-European family of languages was postulated. For the first time, it was clear that the history of European man had connections far beyond Europe's geographical confines, with peoples who did not count Athens and Rome among their intellectual forebears, and with times unmentioned by ancient historians or medieval chroniclers.

Men were aware that philology gave them a unique key to understanding the past, that language and dialects could be analyzed as historical sources going back in each region before the earliest written records. Under the influence of Friedrich Wolf (1759–1824), structural laws of grammar and syntax were combined with mythology, public and private law, religion, archaeology, and other sources of historical data that assist in the verification and interpretation of texts. Wolf called the resulting nexus of skills, in which philology was normative, *Altertumswissenschaft* (the science of antiquity). This broadly conceived approach, modified by evolutionary doctrines and the science of phonetics in the nineteenth century, has dominated work in medieval philology until the present day.

Medievalists owe much to recent philology: for example, in the evaluation of place names as evidence, in the attribution and dating of anonymous treatises, and, supremely, in the editing of texts. In fact, the debt began to accumulate as early as the fifteenth century, when Lorenzo Valla proved that the document called the Donation of Constantine, in which Constantine the Great purportedly gave Western Europe to the popes, was a forgery. The language of the document, he showed, was not that of Constantine's day, as preserved in unquestionably genuine documents; some allusions to historical and ceremonial details were anachronistic; thus, the grant must be false. DuCange also practiced *Altertumswissenschaft* before it had a name; for his two *Glossaria*—one for medieval Latin and the other for medieval Greek—are, far more than word lists, short treatises on terminology that adduce evidence from every branch of knowledge later adduced by Wolf. DuCange's purpose was to grasp the mechanics of medieval institutions by studying the words used to describe them, and his achievement in social and constitutional history was enormous. His elder contemporary across the Channel, Sir Henry Spelman (c. 1564–1641), working along similar lines (*Archaeologus in modum glossarii*, 2 vols. 1616, 1664), achieved perhaps the most brilliant and elemental result ever attained in constitutional history: he demonstrated on philological grounds the existence of feudalism in England, and of royal government as a feudal state, fundamentally different from the institutions of his own day; and thus he made possible the tripartite division of English history—prefeudal, feudal, and postfeudal—that historians now take for granted.

The work of philologists obviously supplies the modern historian with rich interpretive materials. It has still greater value. The point that Valla, DuCange, and Spelman held in common was that language reflected cultural usages, and thus that it revealed how men in past societies understood their institutions and mores. Since the nineteenth century, there has been an important and lively debate between scholars who hold that language merely conveys ideas and others who argue that it also molds them. But it is beyond dispute that, as much as architecture, linguistic usages mark off historical and cultural periods.

It is clear that there is one essential element behind the phenomenal growth in knowledge of the past experienced in the last 150 years: namely, the discovery of increasingly efficient techniques for communication both among scholars at a given moment, and from one generation of scholars to another, perhaps remote in time. Printing, photography, photoengraving, manuscript facsimiles, microfilm, and other modes of communication in bulk have been the essence of modern scholarship, largely because they facilitate the comparative processes on which all branches of historical knowledge rest.

In our own day, scholars turn increasingly to a radical new method of classifying materials: computer analysis. There is no longer any question that computers can greatly assist scholars, and the nose of the computer *qua* camel is already under the medievalist's tent. Scholarly use of the computer began in the 1950's, when it became apparent that the machine had skills in quantification far beyond those of a loyal band of graduate assistants. Perhaps the most ambitious project in medieval social history actually under computer processing is the analysis of the Florentine cadastral register of 1427–1428 being performed by an international commission. Preliminary work on this project has provided very important evidence about life cycles and class structure in Florence at the time of the census, and publication of its report will have first importance.

Medievalists already owe a large debt to the machine in the field of literary studies. Indeed, medievalists were among the first to test the advantages of computerized philology; the Middle High German Center at Cambridge University was a pioneer and remains a leader in the enterprise. The repetitive tasks of philologists — attribution by word frequency counts, stylistic analysis, dialectical studies, and the composition of dictionaries, word lists, and concordances — have now successfully been assigned to the computer. Concordances to Tertullian and to St. Thomas Aquinas' poetry have been compiled by machine. A computer-programmed concordance to St. Thomas Aquinas' *Summa Theologica* is scheduled to be printed in eighty volumes in 1971. There are plans for processing concordances for the Church Fathers and medieval writers of great influence. Content analysis has been applied to literary works, including *Beowulf* (of which, after long and difficult work by programmers, a concordance has also been produced by machine in fifteen minutes), and the masses of Josquin Desprez have been processed by structural analysis.

Research tools, such as concordances and comprehensive, fully up-to-date bibliographies, critical editions showing explicit and implied quotations and textual variants, tables statistically demonstrating canons of literary and artistic taste implicitly held by writers and craftsmen of a given age, and charts collating vast quantities of vital statistics from such sources as parish registers are within the grasp of the medievalist and his mechanical friend, an assistant for which a capability of one billion computations per minute is now planned.

Use of computers may prove as momentous in the field of medieval studies as did, in its time, the invention of printing. But essential as its services will no doubt become in many areas, the computer will enhance the auxiliaries of historical research rather than supersede them. Much of the medievalist's evidence is not significantly voluminous to be statistically meaningful; ethical and esthetic sensibilities cannot be measured; and, in the final analysis, conceptualization of the past can only remain a function of the human mind.

Chapter 5

Religion: Christianity as Life

Religious institutions are both tools and symbols. They establish grades of authority, divisions of labor in performing cult practices, and ritualistic standards of right and wrong that apply to every aspect of life. That is what they do. What they represent is just as important. They express the relation between divinity and man as a bond, even a world, of law in which gods keep their servants and blight the disobedient. The forms that the institutions take and the particular kinds of formalism they perpetuate vary from one society to another.

There is more to religion. Formalism seldom illuminates man's heart or fosters great spiritual aspirations. It comes from and speaks to the mind about which it builds as a cocoon or mausoleum a great protective structure of law. Other parts of the human spirit also rise to God — instinct and mystical intuition — and they evoke a world of order very different from the formalistic one, a world in which obligation is neither pure restriction nor a device of primitive group therapy, but a private way to freedom.

We have been asking how medieval Christianity was administered. We must now ask how it was lived. Formal institutions were like a channel in a great river of religious anxiety and devotion, part of a wider natural phenomenon, one course among many. This was especially true in an age when lay communion was rare and legislation was needed to force priests to perform the Mass at least four times each year.

DEVIANTS

Just as there were people for whom the essence of Christianity lay in regulations and administrative order, there were others who argued, perhaps as anarchists, that Christianity could not be administered at all, that it must be lived. For these latter, and for men who fell somewhere between the two classes, the institutions of the medieval Church failed to symbolize adequately the problems of man's search for salvation, his need for participation in the sacrificial death.

Such men did not agree that authority held the faithful together and separated them from outsiders. Formalists held to the strand in Christian thought that demanded obedience to offices, no matter how unworthy the officeholders, since the offices belonged to a divinely established pattern of authority. Because they were bishops or priests, even the morally blind could hold aloft the lantern of salvation. "Anarchists" took up another strand, ascetic and dissident. Had not Christ Himself driven impure men from the Temple and reproached the Scribes and Pharisees for killing the spirit of the Law by insisting on its literal meaning?

Anxiety—awareness of man's inadequacy before the dangers of this world and the next—brought both classes to seek holiness; to perceive God's wisdom through mystery; to strive for personal regeneration by observing forbidden things in taboos, fasts, and sexual abstinence; and, finally, to aspire to participate in divine power, the power that came upon the Apostles at Pentecost, the power in the preaching of the Cross that was foolishness to them that perished, the power of the Resurrection, the power to become sons of God.

What divided formalists from "anarchists" was the problem of how to participate in the sacred. Could man enjoy God chiefly by adhering to ritual acts, performed in set ways and places, by men, and with cult objects that had all been consecrated to sacred uses? On the other hand, could he become a tabernacle of holiness through "election"; that is, by a special choice of God, or even by his individual efforts, by exercising innate gifts? Was man to seek sanctification as part of the aggregate of all believers, or as an individual? Which was greater: the duty to obey or the power to dissent? That was the supreme question.

The whole current of social development determined the answers. For individual men the answers were often paradoxical. That was the case for the orthodox King Peter of Aragon, victorious assailant of Islam, who was crowned in Rome by the pope but died fighting for his relatives and vassals, the Cathari of Provence. For Europe as a whole, the answers were part and parcel of the growth of a literate and articulate lay society, the reason that cultural advances in the twelfth century were mainly ecclesiastical, and those in the sixteenth, secular. In more than one sense, society in all its branches was the model of religion.

Some currents found followers only in one elite or another. Such were thrusts in philosophy inspired by the new knowledge of Greek and Islamic texts. Even Abelard and the founders of the scholastic method had shifted the foundations of formal religious thought by brushing aside unquestioned formulas and clichés and substituting taut, critical reflection on the very principles of faith. This, the beginning of the West's first true philosophy, raised tensions between modes of reason which thinkers resolved in very different ways. St. Thomas Aquinas produced the most elaborate and, after long controversy, the predominant reconciliation; but in his own day and after, St. Thomas was denounced by many learned and orthodox men as heretical. Aristotle exerted crucial influence on the "rational philosophy" of Dominicans like St. Thomas, but only tangential effect on "spiritual philosophy" of Franciscans like St. Bonaventura (d. 1274). The differences in categories and modes of thought to which this gave rise explains some parts of the dispute over St. Thomas' synthesis. But not all. St. Thomas had bridged the gap between the worlds of spirit and mind by arguing that God perfects nature and that faith brings man to full understanding of nature and of its God. Even within his own order, men remained unconvinced of this unity. Some Dominicans held to the thought of St. Thomas' teacher, St. Albertus Magnus, who accepted the universe of faith as autonomous but also admitted the universe of nature, a world of mental exercise, as autonomous. Did the "Angelic Doctor" in fact deviate from the faith?

The issue became acute through the work of the Latin Averroists, men who were "masters" of the University of Paris, neither priests nor friars. Heavily influenced by the Averroist interpretation of Aristotle, these thinkers boldly split the realm of theology from that of philosophy. Theology, they argued, rested on myth and the opinions of theologians, on fairy tales. Christian law impeded learning; happiness was had in this life, not in any other. This very extreme doctrine of dualistic knowledge alleged that what was true either in theology or in philosophy need not be true in the other realm.

Although orthodox thinkers did not go this far, the duality of reason among non-Thomists undercut the monopoly over human life that the formalistic organs of the Church claimed. In great parts of life — indeed in all parts of it that belonged to nature and could be perceived by man's natural faculties — faith was misleading and irrelevant.

Thus far, the disputes had been between theology and philosophy, two rational processes. But the Franciscan William of Ockham (d. 1349) carried the debate to another level. Beside the distinction between mind and spirit, and the Aristotelian categories that went with it, another tension entered medieval thought from ancient Athens: that is, the opposition of Platonic idealism to Aristotle's realism. Were there universal ideas, or types, from which individual beings derived their forms and natures? Or was the "universal" an idea that man abstracted from many individual beings, and that therefore depended on the particular for its existence? Christianity necessarily held to the first view. Creation as a whole and all creatures preexisted in the mind of God. All history proceeds from the foreknowledge and providence of the divine intellect.

But even in the twelfth century, the Aristotelian, or nominalist, position began to gather strength. Two centuries later it reached an apogee, its classical formulation, in William of Ockham's writings. Only sensory experience, he argued, can bring absolute certainty, and empirical knowledge cannot prove matters of faith. Theology did not deal with rationally demonstrable matters. The effect of this argument, expanded and developed by later thinkers, went beyond the cloister. In Italy, by 1400, the rational dualism of theology and philosophy mattered chiefly for the clergy. Laymen followed William's radical lead and discounted theology altogether as a rational enterprise. Reason could not demonstrate the existence of the soul and of divine providence, the soul's immortality, the performance of miracles, or the whole scheme and mechanism of salvation as preached by the Church. Other currents enriched this view. At the dawn of the sixteenth century, Pomponazzi was able to hold that uncultivated men had invented angels and demons to explain natural phenomena, and the whole anthropomorphic imagery of God, as in the Scriptures; they used these terms, he said, as a kind of poetic license to express what they could not otherwise define. Miraculous events could be explained in terms of natural forces; however much man might affirm it by faith, the immortality of the soul ran contrary to reason. Christianity did not reveal immutable truth. Rather, having followed natural laws of growth, flowering, and decline, it seemed near its end.

These issues mattered greatly to men in the schools of Paris, Oxford, and northern Italy, and to the intellectual elite that had formed among laymen in the Italian city states. For men dedicated to the contemplative life outside these rarefied atmospheres – in other parts of Europe or in other social classes – they had more distant relevance, or none at all.

Astrology and Paganism

Other religious currents beyond the Church were broader than the highly technical issues we have mentioned; and they appealed both to the intelligentsia and to men outside it.

Of these, astrology had the widest appeal. The effect of seasonal changes on human affairs leads almost logically to the main premise of astrology: that heavenly phenomena foretell climatic changes which help or hinder work essential to life – agriculture, fishing, transport of merchandise, and the like. It seems reasonable to assume that they also predetermine the entire destinies of men and nations. Plato and the Stoics, who elaborated his ideas, saw more than random connections. They argued that man's body contained the same elements as the universe, and that it therefore participated directly in heavenly movements. Man was but a small model of all creation, and in the fibers of his being, he shared the condition of the world about him, the heavens and all the stars.

Medieval thinkers took over this idea; some, like Hildegard of Bingen (d. 1179), added original views. But the full development of astrology as an exact science came after the introduction of Islamic observations and techniques in the late twelfth and early thirteenth centuries.

As in many other ways, the Emperor Frederick II proved himself in the avant-garde by maintaining court astrologers, whom he consulted on all matters of state, a practice that soon found many noble imitators. By the end of the fourteenth century, chairs of astrology existed at a number of universities, such as Paris, Pavia, and Bologna. Parents had lifetime horoscopes cast for their newborn children. Wars and military campaigns moved with the stars. There were sceptics. Still, popes encouraged astrology. Even after our period, that most enlightened prince and tough-minded politician, Pope Julius II, had astrologers fix the day of his coronation and consulted them throughout his pontificate.

Astrology ran counter to Christianity. At best, it betrayed its followers into the sin of pride for seeking to know what lay in God's foreknowledge. Its implications were yet more radical. The power of the stars, the natural correlation of man's being with the elements of the universe, and the mechanical regularity of the science itself removed the need for God or faith.

At the end of the fifteenth century, Pico della Mirandola attacked astrologers as enemies of the Church. Their work, he said, was the root of all superstition and magic, because it held that not God but the stars and planets produced all good or evil; it was the font of immorality, because it removed the basis of faith. Earlier, in the fourteenth century, one astrologer, Cecco d'Ascoli, had made this point crystal clear when he cast Christ's horoscope and declared that every aspect of His nature and character — the birth in a stable, poverty, great wisdom, and crucifixion — were inevitable, the automatic result of heavenly constellations, rather than an extraordinary suspension of natural processes. Condemned and fined in Bologna, Cecco went on to Florence which took a sterner view of his teachings and burned him at the stake in 1327. But the art he had practiced and its implications continued to thrive in the households of laymen, at the courts of princes, and even before the papal throne.

Pagan rituals and beliefs formed a second religious current outside, and in some ways contrary to, Christian doctrine. Though a general phenomenon, its special forms varied widely from place to place according to the special nature of indigenous practices, the length of time since Christianization, and receptivity to other external religious influence. Open or covert paganism colored every level of existence in small things, such as the use of amber amulets, as well as in highly developed bodies of knowledge, such as that handed down in Ireland by bardic schools. In some areas, where Christianization was partial or late, pagan traditions flourished vigorously throughout the Middle Ages. That was the case among the Baltic peoples, where numerous pagan cults survived unchallenged until the late twelfth century, and where, as late as the fourteenth century, the grand duke Algirdas of Lithuania was a pagan. Even where Christianity had long since struck down deep roots, some indigenous practices survived, often officially forbidden; such was the case in England, where King Canute in the eleventh century forbade worship of the sun and moon and where, into modern times, the Beltane fires near Norfolk preserved an ancient and licentious fertility ritual involving at least ritualistic human sacrifice. Some of the variations in liturgical years and practices among churches to which we have referred came from the same source, as did the calendars of saints and the modes of honoring them — in images; by bearing their likenesses in procession about a town or region; or in special forms and times of service. This sort of transference came naturally when Christians eased conversion by raising churches on the sites of pagan shrines, and translated native gods and heroes into Christian saints.

Photo: National Museum of Ireland.

(1) The Ardagh Chalice. This magnificent silver cup, adorned in gold, gilt bronze, and enamel, was made in the eighth century for liturgical use, but the superb curvilinear ornamentation continues decorative motifs of the pagan Celts. (2) The Tassilo Chalice. This copper and silver cup was given by Duke Tassilo III and his wife to the monastery of Kremsmünster (777) in Bavaria, where it is still kept. Though sometimes thought Lombardic, the ornamentation is judged by most scholars to reflect Celtic styles, as does the Ardagh chalice. The Tassilo cup demonstrates cultural diffusion and the persistence of pagan artistic motifs. (3) This door frame from a Celtic sanctuary at Roquepertuse (Bouches-du-Rhóne) dates from the third century B.C.; but it illustrates the sort of pagan rituals, including human sacrifice, that continued in parts of Europe until the time of St. Thomas Aquinas.

Photo: Jean Roubier, Fortress Museum, Budapest

154

Astrology was one of the strong anti-Christian currents in the spiritual life of the late Middle Ages. This diagram shows the correspondence that astrologers thought existed between the elements of man's body and those of the earth and the heavens.

Biblioteca Statale di Lucca, Italy

It became explicit in some cases as in that of the East Anglian king who, Bede says, "tried to serve both Christ and the ancient gods," worshipping them on adjacent altars. Similar attempts to keep one foot in each camp were made on the Continent.

The late Roman period had seen the same thing, when the Fathers themselves declared that the cult of martyrs was dragging the Church into polytheism and idolatry, and when Constantine the Great continued to act as head of State paganism while he called himself "bishop of bishops" and oversaw Church affairs. It was a normal stage of conversion. In the Roman Empire it lasted from Constantine's day past Justinian's, well over two centuries; the time lag between formal conversion and true Christianization was often longer in medieval Europe.

The ancient gods and heroes, with the services that pleased them, survived and continued to claim the reverence of men, as did sacred rivers, springs, and trees. Tacitus tells that the Germans considered springs and rivers sacred places inhabited by gods; an eighth-century source reaffirms that the Franks and the Swabians recited prayers on their banks, lighted torches and left offerings for the water spirits. Visiting Cologne on Midsummer Night's Eve, in 1333, Petrarch saw a survival of this veneration in an elaborate civic ceremony. In the presence of the municipal officials and an enormous body of citizens, a throng of young women robed in white and

155

crowned with aromatic herbs went to the river's edge and washed their hands and arms in the Rhine, murmuring incantations. Petrarch was given to understand that the ceremony averted troubles from the city. One can still see, and make, votive offerings at holy wells of Alsace and Wales. Transference was no less easy from the sacred tree to the Holy Rood.

Indigenous practices continued, sometimes brought into the official observances of individual churches, sometimes forbidden by popes, bishops, and kings. However muted by the religion of rulers and conquerors, the voice of popular imagination and devotion still spoke, in every place a different tongue.

Magic and Witchcraft

Pagan polytheism survived, here as additions to the calendar of saints, there as forbidden and occult rites. Men preserved together with it two different but closely related bodies of beliefs and practices that aimed, not at appeasing gods, but at evading divine power and giving man direct control of the material world. The first of these, magic, invoked no appeal to spirits. Its underlying idea is that like begets like, and consequently that the use of appropriate ritual objects, spells, or charms could produce desired effects in the natural world. For example, official circles feared that magicians had killed Charles IV of France (d. 1328) by casting spells with lead and stone replicas of the royal seal. This was the subject of inquiry by a papal commission. The second set of practices, witchcraft, dealt explicitly with the spiritual world. Its essential work was divination in the name of a pagan god, often performed on the bodies of pets that the witches kept as "familiars." Though enriched by parodies of Christian ritual, such as the Black Mass, witchcraft preserved much of pagan religion: adoration of gods in animal forms, ritual dances, feasts, and chants; a liturgical year derived from the seasons of vegetable fertility and divided by the four great "Sabbaths"; and a class of specialists set aside to keep these spiritual observances and to perform the occult arts.

Witches had far wider powers than magicians, both in divination and in the ability to transform themselves into animals, to remove their spirits temporarily from their bodies, to be in two places at once, and to transport themselves through the air. They practiced a religion; magicians, a craft. But these technical distinctions blurred, and men considered magic a normal, and potent, tool in the witch's arsenal.

Christianity itself offered another version of the same thing. It saw the universe as a field of force between the poles of good and evil, in which angels and demons charged about changing the natural course of events and fighting for men's souls by nothing more virtuous than brute strength. Men could influence the outcome by prayers, incantations, and oblations. The same generation believed that angels moved the Blessed Virgin's house by night flight from Nazareth to Tersatto in 1291, and from there to Loreto in 1295, and that Pope Boniface VIII had an oracular spirit by which, among other great deeds, he brought his predecessor to abdicate and gained the papacy himself. Joan of Arc's belief that she heard heavenly voices was one side of the coin; her trial and execution for witchcraft was the other.

Far from being confined to the unenlightened dregs of society, or to cultural backwaters, witchcraft found believers and even practitioners in the most exalted classes. Boniface VIII was only one in a long series of popes charged with spiritual perversion. In the tenth century, Emperor Otto I accused Pope John XII of moral and physical impurity, of praying to Jupiter, Venus, and demonic spirits for help in gambling. In the Investiture Controversy of the eleventh century, Gregory VII's enemies accused him of divination and necromancy, with the help of an oracular spirit. The charge became a stock in trade for papal foes throughout the period. The satanic arts likewise flourished among the cardinals together with astrology and sheer magic, in which Peter of Spain (Pope John XXI d. 1277) earned international acclaim. With appreciative eyes of connoisseurs, the papal Curia also took up punishment of magic and witchcraft. It acquitted Bishop Walter of Coventry (d. 1321) whom eyewitnesses accused of having rendered homage to the devil and of giving him many times the witch's ritual sign of obedience, the anal kiss. But it convicted Bishop Hugo Geraud on similar accusations and sent him to the stake (1317).

Fascination with the occult also had a long history at secular courts. In the sixth century, the Merovingian court was shaken by a series of deaths, which torture followed by confessions proved to be the work of witches. The Empress Judith, wife of Louis the Pious (d. 840), dabbled in sorcery and divination and made the imperial court a nest of diviners and enchanters. The bond of witchcraft and kingship indeed runs unbroken in France to Philip Augustus, who claimed that witchcraft kept him from consummating his marriage; to the great minister of Philip the Fair, Enguerrand de Marigny, a century later, who sent the Templars to the stake on charges of witchcraft and other horrendous crimes only to suffer on the gallows five years later, convicted himself of conspiring against his kings with the use of wax images. In 1440, Enguerrand had a worthy successor, Gilles de Rais, Marshal of France, who died at the stake as a proven convenanteor with the Devil, a necromancer who had brought hundreds of children to ruin and death through his black arts. Everywhere the story was the same: on the one hand, fear of death or sexual impotence or blighted fortunes through witchcraft and the official repression of the arts' practitioners; on the other, recourse to witches and magicians in time of personal or public danger, as in Germany where Frederick of Austria turned to necromancy after his defeat by Louis of Bavaria.

Europe took witchcraft and its appendage, magic, for granted both as a crime to be punished and as a power to be consulted; in 1398 the theological faculty of the University of Paris, presided over by the great mystic and scholar, Gerson, published a full legal and theological statement on the dangerous potency of witchcraft, the rational vindication that the international belief required.

This was the delusion that gripped popes, princes, and the intelligentsia. How intense must it have been at the level of the village priest or peasant?

Today, horoscopes are to be bought in the most antiseptic drugstores and avant-garde supermarkets; now and then the wife of an Anglican bishop may still consult palmists and seers. But witchcraft for most contemporary Westerners lingers among the underindustrialized and unenlightened. At midnight on January 3, 1968, sixteen Mexican villagers tried, convicted, and hanged in the public square a woman who, they were convinced, had killed a girl by witchcraft. The charge, procedure, and punishment could have been taken from medieval chronicles, and, until recent years, similar courts brought witches to justice in Ireland and Bavaria.

Between these modern events and medieval counterparts stands one great difference: the recent trials occurred on the fringe of the civilized community, while the medieval counterparts brought to bear the whole burden of public opinion and the enormously refined legal procedure both in the Church and in civil governments.

It used to be assumed that the "witchcraft delusion" began in the thirteenth century and ran until the eighteenth century and that belief in witchcraft experienced an enormous growth in the late medieval period. We can now appreciate that this was not strictly true. Magic and spells continued from classical antiquity throughout our period in an unbroken and unaccelerated stream. Covenants with the devil are known as early as the pact that—according to Archbishop Hincmar of Rheims—Charles the Fat unwittingly made with the devil in 873.

All parties did experience development and enrichment of views. But the great change that occurred in the thirteenth century was in the equipment used to hunt out and punish magicians and witches. We know more about the black arts in the thirteenth century and later because detection of them was more systematic and thorough than in the earlier period, not necessarily because there was more to know.

The Ritual of Persecution

The crucial moment came when theologians decided that witchcraft was a form of heresy on the ground that all divination was an invocation of demons, a service that detracted from devotion to the true God. Consequently, it fell into the large class of heresies that exalted creatures above the Creator. With this identification, witchcraft and magic became the business of the Inquisition, newly established in the thirteenth century, to root the Cathari out of southern France. What had earlier passed as ordinary, if objectionable, aspects of popular religion thus became the object of increasingly exact theological definitions, legislation, and trials in Church and civil courts, honed by application of relevant sections from Roman Law. After two centuries this process culminated in the epidemic persecutions of the early modern period.

In his famous decree *Summis desiderantes* (1484), Pope Innocent VIII gave the classic statement of the Roman church on witchcraft's pernicious effects and the juridical measures that must be taken to stamp it out. Little remained to be added except exhortations of the sort Leo X received at the dawn of the Reformation from two Camaldolese monks; as part of the general refurbishing of the Church, they wrote, he must see that all men dedicated to the magical arts were burned alive, and that their friends and patrons were stripped of their property and cast into perpetual exile. The heavy machinery of Church law had prepared for this view from the thirteenth century on.

Witchcraft is a common phenomenon. But this intense persecution of witches is peculiar to the history of Western Europe, especially between the thirteenth and the seventeenth centuries. Nothing of the sort occurred in the lands of the Eastern churches. The spiritual crisis of the age certainly intensified because of the extraordinary sequence of natural disasters that struck Western Europe from the late thirteenth century on. Medieval men could understand floods, blighted harvests, and the Black Death only in supernatural terms, in terms that explained either how the mercy of a benevolent God had been forfeited, or for what reasons God had changed from bounty to vengeance. Witchcraft was a sufficient explanation. Other elements in the Latin West combined uniquely to sustain the delusion: refinement and legalism of theology, elaboration of juridical machinery in the Church, and the impact of theological opinions on actions by civil government.

Professor Kai Erikson has been able to draw some very fruitful conclusions about witch-hunts in New England. Among the seventeenth-century Puritans, he maintains, witches were social deviants. They existed on the very fringe of the predominant grouping. But in a curious way they actually served the majority because they led it, in persecution of them, to define its bonds of cohesion more sharply, to join in common fear and enterprise against one foe. The trial and execution of witches had ritualistic, "almost sacrificial" aspects. Though predestined by God to live in wickedness and perversion, the witch stood under judgment by God's laws before His people. He died for involuntary sins. As he went to the scaffold, society demanded that he give a confession, an act of repentence, to show that even he saw the evil of his ways, that the community was entirely right to kill him, and, consequently, that he absolved the community of guilt in taking his life.

This interpretation deals chiefly with a small, closed society in the seventeenth-century wilderness of Massachusetts. Some aspects of it, naturally, do not apply to the much wider and more variegated circumstances in Western Europe two or three hundred years earlier. The importance that the doctrine of predestination had is one example.

What is very relevant, however, is the sacrificial quality of the witch-hunt. The sequence of trial, confession, and execution set it apart from the similar pogroms of Jews. Both processes were often searches for scapegoats in time of danger; both were punitive; but only the procedure against heretics—of which the witch-hunt was one variety—had the quality of expiatory sacrifice to which the victim assented by his confession. In New England, as in medieval Europe, disaster normally triggered persecution. This is a very common phenomenon.

Long ago, Gilbert Murray commented, in an essay on the classical Greek epic: "Human sacrifices have most tended to occur in a disorganized army or rabble full of fear, egged on by some fanatical priest or prophet." Thus, legend preserved Agamemnon's decision to sacrifice his daughter Iphigeneia when natural disasters kept the Greek fleet from setting sail toward Troy. Livy records that, at Hannibal's approach, the Romans ritually murdered Vestal Virgins and buried men and women alive in the Forum. Even if medieval Europe did not know these precedents, it could read in the Scriptures of the Jewish King Ahaz, who "burnt his children in the fire after the abominations of the heathen" in the hope that the Lord, pleased by these sacrifices, would beat back the advancing Assyrian host. God commanded Abraham to sacrifice Isaac, and the patriarch was prepared to obey. Obedient to a vow made in the heat of battle, Jephthah, a Hebrew Agamemnon, sacrificed his daughter. God sacrificed His only begotten Son for the sins of the world.

Human sacrifice was not merely a distant matter of bookish learning for the people of medieval Europe. It was a historical practice of their own tribes. Some Baltic tribes continued to practice it into the late twelfth century. St. Boniface in the eighth century objected that Christians were selling slaves to pagans for sacrificial purposes. Tacitus carries the Germanic tradition back into the days of the Roman Empire. Even where Christianity triumphed, human sacrifice survived, just as the pagan gods sometimes survived to be worshipped with Christ in the same sanctuary. When the newly converted Franks swept into Italy, they performed such a ritual on crossing the Po. And throughout the medieval period, one hears that small children or women were sacrificed—by being hurled into rivers or immured in foundations—to cure or avert leprosy or to protect city walls and bridges, a violent analogy to burial of saints' bones in foundations and pillars. Men also nourished vestiges of actual executions when they tried to eliminate demons of pestilence through mock human sacrifice in mummery or in the destruction of images.

When disaster struck the villages and cities of medieval Europe, it was therefore natural to think that human blood could in some way restore prosperity. Perhaps men who hunted witches as the most pernicious of heretics wished to appease God by punishing those who had angered Him in violating His laws; perhaps on a more primitive level, they wished to stamp out the actual workers of disease and misfortune.

Because disaster was local, persecution tended also to be a local matter. Forms of witchcraft also varied. The nest of witches near Norcia in Italy differed in purpose and technique from that near Salzburg. They represented different "schools," addressed different problems, and thus had very different roles in society and roused different responses in times of crisis. Localism prevailed also for other reasons. On the one hand, it is true that witch-hunting went on throughout Western Europe and that, by the international network of their order, the Dominicans carried the Inquisition's centralized work everywhere. On the other hand, persecution in most areas was a matter of isolated incidents, the occasional mass lynching, rather than the regular, relentless legal process continually under way in every town and village. Indeed, fear and persecution of witches became a normal part of life chiefly at the Elbe's mouth, along the Rhine, and in some Alpine valleys. When Innocent VIII legalized the persecution of witches as heretics with *Summis desiderantes*, he addressed specifically conditions in "some parts of upper Germany," the ecclesiastical provinces of Mainz, Cologne, Trier, Salzburg, and Bremen. In those areas, he said, persons of both sexes had allied with demonic spirits to blight normal reproduction in human beings, in livestock, and in vegetation. Not only did the white heat of persecution concentrate in these regions, but the power of the Inquisition to proceed varied widely from place to place. We have already seen that Alfonso the Wise nationalized the inquisitorial office of Castile in the thirteenth century; it lapsed, to be revived under Ferdinand and Isabella toward the end of the fifteenth century. The Inquisition never took root in England. In France, from the mid-fourteenth century on, the *parlements* acted as appellate courts for persons convicted by the Inquisition, and the faculty of theology at the University of Paris was specifically excluded from the inquisitor's sphere. In Germany parallel operations of individual bishops' courts severely checked the effectiveness of the papal inquisition. Beyond these official limitations, inquisitors labored against the stream of popular hatred, which led to murders of conspicuous inquisitors and to some urban revolts.

The ponderous legal apparatus that the Church developed from the thirteenth century on for suppressing heresy, and therefore witchcraft, was part of broad repression. The hierarchy's authority to scrutinize doctrinal writings burgeoned where it could into an aggressive and harsh censorship. The invention of printing with movable type compounded the problem, and, as early as 1479, Pope Sixtus IV issued the first papal declaration concerning what we would call freedom of the press. In 1515 a Lateran Council forbade printing books without prior examination and approval by delegated ecclesiastical offices; the course was set toward the formal establishment of the Index of Forbidden Books at the mid-sixteenth century. Territorial princes shared in the general tightening of religious standards. The warfare against the Cathari in Provence and the Old Prussians, and the execution of men whom the Church condemned as heretics, were aspects of the drive for religious conformity. Expulsion of the Jews was another.

But in this pattern of repression, in this insistence upon conformity, it would be wrong to see a uniform tendency or a common effort. We have seen that un-Christian, if not anti-Christian, trends in philosophy concerned an elite in definable geographical centers. The other currents had broader appeal. Even so, their manifestations and the responses they aroused varied markedly from place to place and from time to time. Astrology alone had the apparent character of a general miasma spreading over Europe, only because its purposes and techniques depended upon each practitioner. Such diversity in every detail can only throw the student back upon general categories. When we deal with pagan survivals and witchcraft, the problems become, perhaps not less complex, but at least more comprehensible. Localism was the essence of residual paganism. Folk heroes and divinities, sacred groves and wells, and native rituals had no meaning beyond the region where they were honored. Similarly, forms of witchcraft and popular attitudes to it differed widely. Furthermore, once labelled as heretical, witchcraft became subject to the legal process, and thus to the same fragmented patterns of authority that hovered over all Church administration. Territorial princes saw that the Inquisition, no less than papal provisions, subverted their monopoly of power; they resisted it. Repression of Jews can hardly be spoken of as a single process. Two centuries elapsed between their expulsion from England and their banishment by the Catholic Kings from the Spains. They found refuge in Italy, notably in Venice, in Holland, as well as in Poland. Protection of the Jews (for a price) was a prerogative of the Electoral Princes in the Empire. There is no simple pattern. One cannot facilely say that, in the late Middle Ages, the bigoted Christian society of the Latin West expelled the Jews. In the same way, and almost in the same degree, the parallel hysteria over witchcraft as heresy varied as local crises struck and as territorial government allowed. In a sense, the executions of witches were blood sacrifices that each community poured out to its own gods.

DISSIDENTS

Thus far, we have been discussing religious currents outside the Church that people inside the Church could reconcile with orthodox practices. The Averroist philosopher, the court astrologer, the semipagan peasant, and even the dabbler in witchcraft could all with the same tongue praise Christ and the ancient gods, or the mechanistic power of the stars. They had no separate compartments in their religious lives for "non-Christian" and "Christian" beliefs and practices. Popes consulted astrologers and magicians. Great officers of France devoutly prayed before their crucifixes, with enchanted images in their hands. A prior in Bologna was condemned (1468) for keeping a brothel in which he offered sacrifices to demonic spirits and let the citizens have their pleasure of demons in the shape of girls. Necromancy, astrology, and even witchcraft claimed adepts among the clergy as well as among faithful laymen.

Within the Church, however, other currents arose that led men to fight against ecclesiastical order or even to repudiate it altogether. These movements did not spring from a wish to enrich the believers' spiritual life by tapping other sources of inspiration and knowledge. They began with the conviction that the whole idea of the Church as a necessary intermediary between God and man was wrong, and that the structure of property and jurisdiction that defined the visible Church was, not the channel of salvation, but materialism and profanation of the sacred mysteries.

These movements had roots in the same ground as Church reforms. In every age, clergy and laymen reaffirmed the ascetic ideals of primitive Christianity and fought against the worldly wisdom, ambitions, and greed of prelates and religious orders. The Church continually renewed itself. Each generation in its own right broke with the immediate, corrupt past and tried to regain the denial of self and of the world, the spiritual purity of the Apostles. Every age had its austere Savonarola and its voluptuous Cardinal Riario. Throughout the Middle Ages, monastic reforms and the establishment of new orders kept the ascetic ideal alive. The Conciliar Movement worked to the same purpose. Indeed, the witchcraft hysteria was essentially a reform movement; its greatest leaders saw it as part of a broader program in which they demanded strict asceticism in the lives of religious orders and preached spiritual discipline and exacting devotional practices among the laity.

But each new order in its turn spoke to the spiritual needs of its age, grew rich, and departed from the severity of its rule. Angry young men became establishment men. Synodal and conciliar decrees went unobserved. Reformers, although clerics, were in the odd position of preaching against consecrated and legally established Church officers whom they considered wanting in virtue. Perfectly orthodox men, such as the great scholar and bishop Robert Grosseteste of Lincoln (fl. 1250) accused the papal curia of laxity in law and morals. Pope Gregory X returned the compliment (in 1274), when he declared that, by their wickedness, many prelates were speeding the world into ruin. Fed by the hatred between secular and regular clergy and among orders, and by factionalism within individual orders, fiery preachers throughout Europe attacked from the pulpit the inadequate education of priests, the secular lives of clergy, the perversion of the spiritual life by wealth and temporal power, venality of Church courts, and priests' extortion of money from laymen for the performance of sacraments. By the early fourteenth century, a German writer observed that, because of such abuses in the papacy, men had begun to hate clergy as much as they hated Jews.

It was good and most necessary that some churchmen in every generation were preoccupied with reform. If it was to steer its way through the shoals of secularism, the Church had constantly to be reminded of its spiritual purpose. But clearly both abuses and the cry for reform inspired anticlericalism ever more widely from the thirteenth century on. Could one claim that a bishop exercised his office wickedly, in defiance of God's will and to the ruin of his people, without also claiming that to honor and obey such a bishop was to concur with and share his sins, and to leave the path of salvation? A thin line ran between reform and revolt, between communion with the visible Church and schism from it.

Reform Sects and Heretics

From the eleventh century on, when records begin to give more than veiled hints about movements of dissent, some arguments appear repeatedly. Salvation lay, not in the Church's mediacy between God and man, but in God's direct election of individual men. Dissenters therefore argued that any impediment between God and the devout was useless and perverse, and thus they condemned the administrative structure of the Church, the liturgical functions it existed to perform, and the whole formalism of the liturgical year, of venerating saints as heavenly intercessors, of cherishing relics and miraculous images as claimchecks on divine favor. The Bible — its literal message or private interpretations of it — was held as supreme authority. The burden of the Scriptures' purpose was to teach man how to live in holiness, and its accounts of Christ's own life and that of the Apostles gave men a prototype to follow. Poverty was the hallmark of the blessed life, not only for heretical movements but for all reform currents in the Church. Christ and the Apostles had neither property, nor powers of temporal judgment; holiness lay in rejecting the world's wealth and authority.

Heroes of primitive Christianity, the Egyptian hermits acted on similar views when they rejected the world and the visible Church and fled to work out their own salvation in desert solitudes. The impulse of monastic reform from that day on until the advent of the friars was to abandon the world and to seek the fountain of life in desert wastes. But these reforms kept the lines of hierarchic obedience intact, and some, like the Cluniac movement, paid special care to matters of liturgy and ceremony.

The first bands of laymen to take this common ascetic heritage and mold it into heresy appeared in eleventh-century France. In 1049 the reform council of Rheims condemned the new heresies that, like a rash, had spread throughout Gaul. Some, even then, had taken root in Rheims itself. What these independent cells of dissidents believed is hard to tell from our biased and fragmentary sources. It is likely that the clergy who condemned the new beliefs imperfectly understood them. It is more than likely that the dissidents themselves had no set, doctrinaire position, but rather that they changed their minds about great issues and that they left wide areas of faith and practice to the individual conscience.

Some of their arguments are known. Long before the Latin Averroists took up the doctrine of the double truth, heretics at Orleans (ca. 1025) denied that Christ was born of a Virgin and refused to accept His Resurrection on the ground that both acts ran contrary to reason. They considered baptism, the Eucharist, and prayers to the saints empty forms. For them, the highest rule of faith and life was not official authority or the literal reading of Scripture, but the special revelations of the Scriptures' inner meaning that they claimed to have received.

In southern France and northern Italy, another view spread that condemned holy orders, procreation (and thus marriage), and consuming anything begotten by sexual intercourse. It demanded a constant reading of the Scriptures, continuous prayer and fasting, and community of property among believers. The Holy Spirit, abiding in the hearts of the faithful, led them individually to salvation; a violent death, crushing the unclean body, the fruit of procreation, was the gate of Heaven. Other groups condemned specific sacraments such as the Eucharist and baptism, and alleged abuses such as the Church's ownership of buildings for worship, veneration of saints and images, and impurity of life among priests.

Though condemned and persecuted, these sects continued to spread and to inspire the growth of others. Generously informative sources from the beginning of the twelfth century show that such groupings lacked tight and permanent organization. In fact, they were held together by the magnetism of great preachers, inspired men like Henry the Monk in northern France and Peter of Bruys in Provence. Fine points of doctrine counted for little. What mattered was that, with the fire of a prophet, the great evangelist had come who confirmed antipathy toward the visible Church and preached a way of salvation requiring no intermediary between man and God, thus removing believers from the power of impure and extortionate priests and leading them in the path of Christ and the Apostles. When the great preacher fell, victim of this world's powers, another rose to be followed, perhaps with different articles of belief but with the same evangelistic zeal, the same insistence on apostolic poverty.

At the same time, the Church's loyal sons addressed precisely the same public and proclaimed the same ideal of poverty. In revulsion against the worldliness of the clergy, Etienne de Muret, at Grandmont, and St. Bruno, at Chartreuse, established religious communities of utter renunciation which were sustained by the alms of the faithful. Robert of Arbrissel denounced the clergy from top to bottom as blasphemers against the divine word because of the impurity and venality of their lives. As a result of their wickedness and that of secular princes, God had abandoned the world, Robert said. Redemption lay only in self-negation and poverty, in following naked the naked Christ on the Cross.

Orthodox and heretic alike were vagabonds, followed by bands of their most loyal disciples; both preached poverty, not as the spiritual ideal that the Benedictines benign in their wealth and privilege had made it, but as a harsh way of life.

The Apostolic Movements

Still, the apostolic life preached by the orthodox existed only in the monastery. The cells at Grandmont and Chartreuse, Robert of Arbrissel's convents, St. Norbert's Premonstratensian monasteries, Cîteaux, and other similar establishments grew out of this wide and profound conviction that the holy life was the life of toil and common goods. Monks, not bishops, were the authentic successors of the Apostles; the apostolic life was the monastic life, and it could be led, not in the active world but in remote, dedicated places of prayer and contemplation.

In this way, the visible Church domesticated the fierce ideal of poverty; it harnessed poverty to its Juggernaut of property and jurisdiction.

But it merely clericalized the ideal. Seeing the Church as essentially a priestly club, it denied that laymen could lead the apostolic life. It preached that the holiness of poverty lived in the cool arcades of monastic cloisters, the refuges of the elite, rather than in the feverish streets of the city, at the weaver's loom, or in the peasant's fields. Repudiation of holy orders and sacraments had been heretical from the start. But the visible Church had now made the basic ideal of the apostolic movements heretical: that laymen could work out their own salvation through good works, especially through imitating Christ and the Apostles in a life of sacrificial poverty.

This ideal refused to die. Laymen denied that the keys to the kingdom of Heaven could rest in the hands of unclean and grasping men, however sacred the oil with which they had been anointed. Surrounded by bands of followers, itinerant preachers of apostolic poverty continued to preach their anarchistic doctrine.

Under great duress, the visible Church made one last attempt to yoke the movements to its own purposes; the result was disastrous. Among the many devotees of apostolic poverty, St. Francis of Assisi (d. 1226) won the approval of Pope Innocent III. Perhaps inspired by a heavenly vision, as legend says, the Pope orally recognized St. Francis and his followers as a legal order in the Church completely dedicated to a life of poverty and to preaching among the poor. At first, members of the fraternity possessed absolutely nothing. Food and lodging came from occasional alms. St. Francis forbade accumulation of food or capital and ownership of land. There was no formal organization. Even in St. Francis' lifetime, the size of the order and the scope of its work increased so greatly that permanent administrative order had to be established. The rule of poverty too was endangered. Like all reforming orders, the Franciscans received the offerings of the faithful. Brother Elias, St. Francis' vicar, undertook to build a great basilica and monastery at Assisi. The original ideal had dimmed. But St. Francis seemed unaware of this. By his Testament, St. Francis commanded that the life of absolute poverty never be violated and that the Order's Rule which enjoined it not be modified by later emendations, or even by papal decrees. Unlike earlier monastic orders, the Franciscans lived, not in desert places, but in the cities, and they worked, not for themselves or for the broad clerical elite, but for laymen. Still, it seemed likely to follow the Cluniacs and the Cistercians down the path from ascetical ideals into wealth and legalism.

But some of St. Francis' original followers survived him, and beside these, there were many in the Order who had entrusted their soul to Lady Poverty and who considered the Saint's Rule and Testament truly the inviolable pattern of Christ's life. Soon after St. Francis' death, a great conflict arose between them and the faction led by Elias who wished to ignore the Rule and Testament and to live as God gave them the means. A third, moderate division soon appeared, urging that the order keep an austere and pious mode of life, but also that it benefit from the experience of other orders in such matters as estate management and pattern of government, and that it go into the world, not only by preaching, but also by participating in the philosophical and scientific learning of the time.

Pope Gregory IX struck the papacy's first blow in this conflict when he declared St. Francis' Testament (and so the rule of absolute poverty) void and not binding on the Order (1229). The rigorists were therefore driven to oppose both the men they considered errant brethren and the papacy itself. The more extreme zealots withdrew altogether from communion with the Roman Church, which they denounced as the synagogue of Satan and the seat of Antichrist.

Pope John XXII gave Rome's definitive judgment in 1322 and 1323, when he proclaimed that it was a myth and a pernicious heresy to argue that Christ and the Apostles had lived in absolute poverty. Indeed, he said, they had property and enjoyed its use by the terms and under the protection of law. As for the rigorists, the Spiritual Franciscans, he judged that obedience was a greater virtue than poverty, and he condemned as criminals the rigorists in Provence, Ancona, Tuscany, and Sicily that scorned his decrees.

These judgments opened a new period in the stormy conflict. The issues that they addressed continued to divide the Franciscans throughout the Middle Ages and well into modern times. But the visible Church had spoken. The way of Christ and the Apostles, it said, was not the way of poverty, but that of property and legal privilege.

By this time, poverty as a sign and means of union with God had ceased to concern the villager and the artisan alone. Here and there outbreaks of popular anticlericalism continued to appear under the slogan of apostolicity, as they had done with terrifying force when the Pastoreaux invaded Orleans, Bourges, Rouen, Paris and other cities in 1251, killing priests and destroying church buildings. But the problems that the apostolic movements raised had now become matters for speculation by the intelligentsia. The coarse and deluded leader of the Pastoreaux claimed to act on direct revelations from God. Reason and a finely balanced sense of justice guided such eminent scholars as Marsiglio of Padua (fl. 1324) and Wycliffe (d. 1384). But, at the crossroads, they made the same choice.

Social Order and Religious Reform

In the days of John XXII, Marsiglio set forth a most extreme view of the Church, not as a priestly oligarchy, but as a true corporation of the faithful. Set apart from the laity by sacred functions, priests still stood on the same footing with them in the general structure of the believing community. Poverty was a sacred virtue, Marsiglio wrote, especially for the clergy. Church property must be secularized and turned to public benefit; tithes must be suppressed, powers of administration and jurisdiction abolished. The Scriptures held the highest spiritual authority; and neither they nor historical precedent warranted papal primacy. Such powers as the community of believers held were to be exercised by general councils.

Influenced by Marsiglio's doctrines, Wycliffe launched his attacks on the visible Church. In combating clerical abuses, he concluded that a priest or a bishop or even a pope exercised the powers of his office only so long as he was morally worthy to use them. A wicked man had no right to the powers of Christ. From this point, he went further to argue that holy orders were in fact useless, since man needed no intermediaries between himself and God. God elected the saved. He bestowed spiritual understanding directly. Thus, holy orders and the whole structure of property and laws that sustained it were little more than a withered member that should be cut off. God's elect composed the true priesthood. Christ, not the pope, was the head of the Church.

From premises such as these, Marsiglio and Wycliffe drew conclusions that had escaped less disciplined and systematic thinkers. They denied that the hierarchy was necessary or even useful to salvation. But how was religious anarchy to be averted? Who should rule the Church? The two authors answered that the Church was but one among many aspects of lay society, all of which were governed by the same power. In Marsiglio's view, supreme powers rested in the community of citizens, which delegated them to a sovereign as its representative. Like every other part of civil life, religious affairs fell under the surveillance of that ruler: admission to the priesthood, disciplining clergy, granting ecclesiastical benefices, summoning a general council, controlling its debates, and executing its decisions all fell within the competence of the temporal ruler. The Church was a department of state. In a similar way, Wycliffe appealed to secular rulers to purge the Church of the abuses that property and jurisdiction had introduced. All believers were priests; a Christian king was "priest and pontiff in his lands."

With these arguments, Marsiglio and Wycliffe carried the implications of apostolic poverty into a new dimension. The earlier apostolic movements had had no social programs, no ideas for the reform of society. From the eleventh century on, their followers sought a living, apostolic religion outside the Church. Because, in one degree or another, they renounced property, they estranged themselves as well from both the visible Church and from society—the system of laws and property tenure—of which the Church was a part. In search of individual salvation, they cast themselves adrift from society without hard feelings toward it. Drawing their members from every level of society, they had no ideas of class struggle or subversion of a "power structure."

But once Marsiglio and Wycliffe raised the issue of poverty to the level of abstract, philosophical thought, its broad consequences became apparent. Rome had condemned absolute poverty as heretical; it would brook no compromise. Only radical methods without Rome could establish the way of holiness. Cut away the Church's property; cut away its jurisdiction designed largely to govern property ownership and administration. The hierarchy would then be useless, since it would no longer have anything to administer. The pope would no longer matter as the supreme judge in the Church; the temporal ruler or the general council would take his juridical powers. The whole pattern of authority that unified the visible Church would vanish. Without some controlling power, each sect, indeed each believer, could become a law unto himself in matters of religion, and, if there, perhaps also in other kinds of social and political action. The choice, as Marsiglio and Wycliffe presented it, was between a national Church and religious anarchy that might well spread and contaminate all social order.

For Marsiglio, master at the University of Paris, recollections of the titanic struggle between Philip the Fair and Boniface VIII may have tipped the scales; for Wycliffe, English antagonism toward the French papacy at Avignon during the Hundred Years' War. Nationalism and religious grievance had sustained the Cathari of Provence against crusaders from the north and strengthened them to fight to the last for their religion as part of the broad culture that identified them and set them apart from, perhaps above, their enemies. The same fateful coupling of national and religious interests surely played in the minds of Marsiglio and Wycliffe. Charged by their ideas, it leapt from philosophy to action in the Hussite revolt.

Except for the Cathari, the poverty movements had all been dissenting minorities. Though modified by Christianity, Catharism remained non-Christian. With Hussitism, for the first time, a great and influential part of an entire nation followed the demands for reform to the point of schism. The University of Prague, a large segment of the Czech nobility, and a host of humbler people demanded purification of Church life, including the establishment of apostolic poverty for the clergy. Conflict began as an academic debate, in which Jan Hus, an eminent Biblical scholar and preacher, defended the ancient position revived by Wycliffe that validity of sacraments depended upon the personal morality of the officiating priests. When the Council of Constance sent Hus to the stake, the dispute widened into a matter of national honor, almost an affair of ethnic conscience. The Germans had provoked an enduring hatred by dominating life in Czech cities, courts, and learned institutions. Papal representatives drew scorn and bitterness upon themselves and their masters by greed and immorality. Hus' death (1415) activated both these fields of animosity; with the connivance of King Wenceslaus and the open encouragement of his Queen, protest gathered momentum. The irreversible crisis broke when Wenceslaus, yielding to pressure from Pope and Emperor, commanded that non-Hussite priests be restored to their churches (1419). Prague revolted. The King died of apoplexy. His brother succeeded him, the Emperor Sigismund, the very man who had violated his own letter of safe-conduct in burning Hus. Revolt broadened into general warfare that was not to end for eleven years.

Though now divided into rigorist and moderate factions, the Hussites beat back crusade after crusade. The radical wing, the Taborites, ravaged the countryside, preaching apostolic poverty and community of goods for all men, destroying churches and monasteries, killing monks, nuns, and priests. They began with the teaching of Wycliffe and Hus, but they went far beyond those doctrines. To a different degree, the same was true of the moderates. Perhaps for other than doctrinal reasons, the nobility confiscated most of the enormous lands of the Bohemian churches and exercised decisive powers over the consecration and placement of clergy.

They all disclaimed Sigismund, Hus' betrayer and executioner, as true king, and the Roman church as the vessel of salvation.

Radicals and moderates alike argued that the true church existed only in their community. The Taborites went further and rather ahistorically claimed to have revived the primitive Church as it was in Christ's time, completely autonomous, independent of all other institutions, and, above all, Czech in ethnic composition, in language, and in forms of religious observance.

The Hussite Wars ended; with qualifications, the claims of the moderate party were acknowledged and reconciled with those of Bohemians who had remained loyal to Rome; Sigismund was accepted as king. But religious grievance had found nationalistic expression, especially in the community of Tabor, and the convictions that this extraordinary fact engendered lived on for two centuries in Bohemian separatist movements.

All earlier currents of religious protest had been highly localized. From the eleventh century on, dissent marked life chiefly in urbanized and thickly settled areas, which were also the classical regions of manorialism and feudalism: northern Italy, the Rhineland, and the Great Plain of Western Europe. England, for unknown reasons, did not share heresy with this region, to which it was closely drawn in so many other ways. When they occurred for short periods in other areas, such as Provence, the heretical movements also had an urban character. Most incidents of protest were isolated. Even widely dispersed and carefully organized movements—such as the Waldensians—were more fraternities of allies than organic institutions, and they fell into clearly defined regional groupings. None spread throughout Europe or even throughout an entire kingdom. The Lollards, who once seemed likely to become a national movement, were repressed by the beginning of the fifteenth century and driven into a few pockets around Lincoln, Worcester, and Hereford.

Only Hussites came within sight of taking up the options that Marsiglio and Wycliffe had framed in philosophical terms. They too broke into factions, and ended their struggle in compromise with the emperor and the Church. But their revolt and the abstract theories that first inspired it had carried the familiar tension between conservatism and change, the distinction between reform and schism, to a new level. Parallel in many ways to the claims of national churches, their movement united dissident religion with nationalism, spiritual reform with ethnic cohesion, and forecast the socioreligious upheavals of the Reformation.

SUMMARY

We have been discussing two kinds of religious experience that lay outside the visible Church. One, represented by the Latin Averroists, astrologers, and witches, was non-Christian and supplemented the formal exercises of the Church. The other, represented by the various movements of religious dissent, arose within and rejected the Church for having perverted the doctrine of salvation. The astrologer could remain inside the Church; the heretic Waldensian could not. They differed in many ways, but on one critical point they said the same thing. For them all, the visible Church was an inadequate vessel of truth. The Averroist or the astrologer argued that there were truths beyond and independent of those that the hierarchy preached. They even implied that their realms of verity controlled or rendered meaningless the Church's irrational and undemonstrable doctrine. The disciple of religious dissent had a more extreme view. In his eyes, the hierarchy was obstructive and repressive, obstinate in its errors, blind to Christ.

Neither as symbols nor as working institutions did the offices of the visible Church fulfill the hopes of these men. For some they denied man control or even knowledge of his destiny. These took refuge in the pseudosciences, in magic, and witchcraft. For others, they obstructed direct communication between man and God; they denied God the power to enlighten the hearts of those who loved and wished to follow Him, and gave the keys of Heaven to fallible, even wicked, men. These found solace in mysticism or in religious dissent.

In yet another way, the Church's formal structure ran counter to human aspirations. The high degree of localism that we have seen throughout—both in discussing formalistic orthodoxy and in describing religious currents outside the Church—shows that medieval men did not sense spiritual needs in an ecumenical way. They sought individual salvation; they grasped spiritual crises from the center of the universe, not from its outer edges. Their search for comfort and illumination had relevance only to local, indeed personal, impulses. The village, the town, or perhaps the province was their world; and the same limits that defined their immediate concerns and gave them ethnic identity also defined their spiritual needs and aspirations. They could extend their hopes and fears into eternity, reaching upward to divine communion. But the souls they raised to God were national—Czech or Florentine or Aragonese. A sardonic linguistic hierarchy ascribed to Charles V expresses this union of ethnic and religious identities, and thus also of prejudices: "I speak Spanish to God, Italian to women, French to men, and German to my horse." The Welsh put it with more grace in their triad: "English is the language of men. French is the language of birds. Welsh is the language of angels."

In the Middle Ages, patterns of Church order were insufficiently developed to embrace all these diverse social expectations, interwoven as they were with spiritual struggles and acts of worship. Man's heart and body were creatures of time and place. For many men, the medieval Church with its vain insistence on standardized order and discipline, its never-ending demands for money to support distant wars, and its suppression of men who preached the apostolic life, was little more than a dead star.

The history of medieval religion is in large measure an account of local or national differentiation, but it also shows important impulses toward universalism. The whole many-branched growth of papal monarchy did provide a common background for religious history. Opposed in every corner of Europe, the sweeping power that popes claimed over ecclesiastical property and offices still set a standard with which every territorial prince and every dissident religious movement had to contend. Indeed, philosophical and religious nonconformists shared more than parallel responses to the same challenge. The debt of Hus to Wycliffe, and of Wycliffe to Marsiglio, and the close relations between the Hussites and the Waldensians around Dresden illustrate the sort of interchange that did occur and the cumulative indebtedness of later movements to earlier. In a more dramatic way, the debt of the Cathari to the Bogomiles of Bulgaria shows the same thing. Through the orthodox laity a wave of extravagant devotion and mysticism swept from one end of Western Europe to the other in the fourteenth and fifteenth centuries. Stations of the Cross, the Feasts of the Trinity and of the Immaculate Conception, the use of the Rosary, and popular devotional literature of every description became part of Europe's common property. They were spread through the international networks of religious orders such as the Dominicans and the Franciscans, through the work of great itinerant evangelists, and by merchants and warriors along their lines of march.

But what theme was predominant, stratification or mingling? If we are to talk of a homogenous medieval religion, who represented its true character: Gregory VII or the German bishops who condemned him, Boniface VIII or Marsiglio of Padua, St. Bernadino of Siena or the priests of Tabor? What emblem can we take to represent medieval Christianity: the cross of Gero or the Eros in Auxerre cathedral? Again, since society is the model of religion, which society, which religion, may we choose as the end result of general mingling? Whose norms set the standard of religion as a way of life? We saw earlier that Europe knew not one society, but a complex set of independent, interconnected, societies. The religious diversities and similarities that we have now added to the picture conform to that intricate pattern. Only the comparative history of medieval religion—which the work of scholars now appears to forecast—can define the degrees of spiritual affinity that united men and of disparity that divided them. But behind all the doctrinal conflicts and social turmoil lay one immeasurable element beyond the powers of reason to define: the human conscience, the ultimate battleground where each man wrestled with dark and incomprehensible forces, the inner contradictions of his nature, and, at the end, beheld the hidden God.

SUGGESTED READING

Reference should be made to the following lists.

On Roman and Canon Law:
Mortimer, R. C. *Western Canon Law.* Berkeley, 1953.
Post, G. *Studies in Medieval Legal Thought: Public Law and the State, 1100–1322.* Princeton, 1964.
Vinogradoff, P. *Roman Law in Medieval Europe.* Oxford, 1929.

On Theology and Philosophy:
Carré, M. H. *Realists and Nominalists.* Oxford, 1946.
Gilson, E. *History of Christian Philosophy of the Middle Ages.* New York, 1955.
Leff, G. *Medieval Thought: St. Augustine to Ockham.* London, 1958.
Obermann, H. A. *The Harvest of Medieval Theology.* Harvard, 1963.
Pine, M. "Pomponazzi and the 'Double Truth,'" *Journal of the History of Ideas* 29 (1968): 163–176.
Richardson, C. C. *Early Church Fathers.* Philadelphia, 1953.

On Dissidents:
Erikson, K. T. *Wayward Puritans: A Study in the Sociology of Deviance.* New York, 1966.
Heninger, S. K., Jr. *A Handbook of Renaissance Meteorology.* Duke, 1960.
Hopkin, C. E. *The Share of Thomas Aquinas in the Growth of the Witchcraft Delusion.* Philadelphia, 1940.
Huizinga, J. *The Waning of the Middle Ages.* London, 1924.
Kaminsky, H. *A History of the Hussite Revolution.* Berkeley, 1967.
Lea, H. C. *A History of the Inquisition of the Middle Ages.* 3 vols., New York, 1888.
Leff, G. *Heresy in the Later Middle Ages.* 2 vols., Manchester, 1967.
Russell, J. B. *Dissent and Reform in the Early Middle Ages.* Berkeley, 1965.
Throop, P. A. *Criticism of the Crusade: A Study of Public Opinion and Crusade Propaganda.* Amsterdam, 1940.
Williams, C. *Witchcraft.* London, 1941.

On Other General Problems:
Auerbach, E. *Mimesis.* New York, 1957.
Boas, G. *Essays on Primitivism and Related Ideas in the Middle Ages.* Baltimore, 1948.
Duchesne, L. *Christian Worship: Its Origin and Evolution.* 5th ed., London, 1923.
Dvornik, F. *The Idea of Apostolicity in Byzantium and the Legend of the Apostle Andrew.* Harvard, 1958.
Eliade, M. *Images and Symbols.* London, 1961.
Hardison, O. B., Jr. *Christian Rite and Christian Drama in the Middle Ages.* Baltimore, 1965.
Murray, G. *The Rise of the Greek Epic.* 2nd ed., Oxford, 1911.
Wach, J. *Sociology of Religion.* Chicago, 1944.

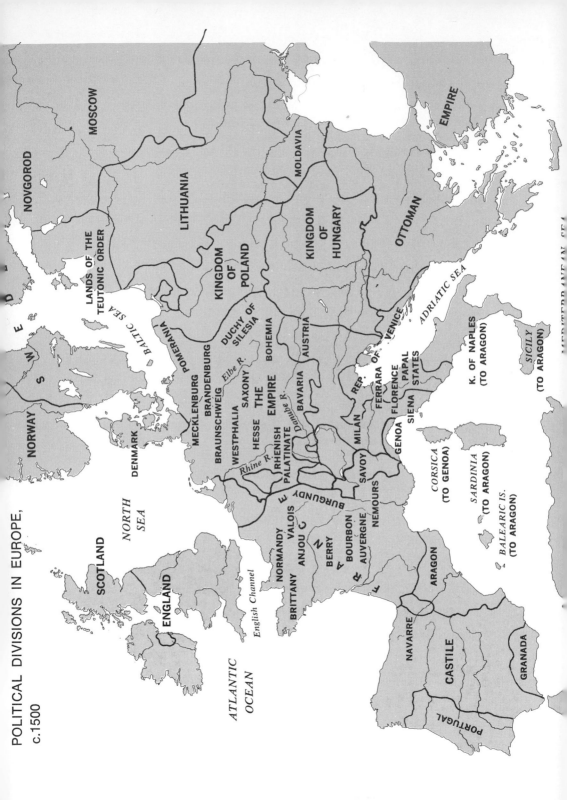

POLITICAL DIVISIONS IN EUROPE, c.1500

NORWAY

SWEDEN

SCOTLAND

NORTH SEA

ATLANTIC OCEAN

ENGLAND

English Channel

DENMARK

BALTIC SEA

NOVGOROD

MOSCOW

LANDS OF THE TEUTONIC ORDER

LITHUANIA

KINGDOM OF POLAND

MOLDAVIA

KINGDOM OF HUNGARY

OTTOMAN EMPIRE

POMERANIA

MECKLENBURG

BRANDENBURG

BRAUNSCHWEIG

DUCHY OF SILESIA

Elbe R.

WESTPHALIA

SAXONY

THE EMPIRE

BOHEMIA

AUSTRIA

ADRIATIC SEA

HESSE

RHENISH PALATINATE

Rhine R.

BAVARIA

Danube R.

REP. OF VENICE

FERRARA

FLORENCE

SIENA

PAPAL STATES

MILAN

SAVOY

GENOA

CORSICA (TO GENOA)

SARDINIA (TO ARAGON)

K. OF NAPLES (TO ARAGON)

SICILY (TO ARAGON)

MEDITERRANEAN SEA

BURGUNDY

NORMANDY

VALOIS

ANJOU

BRITTANY

BERRY

BOURBON

AUVERGNE

NEMOURS

FRANCE

NAVARRE

PORTUGAL

CASTILE

ARAGON

GRANADA

BALEARIC IS. (TO ARAGON)

174

Conclusion

It is clearly wrong to think of "medieval history," "medieval civiliza-tion," or even "medieval Europe" in terms of social unity. We do, however, find convenience in bracketing a long time span in European history as "medieval"; more than that, we find it natural.

But the comfortable familiarity of this "natural" usage comes merely from the hypnotic effect of frequent repetition, rather than from history itself. It is comparable with the idea that the Byzantine Empire was in its death throes for 1000 years. Because this premise was repeated often enough, it held general credit, although it flew in the face of logic and evi-dence, until demolished by recent scholarship.

In dissecting the idea of "medieval Europe" we must take great care not to overemphasize division, to raise the myth of cultural pockets in place of the myth of cultural unity. Even if Rome lacked Gothic architecture, it still practiced a form of Christianity that believers in the area of the Gothic shared in very many details. Are we not dealing with one vast social mechanism, like a clock, with its many parts highly diverse in form, but brilliantly articulated to make one smoothly operating instrument?

By many standards of logic and historical judgment the answer seems to be negative. Scholars of the eighteenth and nineteenth centuries invented the terms with which we analyze life in Europe between Boethius and Luther: "manorialism," "nationalism," "commercialism," "Scholasticism," "Humanism," "Romanesque," "Gothic," "Renaissance," "civilization," "cul-ture," and most of the other terms that we use as a kind of classificatory shorthand sprang from the knowledge and the synthesizing instincts of an earlier age. We may fall short in elegance of expression and breadth of view when compared with the scholars who framed these terms; but our knowledge is so much greater than theirs, both in quality and in quantity, that it renders their categories little more than empty slogans. The terms are anachronistic in two ways: first, they were not used in the period under review; and, second, they no longer suffice to describe the relevant subjects. From this follows a dangerous consequence: they carry a heavy burden of associations and implications placed on them by their inventors. The current pique at "feudalism," an older term than the ones we have mentioned, should spread to the whole taxonomy of our subject.

We now see that to speak of "the Middle Ages," "medieval society," "the medieval town," and the like as types is to yield to deception, the beguiling deception of an outmoded synthesis playing its familiar *tours de force* on the facts. The first step toward this end might well be discarding the terms "Middle Ages" and "medieval." Classical archaeologists identify stages in Cretan civilization by number – Minoan I, II, and III, each having three component periods – and, accepting Toynbee's periodization for the sake of example, we might prefer to think of European I (c. 675 – 1075), II (c. 1075 – 1475), and III (c. 1475 – 1875). Our fullest view of reality lies, perhaps, not in a detailed and mechanical synthesis, but in faint contour lines drawn from, and not imposed upon, the evidence. Avoiding misleading typology would make it easier to gain this view, to give regional identities their proper emphasis.

The rational mind shrinks from chaotic diversity. It needs to organize disparate facts in order to understand them; it looks for the structural scheme. Lives of individual men cannot provide a unifying thread for descriptive analysis. Often they are too obscure, and, when known, they are too diverse. If we are to understand the phenomenon of man in social terms, we must therefore turn to man in the agglomerate, his political and social life. What brought men together? By what rituals or languages or artistic devices or political institutions did they mutually express common hopes, needs, and fears? Many diverse strands flow together in any society. The basic analytical question is: what clamps them together?

Preoccupied with abstract forms, the philosopher has no way of avoiding this question. Even for the historian, preoccupied with individual facts, it is more than a utilitarian irrelevance. Any unified society moves by the tension between conservatism and change, the functions of memory and desire. What range of possibilities do history, technical virtuosity, and aspirations lay before a people? To define on the one hand what a society holds to as signs of its distinctiveness and, on the other, the new powers and possibilities it foresees and can develop is in great measure to say what gives it cohesion and identity.

Between 500 and 1500, Europe had no common drives and thus no institutions to express them. There were, to be sure, some impulses toward universalism. Ideologically, the greatest of these was the concept of papal monarchy and the administrative mechanism that the Roman church developed to enact it. A second was the emergence of cities as autonomous units, centers of long-distance trade and interregional finance. But such forces as these failed. Local sensibilities and loyalties crystallized in the hands of princes and obstructed all thrusts toward pan-Europeanism. Thus, cultural mingling reached a level compatible with the interests and potentialities of princely government, the stage beyond which forces of communication could not override local ties. Students of early modern Europe frequently contrast the particularism of the sixteenth and seventeenth centuries with the cohesiveness of a "medieval synthesis," which they take for granted. We now see that the state of affairs in the age of Louis XIV did not contrast with the medieval conditions but prolonged them.

At the end of our period, Europe's isolation was greater than ever before. Byzantium had fallen. The Turks, interposing themselves as an impenetrable barrier between the West and the Orient, expelled the Genoese and Venetians from their Levantine posts. The Mediterranean ceased yet again to be a channel of communication and became a barrier, a stage of warfare. It is true that the first great international alliances had begun, in the Holy League and the League of Cambrai. These *ad hoc* enterprises at the glittering level of high politics did not blot out the profound social and cultural cleavages we have suggested. And yet, Europe was on the verge of world domination. How did the West concert its forces sufficiently to achieve this, if it was a complex of splintered societies?

The answer to this supreme question must lie in the fact that "Europe" did not achieve world dominion, but that some states in Europe gradually did. Losing the Levant as a center of international commerce threw the initiative into the hands of the nations that were already exploring Atlantic routes: Portugal and Spain. As non-Oceanic states declined, those bordering the Atlantic rose, whipped on by competition for the richest prize that the world could offer. It was the consummate hour of what Professor W. H. McNeill has called "the incessant mutability of European (more recently of Western) civilization," the characteristic which above all set the West apart from other regions.

The ground of this volatility is now clear. Opportunity, need, and inventiveness coincided within a network of societies which lacked uniformity of mores, history, government, and communal myth, but which still had much in common, enough to confront the same broad issues at the same time and to generate the friction of rivalry. The dual tendencies of mingling and stratification that stalked medieval Europe had created irresoluble tensions; their outcome was, on one hand, the Reformation, and, on the other, exploration, discovery, and world conquest.